THE 50 MGM FILMS THAT TRANSFORMED HOLLYWOOD

THE 50 MGM FILMS THAT TRANSFORMED HOLLYWOOD

TRIUMPHS, BLOCKBUSTERS, AND FIASCOS

STEVEN BINGEN

ESSEX, CONNECTICUT

An imprint of Globe Pequot, the trade division of The Rowman & Littlefield Publishing Group, Inc.
4501 Forbes Boulevard, Suite 200, Lanham, Maryland 20706
www.rowman.com

Distributed by NATIONAL BOOK NETWORK

British Library Cataloguing-in-Publication Information Available

Library of Congress Cataloging-in-Publication Data
Names: Bingen, Steven, author.
Title: The 50 MGM movies that transformed Hollywood : triumphs, blockbusters, and fiascos.
Description: Essex, Connecticut : Lyons Press, [2022] | Includes bibliographical references. | Summary: "Discusses the films that, for one reason or another, changed the trajectory of MGM and the film industry in general"— Provided by publisher.
Identifiers: LCCN 2022014216 (print) | LCCN 2022014217 (ebook) | ISBN 9781493067008 (hardback) | ISBN 9781493070893 (epub)
Subjects: LCSH: Metro-Goldwyn-Mayer—History. | Motion pictures—United States—History—20th century. | Motion picture studios—California—Los Angeles.
Classification: LCC PN1993.5.U6 B54 2022 (print) | LCC PN1993.5.U6 (ebook) | DDC 791.43/750973—dc23/eng/20220517
LC record available at https://lccn.loc.gov/2022014216
LC ebook record available at https://lccn.loc.gov/2022014217

Contents

Acknowledgments

This book grew out of my earlier *The MGM Effect* (2022), so it shares many of the same collaborators and contains wisdom culled from many of the same interviews. Likewise, some of the opinions that I have here affected as my own probably were actually requisitioned, inadvertently or not, from the names listed below, and from others I have since forgotten that I also stole from. So, if your name is listed here, or if it should be listed here and isn't, I owe you both my thanks and my gratitude, and in some cases an apology too.

I'd particularly like to share my appreciation to Stephen X. Sylvester, who contributed the *Man from U.N.C.L.E.* essay, and who did a better job with it than I ever could have.

Hollywood's ace historian Marc Wanamaker also added immeasurably to both the look and the content of what is printed here. Marc, of course, is well-known and much appreciated by myself and by every Hollywood historian for his many services to our little community.

I'd also like to single out for praise Greg Gormick and Donnie Norden, both of whom were on the backlot during its last days, and both of whom have made valuable contributions to MGM itself and to this volume in particular. Donnie's book *Phantom of the Backlot Presents . . . Hole in the Fence* has recently been published, and Greg's, *The Lion's Serenade,* is on the way. Look for them both. Likewise, at the Academy of Motion Picture Arts and Sciences Margaret Herrick Library, librarian Kristine Krueger, who, in spite of a worldwide COVID-19–inflicted shutdown, managed to sleuth out valuable information about these last contentious days on the lot. She has my gratitude for her good work regarding, and during, two very different—and very difficult—times.

Additional, and no less valuable contributions to this volume were contributed by the following MGM-related experts, enthusiasts, ex-employees, historians, supporters, and fans. So, thank you Richard Adkins, Marilyn Allen, Ron Barbagallo, John Bengston, Michael Benson, John Bertram, Danny Biederman, Michael F. Blake, David Bowen, Scott Brogan, Krista Christofferson, Ned Comstock, David English, Mike Escarzaga, John Escobar, Christian Esquevin, Rob Feeney, Robert Florczak, Rob Gold, Darryl M. Haase, Danny Hancock, Jon Heitland, David Heilman, Carl Hymans, Rob Klein, Robert Lane, Steve Martin, Alicia Mayer, John Mcelwee, Naomi Minkoff, Scott Moore, Larry McQueen, Jan Murree, Les Perkins, Ana Maria Quintana, Sharon Rich, Rick Rinehart, Robert Short, Richard W. Smith, Steven C. Smith, Mike Stein, John Stephen, E. J. Stephens, William Stillman, Stan Taffel, Karl Thiede, Frank Thompson, Nicholas Toth, Michael Troyan, Martin Turnbull, Gary Wayne, Werner Weiss, Robert Welch, Mike Wetherell, Josh Young, Charles Ziarko, and Deana Zvara.

Lastly, this book is dedicated to Zoe and Beth; like Leo the Lion, long may they roar.

Introduction

I never believed that movies were what really mattered.

A pretty confounding thing to say in a book about movies, isn't it? Make no mistake, I *love* the movie industry. And I've devoted huge swatches of my life to working in it and to writing about it. But that's the whole point. My own personal obsessions on the subject have usually regarded the movie *industry*. I've written extensively about film, but not about *films*. When I watched a movie, I tended to do so for technique rather than for narrative, for craftsmanship rather than emotion.

It is because of all this odd baggage that when it was suggested that I write about the "fifty best" movies from MGM studios, I initially felt like my publishers were asking the wrong guy. Yes, I have obsessed over and written about that studio pretty extensively, most recently in *The MGM Effect*, published in 2022. So, I guess it was assumed that, with my very extensive knowledge of MGM's very extensive library, I would probably be both well up to and well qualified for the task.

I wasn't so sure. But that initial hesitation didn't stop me from digging through my files for a list I have of every Goldwyn—and then every Metro-Goldwyn-Mayer—movie title, listed chronologically by production number, from 1917 into the 1970s. I should mention that there are almost fifty titles per page on that list, that the thing is forty pages long, and that it is forty years old, so obviously a lot of MGM films had come out of the gate after my list had stopped counting them.

Even assuming I could cull fifty masterpieces from that list, and beyond that list, I had to wonder if the world really needed me acting as a one-man Rotten Tomatoes, asserting that *The Thin Man* is somehow better than *No Time to Die*, or which

Howard Keel explores the legendary MGM vault and the legendary MGM library for *That's Entertainment III* (1994).
Marc Wanamaker/Bison Archives

Jeanette MacDonald–Nelson Eddy picture has the most tuneful songs, or whether *The Haunting* really is scarier than *Poltergeist*. Surely someone else would be better at that than I?

Anyway, after riffling through all those titles for a couple hours, I did a quick search and discovered there were already several books out there with the name *The Best of MGM*—all written, although decades ago, by respected scholars with much sharper critical faculties than mine. So, a little relieved perhaps, I set that now dog-eared list aside, thinking it was over.

Needless to say, it wasn't that easy, and it wasn't over. A few minutes later, I picked that list up again. This time with a pencil with a good eraser, I started going through those thousands of titles, not at all sure what I was looking for. But I was now certain there was something I was missing—something tethering some of these films together that stood apart from Leo the Lion's roaring in their openings. But what was it?

I finally saw it. Movies don't exist in a vacuum. Each MGM movie is a tiny piece of a large, colorful (although often black-and-white) quilt, with threads tying it into all the rest of that studio's product—going forward, yes; but also backward, horizontally, and three dimensionally across its entire landscape. And like a quilt, when all these disparate patchwork pieces are combined, a pattern, or a hundred patterns, can often emerge.

To create patterns on a quilt, seamstresses use what they call foundation pieces, which stabilize the surrounding areas. Could it be possible that MGM's library had these foundation pieces as well? And if they could be identified, could those pieces then give us a new and novel examination of both a company and of an industry?

Eventually—well, over the first of many hours—a list, a summation if you will, of the foundation pieces, of the films that epitomized, affected, effected, or altered the course of the studio's overall story emerged. Some of those films were successful; others were failures, either financially or artistically. But they all, be they blockbusters or bank busters, changed the course of the studio, and of Hollywood going forward, or symbolized a change, whether that change in course was evident at the time or not.

This sort of a "best of" list, if you can still call it that, hasn't really been attempted before. Movies are judged, as they should be, based on their artistic merits, on if they are any *good*. But we tend to forget, especially decades after the fact, that show business is as much, and maybe more, about the first word than it is about the second. So, in this case, financial success, as philistine as it may sound, was often a major and deciding factor in determining this list. Although—to my credit, I hope—not the only determining factor. It should be noted that some MGM films also changed the studio internally or corporately or, in some cases, even changed that film's eventual audience, which consequently, inadvertently, and often years after the fact, again reflected back upon and then changed the studio that birthed them.

Think about it. That the movies *can* change an audience is indisputable. *Ben-Hur* (both versions) undoubtably brought nonbelievers into churches in large numbers. *Mrs. Miniver* led to increased empathy for our World War II British allies. Similarly, rock and roll, art deco, foreign cultures, history, science, and literature, as well as countless trends in art and fashion, were all introduced to American audiences, in many cases, through the cinema. But only sometimes has that influence been reflected back into the studio. For example, Hitchcock's *North by Northwest* is masterful, of course, but it shouldn't be ignored that it also led to the creation of other thrillers and ultimately to the *Man from U.N.C.L.E.* and to the James Bond franchises, all of which changed the world and, more directly to our point, changed the studio that made them.

It should also be acknowledged that there are some MGM movies that changed the world but *not* the studio. *A Christmas Story* (1983), in particular, is one of MGM's most successful productions. It seemingly meets the criteria for this list in that it is one of the most beloved films of the past fifty years. But upon its original release, the picture was not a particularly lucrative movie, even during an era when most MGM movies were not particularly lucrative. But three years after its release, the film was acquired by media mogul Ted Turner, and it was through his airing it hundreds of times on his cable channels that the movie achieved its success, and its vast following—none of which MGM was able to benefit from. Sadly, this same scenario has happened to other films once part of the MGM library as well, many of which are now owned by Warner Bros. But seldom has it happened so quickly. Most sorry about that, *A Christmas Story*.

Another example, *They Only Kill Their Masters* (1972) attracted a lot of publicity in its time because the studio announced that it would be the last film ever shot on their storied backlots. Consequently, parties were thrown and interviews given, and publicity was generated to that end. To this day, reference books and websites that really should know better still assert that this was the case—when, in fact, that backlot would be utilized by MGM, and others, for nearly ten more years. The story of the *actual* last films to be shot on those haunted acres, whether you've heard of those films or not or are aware of their significance in this regard, will be duly described here, however.

There are also movies that forever, and often sadly, changed the career of an individual artist. Buster Keaton and John Gilbert, for example, were destroyed—and "destroyed" is the only honest word one could use to describe what happened—by the studio. The Marx Brothers, William Haines, Erich von Stroheim, James Murray, Karl Dane, director Douglas Trumbull, and even Elvis Presley could, with some justification, be added to the same sad list. But their being ground into grist for the factory ultimately caused that factory, let's be honest here, not a moment of regret or reflection. Because this book isn't about them, these sad sacrifices will not be addressed here.

All of this leads to the question, of course, as to what constitutes an MGM movie at all. To some fans, only films made by, or in, the Culver City studio, preferably by Louis B. Mayer, and/or by Irving Thalberg, are "real" MGM movies. I get this. There is a tremendous and nostalgic pull to old Hollywood and all that old Hollywood represents, and that pull cannot be ignored. So *Gone with the Wind, The Wizard of Oz,* and *Singin' in the Rain* are of course here, given their deserved—and frankly, somewhat tiresome—expected prominence. Even though, truth be told, neither Thalberg nor Mayer, owing to politics or mortality, was much involved with any of these titles.

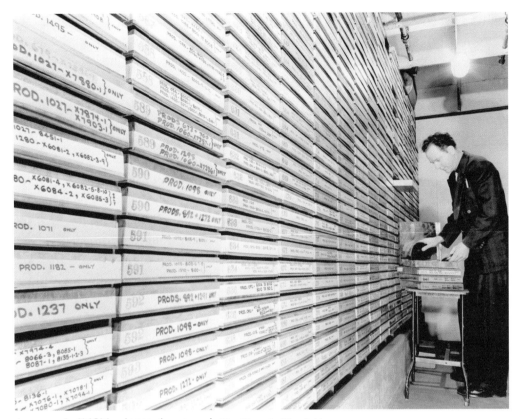

An overworked MGM archivist in the catacombs *Marc Wanamaker/Bison Archives*

I've decided to cast the net as widely and in as many directions as possible here in order to illustrate different facets of the studio's many-faceted story. Consequently, films made elsewhere and by others, but financed and/or ultimately distributed by MGM, are included as part of the family tree (hello, *Gone with the Wind*). As are films made for television, cartoons, documentaries, short subjects, and even properties merely acquired by the studio, sometimes years after their creation—provided that these properties (hello, James Bond) influenced or augmented our story in some way. All of these works, like it or not, are part of the MGM story.

Some, of course, would claim that as the studio approaches its centennial, there is no longer any connection, except in a legal sense, between the MGM of its "golden age," and the entity with that name that exists today. This is patently untrue. Even though it is no longer possible to find current employees, or even former employees, who remember Thalberg or Mayer or their times firsthand, there is such a thing as corporate, as *institutional* memory, which can be just as tangible as personal memory is. Surely then, with this in mind, the studio's on-screen self-shout-outs to its own past or stars in films like *Party Girl* (1958), the *That's Entertainment* series, *Garbo Talks* (1984), *Rain Man* (1988), and *De-Lovely* (2004) could not have been unintentional.

I also hope that anyone first jumping into these rich cinematic waters will use these fifty films as an entrée and a guide into a better world than ours, a world I hope they will then explore beyond the scope of this volume. For those readers wondering where to go next, I have included *another* fifty MGM pictures, with much-scaled-back coverage, in an appendix. MGM's film library certainly is one of the great, vast, essential, and culturally priceless crown jewels of our era, of any era, so further exploration of its gemstones and rhinestones is both highly recommended and well worthwhile. Plus, for different reasons, most of these movies—sometimes old, sometimes new, sometimes triumphs, sometimes embarrassments—are also a hell of a lot of fun to watch.

Decades ago, in a very prescient documentary called *Hollywood: The Dream Factory*, Dick Cavett wryly addressed this very point. His words are more poignantly apt today than they must have been even at the time:

> Like the amphitheaters of ancient Greece or the stages of Shakespearean England, the major Hollywood studios produced the popular entertainment of their time. But unlike them, the dream factory has left its legacy intact, the producers' grand conception, the writers' subtle art, the magical realization of brilliant directors and actors, these are beyond mortality. They remain for future generations to study and enjoy.

My final comment here on a subject that I have now devoted many words and many years to is, oddly enough, also a confession that much of what I have believed to be true for so long has instead largely turned out to be incorrect.

Yes, I was wrong. In the final accounting it is not the studio at all, it is rather the movies themselves that the studio has gifted upon us; ghostly algorithms of shadows and projected light that really matter. It is these elusive phantoms; Garbo's laugh, Gable's cocksure grin, Garland's trembling voice, Gene Kelly's gleeful dance in the rain, these images, and a thousand others that, trust me, if we only deign to let them in, can forever continue to haunt us.

—Steven Bingen
Hollywood, California, 2022.

1

He Who Gets Slapped (1924)

He Who Gets Slapped is regarded as the first MGM movie. An unusual title card in the credits boasts that the film was "produced by Metro-Goldwyn-Mayer" and "released by Metro-Goldwyn Distributing Company," as the new studio was then trying out different variations on their name, and Louis B. Mayer—or rather Louis B. Mayer Pictures—was definitely the junior partner in the tangle.

It's all very complicated. The earliest predecessor to what would finally become, with this production MGM (I'm here and henceforth omitting the hyphens in that name, although you will still find them within these pages when used in quotes by others) was first called Loews Consolidated Enterprises, which went public in 1910 after several years of successfully operating arcades and theaters. Marcus Loew, the company's namesake, was president; Nicholas Schenck was his assistant. This new company, in this new industry, was thunderously successful. By 1919 Loews had built, owned, or was operating theater holdings amounting to $100 million in assets.

The first word in the logo, but the second company founded, Metro Pictures, originally a film distribution and production syndicate, was formally organized as such in New York on January 27, 1915. In 1920, when Metro was purchased by Loews as a way of ensuring a consistent supply of films for their theaters, the factory to produce this product, significantly, was based in Hollywood, California.

The second word in the name, "Goldwyn," came from Goldwyn Pictures Corporation, which was formed in New York in 1916. By 1920 it had already been reorganized several times, endured several minor name changes, and been spun off into

Illustrator Alvin Wolfson's acclaimed artwork for *He Who Gets Slapped* (1924) starkly succeeds in illustrating both the pathos and artistry of MGM's inaugural effort. *Author's collection*

several subsidiaries. Cofounder Samuel Goldwyn, who had understandably changed his name from Szmuel Gelbfisz in 1918 to one that better mirrored his company, would himself be spun out of that company in 1922, lending it that adapted name and little else.

The third partner in that name, and the third word in its logo, came from Louis B. Mayer Productions, which had been founded in 1918 by Mayer, who in 1922 hired a dynamic young producer named Irving Thalberg to oversee his productions.

Two years later, in 1924, Loew bought out both Goldwyn and Mayer. Although, as noted above and as then noted in the logo, of the three players in that merger,

Norma Shearer appears fascinated, and frightened, by Lon Chaney; 1920s audiences often felt the same way.
Michael F. Blake

Loew/Metro, Goldwyn, and Mayer, the Mayer company was by far the most insignificant. Goldwyn, for example, already possessed a modern studio in Culver City, as well as contracts with notable stars and production companies like Cosmopolitan Productions. But Mayer only had Mayer himself—and Thalberg, of course—to offer. In light of the later battles Mayer would wage with his superiors, it is ironic that Loew (who would die in 1927) and Mayer's future nemesis, Nicholas Schenck, in particular, were then apparently so eager to bring him into their midst.

Perhaps because of Louis B. Mayer Productions' junior status in the merger, it would be several months before the name "Mayer" would become permanently affixed to the company and its product. Internal records indicate that the "Metro-Goldwyn-Mayer Corporation," which was also organized in 1924 in order to run the Culver City studio, was the first time those three words were corporately so-combined.

Another oddity about *He Who Gets Slapped* (which, remember, is what is actually being discussed here) is that, again according to those internal records, this "first film" was actually made as "production number 192"! It seems, perhaps arbitrarily, that it was the Goldwyn library, at least that part of it going back to 1918, that was officially credited as the earliest predecessor. So, by this tally, *Fields of Honor* from 1918 was "production number 1." Incidentally, *Ben-Hur*, as production 200, was the first title officially released, if not fully produced, under the entire and presumed to be final Metro Goldwyn Mayer banner.

He Who Gets Slapped is, however, the first film to include the familiar Leo the Lion logo, again carried over from Goldwyn, and with the complete name already above his head, although it should be noted that Leo does not roar, even silently. He keeps his mouth closed here.

It should also be noted that like other famous, future MGM movies like *The Wizard of Oz* and *Quo Vadis*, *He Who Gets Slapped* also includes a lion as an important part of the film's plot. Here, and maybe tellingly, two evil characters are eaten by one of the felines during the climax.

That savage lion climax caps off a film that, despite its theatrical origins (Russian playwright author Leonid Andreyev wrote the 1915 play, which Carey Wilson here adapted for the screen), feels like it could have been written specifically as a vehicle for its popular star, Lon Chaney. Chaney plays a scientist who loses his research and his wife, both to the same evil baron (Marc McDermott). Chaney then becomes a circus clown known as "HE" whose act involves getting slapped and humiliated by his audience and his fellow clowns. He, or HE, also falls in love with a bareback rider (Norma Shearer), until his former tormentor again enters his life and sets his eyes on her too.

The circus backdrop; Chaney's unhealthy, and unrequited, infatuation with a much younger woman; the revenge themes; and the somewhat kinky psychology of the film also make these trappings feel familiarly like a collaboration between Chaney and his favorite director, Tod Browning.

But it isn't. *He Who Gets Slapped* was actually directed by the much classier and more respected Victor Sjöström. Sjöström's stylistic touches, which the slapdash Browning wouldn't have bothered with, include Chaney imagining his circus audience all dressed in clown suits.

Sjöström also includes a reoccurring visual of Chaney with a spinning ball, originally represented as a globe, which HE, symbolically, can never quite manage to dominate.

Considering MGM's later reputation as the most wholesome of studios, it's interesting how this first film in the new Mayer regime is so resolutely unhealthy and cynical about the world it inhabits. Early on, a title states that: "There's nothing that makes people laugh so hard as seeing someone else get slapped." Furthermore, Chaney's

Swedish director Victor Sjöström, left, is treated to a look inside the makeup box from which Lon Chaney, the "Man of a Thousand Faces," created his magic. *Michael F. Blake*

circus act, in addition to the aforementioned physical abuse, also involves him literally having his heart (represented by a felt cutout) ripped from his body, after which HE—and it—are symbolically buried, apart from each other, in the center ring (yes, more globe imagery). What's more, the audience watching these humiliations (and, by projection, the audience watching the movie?) is constantly depicted as fat, braying, almost subhuman grotesques.

Later on, Shearer and her actual lover (a charismatic young John Gilbert) go on a picnic, where hungry ants immediately infest their sandwiches and the cuckoo bird that trills to them behind this scene turns out to be a crazy derelict. It also is revealed that Shearer, whom Gilbert loves and Chaney fetishizes, is not herself above being sold off as a bride, and by the baron yet. If this is MGM wholesomeness, then it is no wonder that it was Browning, and not the refined Sjöström, who would become among the biggest directors of the studio's first half decade.

That said, it should be noted that this era was not nearly as wholesome as our great-grandparents later liked to believe. As would again happen after the Second World War, veterans returning from the first often found much that they had fought for in the trenches to be ersatz and shallow when they returned home. Furthermore, many who would have died of their wounds in earlier wars were, due to medical advances, instead repaired and then unleashed upon society, often with facial wounds and amputations that made them outwardly into real-life Lon Chaney horrors.

Even when those wounds were internal, as in *He Who Gets Slapped*, Chaney was able to capture, again and again, the internal horrors of a soldier or, here, a scientist who, shunned by his people or by what he loves, is then justified in using even something as drastic as a caged lion to enact his revenge upon those who slapped him. In 1924 many a marginalized veteran must have, at some level, sympathized with his lonely plight.

He Who Gets Slapped also reflects an odd trend at the time for depictions of middle-aged men repeatedly being humiliated and shamed by richer or younger men or, worse, by richer or younger women. Emil Jannings made something of a career of such roles, but Chaney and subsequent stars like Erich von Stroheim, Charles Laughton, Wallace Beery, Claude Rains, and Lionel Barrymore often played to this same archetype later. The archetype didn't start here, but as it branched off into melodrama and horror, its roots could be traced to here and to other early MGM pictures, like the same year's *Greed* and to Chaney's own *Laugh, Clown, Laugh* (1929).

Both of these conveniently forgotten archetypes were reinforced and perpetuated for the next several seasons, and beyond, when *He Who Gets Slapped* became a major box office and critical success, launching Metro-Goldwyn-Mayer, or whatever they were calling it, into the Hollywood stratosphere from its very first release. Yet within a very few years, when singing and dancing and wholesome Andy Hardy were dominating the studio's slate and filling its coffers, this early, darker post–World War I MGM would largely be forgotten.

As noted, the same thing would happen after the Second World War, when once again veterans would return home feeling alienated and betrayed. But this time, all the studios, especially MGM, covered the postwar darkness over with more musicals and comedies. As a result, that war's damaged souls never had a Lon Chaney to mirror their sad frustrations.

2

Greed (1924)

Greed is nothing less than the original sin of the American studio system. All the evils attributed to Hollywood—suppressing the rights of artists, the defacing of works by those incapable of understanding those works, even the perceived impossibility of true art ever being created by a committee—can thusly, and bluntly, be attributed to this single title.

Erich von Stroheim claimed that he read Frank Norris's novel *McTeague*, published in 1899, in the teens at a hotel in San Francisco, where the gothic, squalid story of a dentist's downward spiral made him determined to eventually bring it to audiences, even though the story had then already just been filmed, as *Life's Whirlpool* in 1916. He got his opportunity in 1922, after being fired by Irving Thalberg, then at Universal, for cost overages on *Merry-Go-Round*, which had finally been finished by another director, Rupert Julian, and released in 1923.

Von Stroheim ultimately ended up at Goldwyn Pictures, which was receptive to the project, especially when the director promised to use existing locations rather than build expensive sets, which had gotten him in trouble before. In hindsight, then, it is rather ironic that studios, especially MGM, which then often kept projects at home to control their costs and their directors, here specifically instead tried to get von Stroheim to utilize real-world locations.

Consequently, as instructed, von Stroheim went off and shot for some four months in San Francisco. The unit then traveled to Death Valley—in midsummer of all times, when midday temperatures averaged over a hundred degrees. Although the sequences

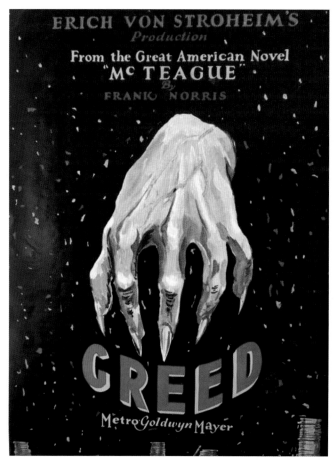

Artist Fred Powis's 1924 vivid *Greed* illustration captures all the horror and despair of the film itself, which was not necessarily a good thing. *John Stephen*

set there, at least as described in the book, were relatively brief, his unit did not return from wandering in the desert for two months!

Von Stroheim's producer at Goldwyn, Abe Lehr, perhaps to his credit, indulged the director during this period, even going so far as to, apparently willingly, increase the budget. Consequently, *Greed* eventually wound up costing almost half a million dollars, although it should be noted that this was not an unrealistic amount for a big-budget film, and certainly not for a von Stroheim film. *Foolish Wives*, which the maestro had shot on a Universal backlot in 1922, had ultimately cost more than twice that.

On January 12, 1924, von Stroheim offered up what was reportedly a nine-hour cut of his film. In addition to studio executives, there were a dozen others in the screening room for the unveiling. At least three of those who were there—writers Harry Carr and Idwal Jones and director Rex Ingram—all agreed for the rest of their lives that it was the greatest movie they had ever seen.

Unfortunately, during postproduction, in April 1924 the Goldwyn company merged with Loews/Metro Pictures, which subsequently made von Stroheim's new bosses the formidable Louie B. Mayer and von Stroheim's old nemesis, Irving Thalberg. Metro and Goldwyn and Mayer then took a reportedly five-hour, fifteen-minute cut of *Greed* and proceeded to eventually carve it into a little more than two hours. Thalberg was later quoted in the *Los Angeles Times* as saying that the cuts "made the picture stronger."[1]

Mayer was more direct. He hated the squalid nature of the film, and reportedly physically assaulted von Stroheim after the director, in a surely memorable confrontation in Mayer's office, referred to all women as whores, including his own mother—to whom, incidentally, von Stroheim ultimately dedicated *Greed*.

The MGM-sized *Greed* opened in New York on December 4, 1924. Reviews were mixed, but bordering slightly toward the negative. The box office was disastrous, although the film's failure did not immediately affect the studio or even its director, who immediately rebounded with a success: *The Merry Widow* (1925); yes, for MGM. After that, however, and not at all surprisingly, von Stroheim migrated to Paramount, followed by RKO, then Fox, usually only for a single film. But his continuing on-set excesses, cost overruns, and battles with studio brass always eventually got him into familiar trouble. In 1935 von Stroheim returned to MGM, not as a director but as a lowly staff writer, a position he would hold for almost two years. After that there would be only acting roles, in which he often played overtly Teutonic parodies of himself, and eventual martyrdom.

That martyrdom might well have been what Erich von Stroheim had always wanted. Cinematographer Karl Brown once speculated to historian Kevin Brownlow about von Stroheim that perhaps

somewhere in his early life he was visited by such very great humiliation, such deep inward psychic wounds, that there came in him an insane desire to use his genius as a weapon. And that he would use the beauty of his work as bait, to make them put out thousands, then hundreds of thousands, then millions and then more millions until he had a beautiful, magnificent monstrosity that is worthless except as a curiosity piece and he had his vengeance, he had proved his genius and he had his revenge all at one fell swoop.[2]

Those who would blame the studio system for destroying an artist, or for compromising an artist's vision, might do well to remember Brown's words.

What is one to make then of the scar-tissued thing that is *Greed* today? Tragically, the original footage was lost—or destroyed—so the existing version is the only one available. If MGM is guilty of destroying the film, then its greater sin is in not keeping those hours of excised scenes for later evaluation. Long-held rumors that MGM kept an uncut version in their vaults, sometimes reported as being labeled "McTeague," continue to surface occasionally.

Producer/actor John Houseman was once reported to have screened an uncut, or nearly uncut, version of the film on the lot, although he was maddeningly short on details about when this happened and what he saw. Von Stroheim's son Joseph once claimed that while he was in the Army during World War II, he saw a version of the film that took two nights to screen fully. And his father once said, perhaps jokingly, that Benito Mussolini had his own complete print as well.

In 1999 the Turner company funded a restoration, of sorts, of *Greed*. Although no new footage was available, there were extant production notes and publicity photos involving the lost sequences. As had been done for missing scenes in *Lost Horizon* (1937) and *A Star Is Born* (1954), these stills were used to bridge gaps in the narrative. Unlike the aforementioned films, however, where the cut sequences involved but a few minutes of screen time, restoring the missing *Greed* sequences potentially involved visually representing up to seven hours of missing material!

Fortunately, the lead film preservationist on the project, Rick Schmidlin, had access to Herman G. Weinberg's earlier and well-researched book on the subject; he was also able to make extensive use of von Stroheim's still-surviving notes. Schmidlin also had Norris's original novel, which, aside from some minor updating, the director had followed slavishly.

This "restored" *Greed*, at approximately four hours long, is fascinating. It's hard not to feel admiration for Schmidlin's resourcefulness in finding ways to visualize hours of missing scenes. In 2002 Schmidlin would face an arguably even greater challenge with MGM's *London After Midnight* (1927), for which there is *no* surviving footage.

The restoration also proves that the studio was correct in doing what it did.

Yes, it may seem heresy to say that, but if we are to trust Schmidlin's reconstruction, the long version—the one supposedly best representing von Stroheim's vision—is, as Thalberg once alluded, and as Brown overtly stated, somewhat redundant.

For example, there are subplots in the reconstruction involving two sets of McTeague's neighbors. One, like he, is destroyed by greed; the other, a timid elderly

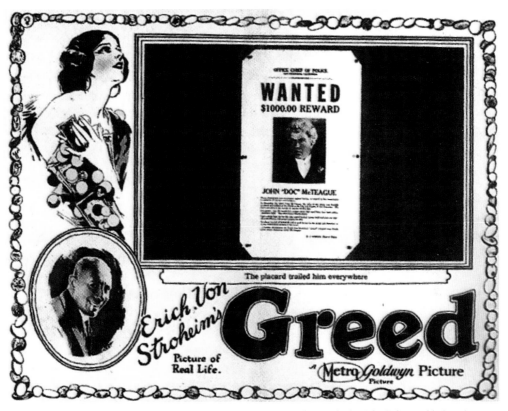

This *Greed* lobby card is indicative of the new company's indecision as to how to deal with both this troubled production and their own name, which here omits Louis B. Mayer. *Author's collection*

couple, manages to rise above these instincts. In a book by Charles Dickens, Theodore Dreiser, or Frank Norris, this secondary material would be welcome, even necessary, to make the point that greed corrupts only those susceptible to that corruption. But on film, having another couple descend into madness and murder over their lust for gold before McTeague and his wife do so distracts from, and then renders less effective, McTeague's own downfall into hell. At least it does in a movie, where the audience's patience is limited by their endurance. Today such long-form, novelistic filmed entertainment is possible, but eighty years before at-home binge watching would become a reality, von Stroheim's mad, brilliant conceit could only be presented in a way digestible, and endurable, to audiences. Thalberg and Mayer, whatever their surely complicated personal feelings toward the director, only did what then had to be done.

Whatever version of *Greed* one is lucky enough to see, it's an overwhelming cinematic experience. And *Greed* truly is a *cinematic* experience. Von Stroheim's mastery of the medium is apparent in every shot. For example, the wedding between McTeague (Gibson Gowland) and his bride, Trina (ZaSu Pitts), is presented by the director as a grotesque farce of matrimony—the photographer is a hunchback, and the children scurrying about their feet are presented as vulturelike harpies. The adult guests get off no better, being framed and shot as piglike and feral. Outside, a funeral procession passes by, further foreshadowing the unhappy union.

McTeague buys a yellow canary early in the story; this is barely mentioned in the book, but von Stroheim seizes upon and develops it throughout the narrative. He gives the bird a female companion on his wedding night—a ham-fisted and much unappreciated gift for Trina. And he proceeds to stubbornly carry this hapless animal, which is both yellow (gold!) and imprisoned, with him even into the hell of Death Valley. At the climax, McTeague releases the canary, but even this good-seeming impulse is immediately mocked when the bird flutters for a few feet and then drops dead on the desert floor. Not a good omen.

The cast gives von Stroheim exactly what he wants. Pitts and Jean Hersholt, who plays the rival for Trina's affection, both had long careers (Hersholt even has an Academy Award named for him), but they were never better than here, albeit in atypical roles. Alternately, Gowland's very unfamiliarity (Can anyone name another film he was in?) works to his advantage. McTeague comes across initially as an empty vessel, which the film, rather than any previous or future associations, has to fill up for us. Von Stroheim does this immediately by having his "hero" toss a fellow miner off of a trestle in the opening scene. It also must be said that both Gowland and Pitts certainly have interesting hair. He looks like a grumpy, dangerous Harpo Marx. Her tied-down, pulled-back Gibson-girl locks get progressively more manic and unhinged as she does.

For such a well-directed film, there are a lot of disconcertingly unmatched shots and misdirected actor's eyelines, however. For example, in the climax, when Gowland and Hersholt are finally at each other's throats, in the long shots McTeague is seen striking his rival in the face. Yet in the intercut close-ups, we see only that unconscious, bloody face; McTeague's fists are nowhere to be seen. At least until the next wide shot, and this sort of missed continuity happens all the time in *Greed*. These glitches are rather inexplicable, and relatively unprecedented for a studio-made late–silent era picture. Before sound forced a reinvention of all the rules of cinema, the late 1920s was a period in which cinematic technique was, arguably, more advanced than it ever would be again.

Chester Conklin, Jean Hersholt, William Barlow, Joan Standing, Austen Jewell, twins Oscar and Otto Gottell, and some of director Erich von Stroheim's other grotesques gather for the nuptials of Gibson Gowland and ZaSu Pitts (center). The honeymoon would soon be over. *Photofest*

Maybe these sloppy-seeming mismatched edits can be blamed on the number of cuts, and the number of people making those cuts, *Greed* has been forced to endure over its much-truncated life. Or maybe von Stroheim is toying with his audience; maybe the master is trying to create a sense of unresolved tension by not cutting when and how the rules tell him he is supposed to do so.

Could it be that he is evoking a tension, a sense of unresolved unease amid his audience by intentionally perverting the very language of the movies? Could it be that von Stroheim always knew that MGM—that Mayer, that Thalberg—*would* take his film away from him? Maybe he knew; maybe he even secretly reveled in the fact that they could cut *Greed*, but they could never "fix" it.

3

The Big Parade (1925)

By all accounts, 1925 was the greatest year for silent cinema. The language of silent film had evolved and been refined to the extent that any emotion or plot point, however subtle, could be communicated by a skilled director to his audience. So assured and organic was the form in 1925 that Lillian Gish could, years later of course, be often quoted as saying that silent film should have evolved out of talkies, instead of the other way around. Certainly, one of the highlights of 1925 and of silent cinema, both artistically and, to MGM's benefit, financially, is *The Big Parade*.

The film's critical reputation today, however, unlike some of its more overtly personal or impressionistic contemporaries, is somewhat in eclipse. If mentioned at all in serious studies of cinema, *The Big Parade* is usually damned with the faint praise that it "still holds up" or, even worse, "is good for its time." Although modern audiences (as opposed to critics and scholars), when given the opportunity to see the film in a theater with a live orchestral score, still respond most enthusiastically to its action and sentiment.

The Big Parade's world war setting (the Great War, of course, had not yet been christened World War I) was somewhat unique in 1925. Some of *The Four Horsemen of the Apocalypse* (1921) had a wartime setting, and that film had been distributed, pre-merger, by Metro Pictures (MGM would rerelease that film in 1924). But except for comedies, romances, or aviation epics, where the ground conflict was largely avoided, the war had been ignored by studios for several years—much as post-Vietnam, those same studios would shy away from dramatizing *that* war, at least until a suitable, and safe, number of years had passed and the wounds inflicted had started to scab over.

The *Big Parade* would tell its story of men going to war by showing us three of those men, all from different backgrounds. Jim (John Gilbert) is a member of the idle rich, Slim (Karl Dane) is a construction worker, and Bull (Tom O'Brien) is a bartender. (Decades later, *The Best Years of Our Lives* would invert this paradigm by depicting a similar cross section, only now returning *from* the conflict; this time, World War II.) In France, Jim, although engaged to his childhood sweetheart back home, still falls into a bittersweet affair with a local girl, Melisande (Renée Adorée). Both Bull and Slim are killed in battle. Jim loses a leg but returns postwar to France, and to Melisande.

The first half of the film's 151-minute running time is taken up with establishing the characters, both stateside and while waiting to be deployed, in a French village. These scenes, many of which involve low comedy, are alternately tiresome and charming, and they probably always were, depending on one's tolerance for such material. But this same material does at least force the viewer to invest in the characters.

Artist William Galbraith Crawford's 1925 *Big Parade* insert poster well captures the romance if not the tragedy inherent in the film itself. *Author's collection*

When the bugle finally sounds and those characters receive their marching orders, an intertitle informs us that this march, depicted by hundreds of vehicles driving into infinity on an endless road with biplanes buzzing overhead, is actually the "big parade" of the title, as is the similar row of ambulances and wounded troops later depicted falling back at the end of the battle.

That battle, apparently based on the actual 1918 Battle of Belleau Wood, is vividly depicted by the troops marching through a forest consisting of hundreds of narrow trees. As the bullets start to rain down upon the regiment and the characters as well as the audience see men dropping in the background, it is here that the strengths of director King Vidor, and of silent film in general, are most evident. Vidor apparently used a metronome to time the walk on the set. If the film had had a soundtrack, he would have been forced to let the audience hear a bullet corresponding to each casualty. Instead, in surreal silence, the men just fall away, like pawns being removed from a chessboard. Sometimes, and almost as effectively, the carnage is instead devastatingly depicted by innocent-looking little puffs of smoke, again with no sound effects. Fortunately, in existing prints, which include a fine orchestral score by Carl Davis, no attempt is made to layer in synchronized sound effects after the fact, which would have blunted the battle's surreal silent horror.

The subsequent trench warfare sequences are effectively directed as well, although these scenes have a less shattering impact overall, perhaps, and this is no fault of either Vidor or *The Big Parade*; because similar sequences have appeared in many similar movies since, from *All Quiet on the Western Front* (1930) to *1917* (2019), all of which owe a debt of gratitude to what was presented here first, or nearly first. It isn't that there is little to say about these scenes, and about this type of scene; it's just that it has been said before as wars, actual and cinematic, have continued to be waged.

In 1925, however, none of this had yet been depicted on-screen. So for many veterans who had experienced the war, and for their families, this was the first time their experiences had been dramatized in a reasonably realistic, if romanticized, manner. The screenplay for *The Big Parade* was primarily by Laurence Stallings, a World War I veteran who, like Jim, had lost a leg in battle. Stallings' 1924 play about the war— *What Price Glory?*—would be filmed (for the first time) in 1926 in the wake of *The Big Parade*'s success. So obviously there was a sudden need for stories about the Great War during this time, and for the catharsis these stories could exercise for the millions of people who had survived it.

For most of those involved, however, *The Big Parade* did not bring about long-lasting success. John Gilbert had appeared the year before in *His Hour*, also from MGM and also directed by King Vidor. The success of that earlier film, followed by the total triumph of *The Big Parade*, made Gilbert one of the biggest stars in the world. His spectacular fall from grace with the advent of sound, presumably because his voice did not reflect his on-screen personality, is pretty much all people remember of John

Gilbert today. That is a shame because, well, he deserved better. His performance here is dead-on, and happily unencumbered by phony theatrics or bravado.

Less well known today, although equally tragic, is the fate of two of John Gilbert's costars. Renée Adorée died of tuberculosis in 1933, three years before Gilbert. Karl Dane, who played Slim, died the following year, in 1934. A story that the then-impoverished Dane had been reduced to operating a hot dog stand outside the MGM gates in order to make a living is apparently untrue.

On the other side of the studio ledger, *The Big Parade*'s long-term beneficiaries would include its director. Although King Vidor later admitted that he had unwisely sold his percentage of the picture back to MGM, that picture's success still led to a very long and prestigious Hollywood career. That career would continue for so long that *Guinness World Records* once certified Vidor as having the longest-lasting career as a film director in history—some sixty-seven years in all. King Vidor died in 1982.

But the biggest beneficiary of *The Big Parade* was its studio. In 1925, MGM, in only its second year of operation, was anointed as the most prestigious and successful film studio in the world. That year *The Big Parade* and *Ben-Hur* together brought a windfall of prestige and profits to the company, and certainly silenced any naysayers who had doubted that the new conglomerate with the unwieldy, often-hyphenated name could long survive.

The Big Parade's final budget-to-return ratio, especially when laid side to side with the elephantine *Ben-Hur*'s, was

Studio copywriters in 1925 struggled to describe *The Big Parade* in a way that would attract action-craving male audiences as well as their wives and girlfriends. They needn't have worried. *John Stephen*

The Big Parade turned out to be the biggest hit of the entire silent era. It was also the first movie to play at the Loews Astor Theater on Broadway, where it would run for almost two years. *Photofest*

particularly telling. Produced for less than $250,000, *The Big Parade* ultimately marched back into the studio coffers something between $15 million and $22 million dollars. (Actual numbers seem to vary.) Whatever the final number, it was certainly very impressive.

When silent films are discussed today, *The Big Parade* is consistently referred to as being the single most successful silent film ever made during that era, at least financially. It's probably even true.

Mayer hated the film.

4

Putting Pants on Philip (1927)

Stan Laurel and Oliver Hardy first appeared together in *The Lucky Dog* (1921). They next shared billing, if no scenes, in *45 Minutes from Hollywood* (1926). *Duck Soup* (1927) also featured them both, although it is unclear if the two were intentionally paired here as a team or not. So it was left to *Putting Pants on Philip*, later that same year, to prove how magical the duo really could be.

In addition to being the first true Laurel & Hardy picture, this was also the first of their films to be released by Metro Goldwyn Mayer. It should be noted though, that Laurel & Hardy were not really MGM stars, although they occasionally appeared in MGM movies.

The duo actually was under contract to Hal Roach, an independent producer who made a few dramatic films but whose product, overwhelmingly so, was mostly comedies. In addition to Laurel & Hardy, Roach also made vehicles for Harold Lloyd, Will Rogers, Charley Chase, Harry Langdon, and "Our Gang" during this period and beyond.

Hal Roach's studio was in Culver City, just a couple blocks from his distributer-neighbor, MGM. But unlike the regimented factory that was MGM, the Roach lot—sometimes aptly nicknamed the lot of fun—was spontaneous and chaotic, and the films produced there had a sort of archaic improvised feeling about them that worked well for most of the comedians who worked there. Many of those comedians had come out of vaudeville or burlesque, and already innately knew what was funny and how to spontaneously create comedy out of any situation Roach's gag writers could devise.

Stan Laurel and Oliver Hardy, the most beloved comedy team of all time, as their fans remember them in *Thicker than Water* (1935)... *Stan Taffel*

Another factor besides geography separated Hal Roach's studio from his neighbors. Unlike at the backlot-bound MGM, Roach liked to shoot on the streets, sometimes with his comics making up a scenario as they filmed on those streets, sometimes within sight of MGM's tall white and regimented walls.

MGM had its own comedians of course, but it must be said that, because of the airless, tidy nature of the MGM method, most of those comedians ultimately found it rather difficult to be funny inside those white walls. Buster Keaton, the Marx Brothers, and (later) Our Gang all found the quality of their product dropping, even as the budgets of their films went up, once they consented to work at, and for, MGM.

Fortunately, Laurel & Hardy, then protected by Hal Roach, were pretty much left alone to make pretty much whatever they wanted.

... and enacting earlier, and quite different comic stylings as Philip and Mumblethunder, seen here with Harvey Clark in *Putting Pants on Philip* (1927). *Stan Taffel*

They made magic. There was never a partnership on-screen quite like these two. It has long been said—by people who don't understand—that what made Stan and Ollie unique was that they were both funny, unlike other comedy teams, which consisted of a comic and a straight man.

This is untrue. Yes, on stage the straight man provided a vital function. Usually the only person the comic interacted with, the straight man was a surrogate of sorts for the audience. Therefore, a good straight man would often be better billed and better paid than the comic.

But that's on the stage; in the movies, anyone the comic encounters is, in effect, the straight man. So that role, so important on stage, eventually became a sidelined character on-screen. For example, by all accounts Dean Martin was a brilliant straight man, but he had little to do, at least in his on-screen teamings with Jerry Lewis.

But unlike Martin & Lewis, and unlike Abbott & Costello and Burns & Allen, the only other major movie comedy teams equipped with an internal straight man, Laurel & Hardy did not originate on the stage. Therefore, they did not need a straight man. They were a comedy *team* in the truest sense because they were both comics. And unlike many other comedy teams, never once did one member try to distract from or steal laughs from the other. Theirs was a very caring and democratic partnership. And very unique and very unlike other (straight man–free) comedy teams, where one member tends to get more laughs than the other(s). By contrast, has anyone ever said they prefer Laurel over Hardy? Hardy over Laurel?

Contrary to their equal on-screen partnership, however, it was Stan Laurel who almost exclusively designed the gags, (re)wrote their material, edited their films, and fought with Roach and their directors for the integrity of their characters and their films. All Oliver Hardy had to do was simply show up and trust Stan to take care of him. And Stan always did.

At twenty minutes long, *Putting Pants on Philip* (1927), as their "official" first film, surprises in that it is very much a rough prototype of what would come later. One rather expects that "Laurel & Hardy" would arrive first on-screen, already fully formed, pulling up to the curb in a Model T or getting off a train together while twiddling their ties.

Not so. The first surprise is that here these partners are not really partners. Their characters don't even know each other at the beginning of the film! They don't use their real names either. Instead, Ollie plays someone named J. Piedmont Mumblethunder. As the name implies, he is a member of polite society, just the sort of snob who would want nothing to do with Hardy's later "Ollie" character. Hardy's pompous fussiness and physical prowess do earn him a few laughs here, but in this film, Oliver Hardy is a straight man.

Stan is Phillip, who, as the story begins, is just getting off the boat from Scotland. Stan's kilt horrifies the stuffy Hardy. His getup also inexplicably shocks the rest of the city, with every person on the street gawking and staring at the sight of a man in a skirt. Were Americans really so provincial in 1927 that they had never heard of Scotsmen wearing kilts? Maybe they were.

What's more, this Stan Laurel—quite unlike his later, very childlike "Stan" character—is such an ardent womanizer that he literally kicks up his heels and dashes off in pursuit of every attractive female he sees on the street. This one-time-only char-

Stan Laurel models the latest in Scottish high fashion for *Putting Pants on Philip*. *Stan Taffel*

acteristic has led some fans to speculate that here Stan Laurel was stealing his material from Harpo Marx! Probably not. Laurel admired other comics (who uniformly admired him back), but it's improbable that he would ever have "borrowed" another comedian's schtick outright, especially since the Marx Brothers would not make their (screen) debut for two more years. *Putting Pants on Philip* also predates that iconic scene in which Marilyn Monroe's skirt flies up on a subway grate in *The Seven Year Itch*. Although it must be said that the effect is not as memorable when it happens to Stan Laurel. And certainly, nobody has ever claimed Billy Wilder stole that.

Like most Roach films, this one wiles away its running time, trying to decide on a plot. A subtitle after the credits claims that Philip is in America to look for a half dollar his uncle has lost there. Presumably this is some sort of "funny" reference to Scotsmen's perceived frugality, but no matter—this situation is never mentioned again. Instead, the rest of the story finds Ollie repeatedly exasperated by his future partner's womanizing, kilt-wearing ways, eventually justifying the short's title by trying, unsuccessfully and disastrously, to get Philip into his first pair of pants.

As mentioned earlier, many Roach comedies were shot outside on the streets, specifically in Culver City. It is amusing today to spot the historic, and still standing, Culver Hotel in that neighborhood, for example. Look carefully, a "Harry H. Culver & Company" plaque, named for the actual founder of the city, is also visible on-screen. Later, as Mumblethunder runs after Philip, a local dog, improvisationally and amusingly, chases him across that street. That nice bit of spontaneity wouldn't have happened on a backlot. It also should be noted that future director George Stevens, who would later indulge in hundreds of takes to achieve airless perfection on his serious Hollywood epics, was the cinematographer here—as he would be on many Roach comedies. He certainly would never have allowed this bit of canine improvisation later in his career.

MGM would continue to distribute those Roach comedies, which eventually included feature films as well as short subjects, until 1938. During World War II, while Hal Roach was serving in the US Army Signal Corps, his entire studio was turned over to the production of government training and propaganda films. After the war, Roach returned to film and, later, to television production. His company was eventually dissolved, and his little studio, the lot of fun, was demolished in 1961. Roach himself would live until 1992, passing away in November of that year at the age of one hundred.

Stan Laurel and Oliver Hardy, as Laurel & Hardy rather than Philip & Mumblethunder, went on to become the most famous, and most beloved, of all comedy teams in history. Their partnership only ended with Hardy's passing away in 1957, after which Laurel promptly retired. For the rest of his life, Stan refused all offers to appear on camera without Ollie by his side.

They were, hopefully, reunited in 1965.

5

White Shadows in the South Seas (1928)

Irving Thalberg, whose health had always been precarious, reportedly read Frederick O'Brien's 1919 book, *White Shadows in the South Seas*, during one of his many convalescent periods away from the studio. Despite a tenacious absence of any perceivable plot, the book's romantic Marquesas Islands setting had made it a bestseller and, in Thalberg's opinion, would make it ideal movie fodder as well.

Once the rights to the property had been secured, the director Thalberg chose for the project was Robert Flaherty, the famed documentarian who had just released *Moana* (1926), which had much benefited from similar South Seas settings. Flaherty's hiring was widely opposed on the lot, especially by the film's young "supervisor," future mogul David O. Selznick (Hunt Stromberg would be the film's official producer). Selznick eventually lost this battle, but he did score a major, and expensive, victory in somehow convincing Thalberg and Mayer to shoot the film on location.

That location was to be Tahiti, which, especially in the 1920s, and especially for MGM, was an astonishingly faraway place in which to make a movie. *Moana* had been filmed in Samoa, but unlike Flaherty's earlier film, *White Shadows* was not to be a documentary but a traditional, narrative film with actors and a script. All practicalities aside, the eventual go-ahead from the front office for such a difficult location trip turned out to be a major coup for the ambitious Selznick.

It's hard to reconstruct what exactly happened on that location and when, but ultimately, out there under the South Seas sun, Flaherty was replaced by the very dependable in-house director W. S. "Woody" Van Dyke, who had originally been

The kaleidoscopic ad art for *White Shadows in the South Seas* (1928) very well emphasized the colorful, exotic nature of the film itself. *Author's collection*

sent to the islands on behalf of the studio to "assist" in the production. Van Dyke, whom Selznick made sure everyone realized had been his original choice to begin with, ultimately returned to Culver City with some of the most stunning footage anyone had ever seen. He would ultimately be the only credited director on the picture, although some of this remarkable footage was certainly courtesy of the then-banished Robert Flaherty.

Van Dyke returned to the studio in mid-1928. Meanwhile, Warner Bros.' *The Jazz Singer* had opened in October 1927, and its singing (and to a lesser extent, talking) sequences had made the film a sensation. MGM, however, secure as the biggest studio in the world, expressed no immediate need to jump on the talking picture bandwagon, believing that any product with their name on it would continue to do well, even without the perceived gimmick of sound. This complacency was borne out by the studio's profits, which were $6,737,205 in 1927 and would actually rise to $8,568,162 in 1928. Therefore, while other smaller, hungrier studios were soundproofing their stages and hiring sound engineers, MGM continued to quietly maintain their pre–*Jazz Singer* course.

By the time Van Dyke got back to California with his many cans of South Seas exotica, however, the company had reluctantly decided to dip their toes into the sound revolution. *White Seas*, it was decided, would be a good experimental sound project because it contained little dialogue, although rerecording that dialogue months after it had first been spoken four thousand miles away was determined to be an impossibility. No matter, as the cast had no marquee stars whom audiences would be interested in hearing the voices of anyway. Therefore, sound effects and music would be all that would be required to make *White Shadows* into a "talkie."

To do this, Douglas Shearer, the brother of Thalberg's new wife, actress Norma Shearer, was quickly appointed as the head of the studio's new Sound Department.

Monte Blue goes native for *White Shadows in the South Seas,* although, at least here, he doesn't seem to be enjoying it very much. *Author's collection*

Unfortunately, as of yet there was not even a skeleton operation there to be in charge of. Shearer had no facilities, no equipment, and no staff. Undaunted, he personally took the completed film via train to the Victor (Victrola) Talking Machine Company in Camden, New Jersey, which was in the process of being acquired by RCA, and where music and sound effects were quickly, and rather crudely, grafted onto those beautiful visuals.

White Shadows in the South Seas would be the first MGM film with a soundtrack, but *Alias Jimmy Valentine,* released a few days later in November 1928, would become the first MGM film in which an actor's dialogue was recorded while that actor actually spoke it. But Shearer was still so far behind his competitors that he was rather humiliatingly forced to lease a newly completed soundstage from Paramount for those actors to speak that dialogue. After that, it was deemed that all MGM movies would need to speak. Ultimately, the last all-silent MGM picture would be *The Kiss,* completed in September and released in November 1929. That film starred Greta Garbo, who, Garbo-like, would not deign to speak on-screen until February 1930, with the successful release of *Anna Christie.*

As a talkie, *White Shadows in the South Seas* is an abject failure. It has been oft noted that there is only one word of spoken dialogue in the whole film, "Hello," which is so badly recorded that although the line is supposed to be screamed by an actor (whose back is to the camera, thus avoiding synchronization problems), it is almost inaudible. Perhaps to make up for this, the word is then repeated two more times. Actually, another line, "Stay away," can also be heard on the soundtrack, although it too is so muffled that few have ever noticed it's there.

All of this less-than-abundant dialogue is supposedly delivered by the film's star, Monte Blue. Blue plays an alcoholic doctor, Matthew Lloyd, adrift in the South Seas. Disgusted at the exploitation of Polynesian peoples by his fellow "white shadows," a phrase taken from the book's colorful description of the European encroachment in the islands, he is eventually shipwrecked amid an unspoiled people who have had no contact with Westerners. Unfortunately, those same Westerners eventually arrive there as well, and Lloyd is killed trying to keep them away. The movie ends rather bitterly by showing how that island and its native culture is overrun and corrupted by the arrival of the West.

Lloyd is an intriguingly complex character. Very much cut from the W. Somerset Maugham mold, he is both a product and a victim of colonialism. Repulsed by his countrymen's exploitation of native peoples as pearl divers, he later falls victim to those same evils himself. Ultimately, he brings the white shadow into his own island paradise, destroying both it and himself.

Monte Blue was in his early forties when he made this film, but as befitting his character, he is something of a physical ruin, sweaty and out of shape, which probably blunted the appeal of the movie for some audiences, although that same antihero vibe makes the film feel surprisingly modern today. Selznick, as he probably told everybody who would listen, seemingly realized, even at the time, this potential commercial flaw in the material. Consequently, a 1929 semi-follow-up, *The Pagan*, also shot on location by Van Dyke, offered a buff and youthful Ramon Novarro in the lead. In 1932 Selznick would make a similar tale, *Bird of Paradise*, for RKO. Here the male lead is again played by a younger and more athletic actor, Joel McCrea. *Bird of Paradise* would also shoot (briefly) on location, but this time in the more accessible islands of Hawaii.

As in its characterization of its hero, *White Shadows in the South Seas* is also refreshingly forward-looking in its depiction of the Polynesian people. The script constantly reinforces the theme that in every respect, their "primitive" culture is actually superior to that of the Europeans. The islanders Lloyd discovers are depicted as being harmonious with nature, for example. Yet as soon as Westerners arrive on that island, those supposedly more-enlightened individuals shoot him, one of their own, causing the

White Shadows in the South Seas' official credits and advertising could find no room for Robert Flaherty, its original director. *Author's collection*

natives, who have never heard gunfire before, to flee—and leading Lloyd's completely nonplussed murderer only to remark that he should have used a knife instead! One can only wish that more films of that era depicting Native Americans and African Americans had been so progressive.

Amusingly, the film's only prejudices are focused not against the islanders at all but against . . . octopuses. We now know these creatures to be gentle and intelligent, but here they are described in a subtitle as being "slimy . . . deadly . . . devils of the deep." What's more, they are often depicted on-screen by unconvincing puppets.

As noted, the cinematography, by Clyde De Vinna, is outstanding. De Vinna was already an old hand at photographing nature, be it on location or manufactured on the backlot, and ultimately his work here would win him a well-deserved Academy Award. Sadly, Robert Flaherty's participation, whatever that participation involved, has led to many of the film's more beautiful pictorial effects being credited to him rather than to the cinematographer.

White Shadows also contains some very early, and very fine, examples of on-location underwater cinematography, which was in its infancy. Such scenes were usually faked by shooting in a studio through a glass plate or filming on dry land, with the fish and the divers often floating unconvincingly on wires. Here we are treated to real water in a real ocean and with real fish—except for that octopus.

White Shadows in the South Seas has been somewhat forgotten among other, noisier torchbearers of the sound revolution, although Leo the Lion's first audible roar alone anoints it as a seminal film in the MGM canon, as does that very unusual and mysterious location trip to the long-ago South Seas. And yes, Robert Flaherty's quick, and again mysterious, dismissal still stands as a marker of sorts, for those looking for such markers, as to the studio's apparently already-in-place distrust of "creative" or "artistic" filmmakers and preference for efficient directors like Van Dyke and producers like David O. Selznick.

As a rebuttal to this oft-expressed opinion, though, it should be noted that Selznick, like Flaherty before him, ultimately ended up losing his job because of this film.

Selznick's firing, it was said, was owed to his assertions, either vocalized or typed up in long memos to anyone on the lot who would listen, regarding that studio's perceived mismanagement of *White Shadows in the South Seas*. So maybe being a company man at Metro wasn't always the best tack to take after all.

Or maybe it was. In 1933 Selznick would return to MGM. This time in triumph—and this time married to Mayer's daughter.

Robert Flaherty, unlike the ambitious Selznick, was not so politically savvy. Consequently, his career never recovered. The distinguished father of the documentary would never work for a Hollywood studio again. Instead, he would finish his career toiling on low-budget promotional films for companies like Standard Oil.

6

The Broadway Melody (1929)

Frank Sinatra opens the documentary film *That's Entertainment!* (1974) with a scratchy black-and-white song and dance routine from MGM's first musical, *The Broadway Melody*, featuring, as Sinatra puts it, "Charles King and a line of slightly overweight chorus girls." The number, badly framed and shot, with those girls loudly out of step—somersaulting, tapping, and hopping around on a stage while inexplicably holding one leg in the air—is meant to illustrate how crude early musicals were. It succeeds.

It succeeds, although Sinatra, or his writers, must not have seen the rest of the movie, or must have chosen to ignore the context of that number within the rest of the movie. In the plot of *Broadway Melody*—and, unlike some other early musicals, this picture is indeed in possession of a plot—this dance routine is *not supposed* to be good. It seems that a specialty number featuring our two leading ladies, Bessie Love and Anita Page, has just been removed from the center of the routine, therefore making it *intentionally* awkward. Also, the number is presented in the film as a rough dress rehearsal, which is criticized *in the film* as being "too slow."

But Frank Sinatra does not tell us any of this. In fact, *That's Entertainment!* intentionally lies to us by intercutting this maligned number with footage of a Broadway marquee and an applauding audience—which they have, in fact, stolen from another part of the film in order to convince us that this ham-fisted number represents a polished opening night.

This all seems rather dishonest, doesn't it?

Make no mistake, *The Broadway Melody* can be primitive. It shares many of the faults of other early talkies; namely, limited camera movement, minimal editing within

As its credits illustrate, MGM's first musical, *The Broadway Melody* (1929), would feature more notable musical talent working behind the scenes than in front of them. *Photofest* scenes, and sequences where people describe things that are happening off screen, which we in the audience never get to see.

But let's cut this film a bit of slack. In addition to being MGM's first musical, *The Broadway Melody* was also the studio's first all-talking film (the earlier *Alias Jimmy Valentine* had silent sequences), although there are still a few wholly redundant titles scattered amid the dialogue. Besides, the innovations paid off, as the result netted the studio its first Best Picture Oscar win—the first sound film ever awarded that honor. Finally, and not incidentally, *The Broadway Melody* was the top-grossing film world-wide of 1929.

The film also tries to be innovative, even beyond the existence, and limitations, of its soundtrack. Director Harry Beaumont's filmography is long, and largely undistinguished, but he always got the job done, even when, as here, an entirely new means of storytelling had to be invented. For example, the practice of playing prerecorded music through speakers on the set for the actors to perform to was first utilized here. MGM rewarded Beaumont for his reliability and patience by keeping him employed, at least intermittently, until his retirement in 1948.

The film opens with impressive aerial shots of Manhattan (another first?), which anticipate *West Side Story*'s similar opening by more than thirty years, but then settles into its "talented kids trying to take on the Great White Way" plot, which of course was not such a screen cliché then as it would become. Al Jolson in Warner Bros.' recent smashes, *The Jazz Singer* (1927) and *The Singing Fool* (1928), had already used the same plot, twice. But here, in yet another, and in a protofeminist screen first, those kids are women.

Unfortunately, a potentially interesting sublot of these two, who are sisters, uniting against predatory male producers is not really explored here as it would be in later musicals because our two leads have a protector, the aforementioned Charles King. King plays Eddie Kearns, a song and dance man who pretends to love one sister while secretly carrying a torch for the other, all the while chivalrously protecting them both. It's hard not to wonder if the Kearns character was based on composer Jerome Kern, who was one of the towering figures of the New York stage at the time of the film's production, and whose life MGM would later dramatize as *Till the Clouds Roll By* (1946).

Other characters to be found in *The Broadway Melody* include producer Francis Zanfield (played by Eddie Kane), who probably was based on producer Florenz Ziegfeld, whose life and work MGM would mine well in future years as well. Then there is Jacques Warriner (Kenneth Thompson), a slimy investor. Warriner's name, especially considering how it is pronounced in the movie, sounds suspiciously like that of rival studio mogul Jack Warner, although it might also be meant to evoke that of

Note both the false stage walls behind the Viking chorus being photographed for *The Broadway Melody* and the real stage walls, hopefully not being photographed, behind them. *Photofest*

millionaire John Hay "Jock" Whitney, who at the time was a very prominent backer for Broadway shows and would later help David O. Selznick start his own studio.

Two other names that show up on-screen are that of the film's composer and lyricist, Nacio Herb Brown and Arthur Freed, respectively, who, if you look carefully, are credited by name for the songs from the fictional show in an opening-night program. Both Brown and Freed, presumably playing themselves, also briefly appear on-screen. The two of them, like so many others here, would have a much bigger part to play in the studio's future.

No one noticed it at the time, of course, but *The Broadway Melody* was also the first of what would later be called "pre-code" Hollywood films, referring to the era after sound and before July 1934 when the studios flirted with more risqué material than would be allowed for decades after due to strict enforcement of the Motion Pictures Production Code.

The Broadway Melody's pre-code flag is hoisted early and often. There is risqué dialogue to burn here. The two sisters seem to be even more invested in changing

The notorious title number from *Broadway Melody*, which Frank Sinatra would later effectively, and unfairly, eviscerate in *That's Entertainment!* Marc Wanamaker/Bison Archives

costumes in front of their costars and jumping about in their skivvies at home than they do in conquering Broadway. Unfortunately, the script also goes out of its way to stereotype gay men, lesbians, comic alcoholics, Scotsmen (again), and even stutterers.

The Broadway Melody's status as the first MGM musical makes it an unassailable beacon in that studio's story, but the film itself is something of an anomaly. Plot wise, if not stylistically, it more comfortably evokes cynical Warner Bros. musicals like *42nd Street* (1933) than films that would come from MGM just a little later.

One of the first of those films was *The Hollywood Review* (1929), which premiered the same month that *The Broadway Melody* went into general release. That film would boast more music, more stars, and considerably less plot than its predecessor, and would tend to characterize most of MGM's singing-dancing output better than anything to be found under the shaky prosceniums in *The Broadway Melody*.

Like those later musicals, the stars of *The Broadway Melody* were able to take very little away from the original film. Charles King's name, for example, today means little more than the sarcastic shout-out in *That's Entertainment!*—if that—although King proves himself a respectable hoofer and singer, which could not be said for either of his leading ladies.

Those leading ladies, Anita Page and Bessie Love, are at least both lively and likable, especially Love, whose *Broadway Melody* role scored her an Academy Award nomination. But like Charles King, neither lady ever achieved the stardom this movie's success should have granted them.

Part of the problem was that in the wake of *The Broadway Melody*'s financial windfall, Hollywood oversaturated theaters with all-singing, all-dancing spectacles. Bessie Love, for example, would do five more musicals in the next year—and remember, she lacked the seemingly important ability to either sing or dance (she could, apparently, play the ukulele). Consequently, when audiences unsurprisingly grew weary of musicals and stopped going to them, the studios briefly stopped making them—and stopped hiring the people who had made them.

Both ladies, however, unlike the unlucky King, who died in 1944, would go on to live very long lives. Bessie Love survived long enough to appear in Warren Beatty's epic *Reds* in 1981! She died in 1986. Anita Page survived her by twenty-two years, living to the age of ninety-eight. Her family remembers that, to the very end of her life, Anita enjoyed watching her old movies on television.

The musical genre had more life in it too. In a couple years, Busby Berkeley's virtuoso (and for the first time, cinematic) musical numbers at Warner Bros. would smash the proscenium arch the genre had largely been encased in and fire it back to life, and eventually back to MGM.

The Broadway Melody had more life in it as well. *Broadway Melody of 1936* (1935), *Broadway Melody of 1938* (1937), and *Broadway Melody of 1940* (1940) would follow, as well as the ultimately unmade *Broadway Melody of 1943*, which was reportedly to have teamed Gene Kelly and Eleanor Powell. Therefore, yet another innovation that could be laid at the feet of the original is the concept of the sequel, although these follow-ups only took the name, not the plot or any of the characters from the original. So the lecherous Jacques Warriner never got to make a repeat appearance. These later entries, although less innovative than the original, were also better crafted, better cast, and better produced. In short, they were more like "MGM musicals."

Because of the sequels, the original *The Broadway Melody* is now sometimes referred to as *Broadway Melody of 1929*—presumably to differentiate it from its stepchildren, although stylistically, no one could mistake the original for any of the follow-ups.

The first *Broadway Melody* stands alone.

7

Hallelujah (1929)

Popularly regarded as the first studio feature film with an all-Black cast (although Fox's low-budget *Hearts in Dixie* actually beat it into theaters by a few months), *Hallelujah* is more than that.

After the success of *The Big Parade,* director King Vidor became the fair-haired boy on the Culver City lot and was given plum assignments like *Bardelys the Magnificent* (1926) and *Show People* (1928), as well as riskier projects like *La Bohème* (1926) and *The Crowd* (1928).

Vidor's interest in a film about African-American life (which, of course, is not what such a project would have been called at that time) went back to his childhood in Texas. "Everything in the film I saw when I was a child," he said. "I remember that there was a Black woman in my family. I made this film for her. I should have dedicated it to her."[1] Vidor somehow managed to interest Nicholas Schenck in the project, which is perhaps how location shooting, in faraway Tennessee and Arkansas, ultimately supplemented the usual studio work. Because there were no significant Black stars in Hollywood at the time, Vidor cast unknowns, even as the leads. (There is some evidence that the then well-respected Paul Robeson was at least discussed, although years later he stated that he had turned the role down.)

For his first sound film, Vidor included a great deal of "traditional" music by the likes of Stephen Foster, as well as contemporary songs by Irving Berlin that sounded as though they might have been written by the likes of Foster.

The setting of the film is supposedly somewhere in the Deep South, although nothing of the sort is ever stated. Certainly, the overt presence in the film of slave-era dialect, shanties and cotton fields, and river-boats as a background for the action implies that this is so. Yet because the cast is entirely African American, there is no element of race, or racism, present. Quite unlike Broadway's *Show Boat* (which would be filmed, with Robeson, in 1936), where that very issue is the epicenter of the action, *Hallelujah* is intended to be a timeless morality tale—and so, let's hope, relatable to all.

The plot involves the everyman adventures of one Zekiel, or "Zeke," played by Daniel L. Haynes, whose adventures take him from the cotton fields to the pulpit to the chain gang and back home again. Haynes is better than fine. It's a shame he was not given more opportunities; his last screen credit was in 1936, although he lived until 1954. A very similar

The striking poster art by Al Hirschfeld for Hollywood's first major all-Black feature, *Hallelujah* (1929). *Photofest*

fate would befall most of the very large cast of *Hallelujah.*

The standout in that large cast is Nina Mae McKinney as bad girl Chick, who performs a provocative dance, the "Suwanee Shuffle," and then lures Zeke off the straight and narrow. McKinney is so effective that MGM responded by giving her a five-year contract, the first time that had happened to any African American actor at any studio. Sadly, as would later happen to Lena Horne at the same studio, MGM had no idea what to do with the dynamic and beautiful actress once they had her—theaters in the Deep South would not have played her films, and certainly would not have tolerated any young African American woman appearing opposite white male actors. So, as would happen to Horne, MGM instead featured her in sequences that could be cut for those markets or in disposable short subjects.

Eventually McKinney was forced to move to Europe, where the roles were slightly better, and where she was occasionally referred to as "the black Garbo." In 1935, on *The Voice of Britain*, she became the first Black person ever to appear on British television.

That same year she acted opposite Paul Robeson in *Sanders of the River*. But after returning home when war broke out, McKinney could find only a few supporting roles in films and as a singer in honky-tonks. When Nina Mae McKinney died in 1967, none of the Hollywood trade papers thought her worthy of an obituary.

Hallelujah was successful enough to justify the studio's faith in it. But MGM would not make another film with an African American cast until 1943's *Cabin in the Sky*. Lena Horne, one of the stars of that film, eventually achieved a very hard-fought level of stardom. Her relationship with the studio would continue, in often continuous fits and starts, until 1994.

Ironically, in the twenty-first century, MGM would finally find continuing success with an African American cast in the acclaimed, and amusing, *Barbershop* franchise.

The beautiful Nina Mae McKinney was questionably described in a 1929 *Photoplay* article as "black, but she's got a blonde soul." *Author's collection*

King Vidor's direction of *Hallelujah* is quite innovative, especially for 1929. Much of the film was originally shot silently. So, as with a few other early talkies, like *All Quiet on the Western Front* (1930), much of the sound was added later, allowing the action to be more mobile, a process much superior to the camera-nailed-to-the-floor, stage-bound effect evident in many other early talkies. Unfortunately, with *Hallelujah* the synchronization of some of the dialogue and songs in these scenes is noticeably off, but even with this deficit, the result is still far superior to the alternative.

Vidor's movies always featured a strong sense of the earth itself, presented as both a provider and an indifferent force, ever ready to either reward or destroy mortal man at its whim. Here, as in *Wild Oranges* (1924), *Northwest Passage* (1940), and *Ruby Gentry* (1952), there is a swamp waiting to consume the characters, although Zeke manages to escape from its muddy embrace to return to the bosom of his family.

That family, and all the characters in *Hallelujah*, good and bad, unfortunately largely fit into the predominate "Negro" stereotypes of the era. The lazy, shiftless Negro and the cowering domestic are largely avoided, but the plot is still rank with

William Fountaine and Nina Mae McKinney lead Daniel L. Haynes off the straight and narrow in *Hallelujah*. *Photofest*

con men and whores, and cotton pickers and pickaninnies. And the positive characters speak in the same Huckleberry Finn dialects as the negative ones do. Vidor's insistence on setting the film in some undated faraway *Song of the South* fairyland makes his mining of these clichés easier to understand, at least to some degree, if not forgivable. Perhaps if the same story had been set in the 1920s tenements of New York, for example, rather than a Stephen Foster–inspired Dixieland, it would have been easier for the undoubtably well-intentioned Vidor to avoid the stereotypes. These very stereotypes are probably why Robeson reportedly disliked the film so much when he saw it, and why many who have never seen it continue to dislike *Hallelujah* today.

Even the tragically underused Nina Mae McKinney, who very much liked and always spoke highly of King Vidor, probably realized that she was being asked to conform to a White person's idea of her race. She was once quoted as saying, "You just show me one Negro girl who's made movies who didn't play a maid or a whore. I don't know any."[2]

In *Hallelujah*, at least Nina Mae McKinney didn't have to be the maid.

8

Freaks (1932)

Freaks is the ugly stepchild of the MGM family. For years it was unseen, banned, censured, whispered about, and locked away in the dark.

Louis B. Mayer did not like horror movies. The very idea of cinema designed to frighten its audience was completely alien to a mogul whose idea of a good movie was the cinematic equivalent of a comforting bowl of chicken soup. But in 1931, horror movies were popular due to the triple punch of Universal's *Dracula* and *Frankenstein* and Paramount's *Dr. Jekyll and Mr. Hyde*, all of which would be released that year.

Lon Chaney had been a big star since the earliest days of the studio, and some of his MGM movies were certainly shocking, but it should be noted that the horror genre did not exist as such until the February 1931 release of *Dracula*. Chaney's status as a horror star came only in hindsight. His death in August 1930 meant that he probably died before the genre he is most identified with had been defined and named.

But although none of Chaney's films were referred to specifically as horror movies during his lifetime, that doesn't mean they aren't. The oddest of Chaney's MGM films (although actually acquired rather than produced in-house) was *The Monster* (1925), which could have referred to several, but certainly not all, of the characters he played. This particular specimen, which dealt with a spooky house and a mad scientist, was unusual, however, in that it was a comedy—a spoof if you will—of a genre that hadn't yet been created.

Chaney's favorite director was Tod Browning, whose oft-noted morbid fascination with grotesque characters, both physical and internal, perhaps exceeded even Chaney's. Browning had crashed show business at the age of sixteen, when he had literally run away from home to join the circus—perhaps the sawdust-tainted root of why so many of his films would deal with carnies, con men, and sideshows.

It has long been assumed that Browning wanted Chaney to play the lead in his personal dream project, *Dracula*. If this is true, then the director and his star would have had to find a way for Universal, who owned the property and to which Browning was attached, to somehow borrow the actor from Mayer, which would have been unlikely. Chaney's untimely death led to Bela Lugosi being ultimately, indelibly, directed by Browning in the role instead.

After the success of *Dracula*, and the anticipated eventual success of *Frankenstein* and *Dr. Jekyll and Mr. Hyde* (as well as upcoming MGM homegrown horrors, *The Mask of Fu Manchu* and *Kongo*), Thalberg, who had championed Browning from their days together at Universal, offered the director a chance to make a talking horror film at MGM, and reportedly told Browning to make the most horrible one he could. Thalberg got exactly what he asked for—disastrously, as it turned out, for the studio and for Browning personally.

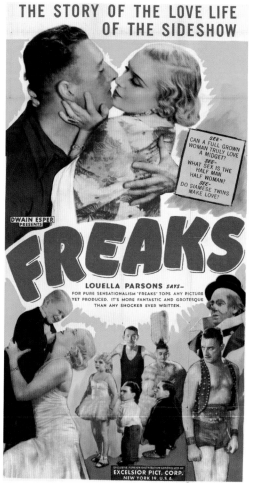

Reissue poster for *Freaks* (1932) poses the eternal question "Do Siamese Twins make love?" yet is too discreet to mention MGM. *Author's collection*

Freaks was based on a grisly short story called "Spurs" by Tod Robbins, who had earlier written the successful Browning-Chaney collaboration *The Unholy Three* (1925). The plot concerned a circus midget who marries a full-size woman who only wants his money. But when the midget and his friends, also circus oddities, discover this, they enact their sideshow-style revenge.

In the 1920s Browning had cast Chaney as assorted amputees, cripples, and monsters. Audiences at the time, although politely horrified, could still take solace in the fact that the "man of a thousand faces," as Chaney was aptly called, could take off all those scary masks at the end of the day. So there was a safety net of sorts to be found in the fact that, despite his mastery, Chaney was, after all, still "one of us." But for *Freaks*, now deprived of Chaney and his makeup box, Browning instead ripped the veneer of comfortable fantasy completely away by casting actual "freaks" to play themselves. He had MGM representatives scour sideshows and circuses around the world in search of their most terrifying oddities, and then he brought them all to Culver City.

Culver City was not ready for them.

Freaks and Browning's freaks represented an anomaly on the MGM lot, to say the least. The most beautiful, the most privileged, and the most appreciated people in the world suddenly found themselves face-to-face with their mirror opposites. Casting the freaks' "normal" costars was difficult, again to say the least. Myrna Loy, Jean Harlow, and Victor McLaglen all refused outright to have anything to do with the movie.

Eventual, and second-string, leading lady Olga Baclanova remembered the experience of working with her costars as "very difficult . . . because I couldn't look at them. It hurt me like a human being. How lucky I was."[1] F. Scott Fitzgerald, working as a screenwriter on the lot, reportedly became physically ill when Siamese (conjoined) twins Daisy and Violet Hilton sat near him in the commissary and one consumed a lunch the other apparently could also taste. Eventually that commissary was declared off-limits to most of the cast of *Freaks*. Mayer, hearing about this discord from his office, was certainly horrified both by the project and by Thalberg's continued, and to him confounding, support of the project, which turned out to be yet another factor in the two moguls' increasingly tenuous relationship.

The discord continued. At a studio preview in San Diego, *Freaks* horrified unsuspecting audiences as no film before or since. Merrill Pye, a studio art director who was there, recalled that "halfway through the preview, a lot of people got up and ran out. They didn't walk out. They *ran* out."[2] Reportedly, and this has never been proven, one woman was so traumatized by the film that she subsequently suffered a miscarriage.

Faced with a film that was un-releasable in its present form, possibly in *any* form, the studio was forced to perform a wholesale castration of Browning's efforts. Much of the footage of the freaks—especially the nightmarish climax with the sideshow denizens hopping and crawling through a thunderstorm to enact their revenge—had to be almost entirely removed. When the editors were finished, the film was more than half an hour shorter than Browning had intended. The version that was actually released, even after some additional scenes were added to pad out the running time, finally clocked in at a B-movie length of sixty-four minutes.

The AMAZING LIFE STORIES of the FREAKS!

By FAITH SERVICE

Top, across the two pages, some of the headliners of "Freaks" at lunch on the set. At the head of the table is Prince Randian, the Living Torso; fourth down the table is Schlitze, the Pin-Head; sixth, Johnny Eck, the Half-Boy; eighth, Frances O'Connor, the Armless Beauty; tenth, Angelo, the Dwarf, eleventh, Koo-Koo, the Bird-Girl; thirteenth, one of the Siam Twins; fifteenth, the Bearded Lady; sixteenth, Pete Robinson, the Living Skeleton; and last, Josephine Joseph, Half-Man, Half-Woman. Right, Daisy Earles, perfectly formed midget—who stopped growing when four

You will be amazed when you see them on the screen in "Freaks," Tod Browning's drama of the misshapen creatures of the circus sideshows. And when you do see them—the Siamese Twins, the Half-Boy, the Pin-Head, the Armless Beauty, the Living Torso, among many others—you will wonder where they came from, how they live, how they feel about their fate. This story of their lives may surprise you!

You have seen Lon Chaney's pictures and "Frankenstein" and "Dr. Jekyll and Mr. Hyde." You have seen every kind of human horror imaginable, on the screen—except the characters you are about to meet in "Freaks." There has never been anything like it before, and may never be again. These are no actors donning cruel make-up for a few hours, to be curiosities that some author has imagined. These are the most tragic people in the world—actors who must wear their grotesque make-up and be curiosities as long as they live. You will get a new outlook on life by reading their life stories!—Editor.

Above, Johnny Eck, the brilliant Half-Boy, born without any lower body. He is the only one of the human curiosities who considers himself tragic

Left, Frances O'Connor, the living Venus de Milo—born without arms. From childhood she has used her feet as normal people use their hands

THE most amazing people in the movies—and that means the world—are those misshapen distorted men and women you will see in M-G-M's "Freaks," the like of which you have never seen before. Out of strange backgrounds, from the four corners of the earth, they have come to Hollywood to show you what the circus sideshow people are really like. It's amazing enough that they are here. Their appearances, in some cases, will make you shudder with amazement—even as you watch, fascinated. But the most amazing things about them are their life stories—and how they look at life.

For seven years, Tod Browning—who directed Lon Chaney in so many of his successes—has had the idea for this bizarre mystery drama about the sideshow folk, and has been trying to get producers to listen to it. Browning, himself, started life

Above, Prince Randian, the Living Torso, shaving himself. Both armless and legless, he has two children and eight grandchildren

in a circus—and he has never got over its fascination. He knows the human beings behind these grotesque exteriors, knows their temperaments, their amazing abilities. After you see how he presents them, there won't be anything more to know about them except where they came from—and you will certainly want to know that. This story tells you.

Are you expecting to find these Strangest People in the World a collection of half-dopey, maudlin, self-pitying wrecks? You are due for a surprise. Some of them are idiots, it is true—but they are happy idiots. Others have normal intelligence, or more, and have managed to make their minds more important than their bodies. With one tragic exception, of which I'll tell you later, they are all exuberantly happy. They are contented. They are glad they are alive. They have no resentment toward whatever Force or Being or biological crack-up

The April 1932 issue of *Motion Picture* magazine took time out from their usual movie star profiles to interview the unusual stars of *Freaks*. *Author's collection*

And even that very-truncated version was a massive box-office disaster. What's more, the critics of the time were generally as horrified as audiences were. *Time* magazine, for example, missed the point—or what was later perceived to be the point—of the movie by cruelly describing the cast of the film as "subhuman animals."[3] The studio also had to face the reality that many local censorship boards would demand even more cuts and deletions before the film could be exhibited in their towns at all. Worse yet, in England, a major market, *Freaks* was banned outright. No one knew it then, but this exile would ultimately stay in effect for more than thirty years!

After an unsuccessful New York opening, and a few other very unpromising engagements in other cities, Mayer finally went over Thalberg's head and had the film pulled from theaters outright. According to historian Mark A. Vieira, *Freaks* set the unfortunate historical precedent of being the only time in the studio's history that an MGM movie was actually yanked from distribution before it had completed its original run. It could be argued then, that the July 1934 decision by all studios to afterward follow a strict standard of self-censorship could be traced to *Freaks*, as well as to other costly pre-code public relations disasters.

In 1932, one might then have expected *Freaks* to rot away in the MGM vault. And yet surprisingly, Dracula-like, the film refused to stay buried. In the 1940s exploitation producer Dwain Esper's Roadshow Productions reportedly paid MGM $50,000 for a twenty-five-year unlimited "lease" on the film. *Freaks* had cost the studio more than $300,000 in 1932, so at this point Mayer was probably glad to make a few dollars on the horrid thing and then be rid of it. And Esper, the ringleader of bottom-of-the barrel atrocities like *Narcotic* (1933) and *Maniac* (1934), which had probably cost considerably less than $10,000 each to make, was undoubtedly delighted to have wrestled a big "Hollywood epic" from a big Hollywood studio.

Esper, probably under the terms of his contract, chopped the MGM logo off the front of "his movie" and replaced it with a badly worded text prologue stressing the film's "educational" qualities. He and, later, companies with names like Excelsior Pictures and Sonney Productions ran the film for years in big-city grindhouses and Deep South drive-ins, using increasingly battered and censored prints of the movie, and sometimes retitling the film with names like *Forbidden Love* and *Nature's Mistakes*—possibly, the worst indignity ever inflicted upon an MGM movie. Even if that movie no longer was.

Something else Esper inflicted on *Freaks*, or whatever alias it was using, was a sort of grimy, undead immortality. *Freaks*, probably inadvertently, ultimately had a longer theatrical run than almost anything else the studio ever produced. And the audiences in raincoats and coveralls who, carny-like, were conned into seeing the film in the 1940s and 1950s by Esper's exploitation tactics—which included bogus doctor's testimonials, mummified remains on display in the lobby, and locally recruited gorilla-suited farmhands on the sidewalk—must have been unprepared for, and then long remembered, what they got for the dime or dollar they paid to experience *Freaks*.

Because of its short original theatrical run, and then its long afterlife and half-life on the exploitation circuit, *Freaks* became a cult film long before the name or concept of a cult film existed, as had earlier been the case with the horror genre itself. Tod Browning, whose career never recovered from *Freaks,* died in 1962, the same year his film was officially resurrected and screened at the Venice Film Festival to glowing reviews from the intelligentsia of the time.

Throughout the 1960s, when being a marginalized "freak" was suddenly considered a badge of honor, the film, now reclaimed from purgatory by MGM (but with Esper's crude prologue usually still included), was suddenly praised by critics for its innate humanism and compassion. After all, in *Freaks*, the freaks—although exploited both

Wallace Ford and Leila Hyams, part of the "normal" cast of *Freaks,* seem to contemplate their costars. *Photofest*

in and by the film—are still the heroes. In 1994 *Freaks* was selected by the National Film Registry as being a film "culturally, historically, or aesthetically significant." A decade later, in 2004, *Freaks* was released on DVD with an accompanying documentary, which, at sixty-four minutes, is exactly as long as the film it celebrates.

Today there is so little left of *Freaks* as it originally looked that it is hard to figure out what audiences at that first, legendarily disastrous preview really saw—and what they imagined they saw. Consequently, the film as it exists today has more missing or malformed appendages than most of its cast. *Freaks* has become what it celebrates.

9

Tarzan the Ape Man (1932)

Tarzan the Ape Man was not the first Tarzan film, but it was the first MGM Tarzan film, so in many ways it is the definitive and archetypal tale of one of the most recognized, influential, and celebrated fictional characters in the world.

What *Tarzan the Ape Man* is not, however, is an origin story for that character. Many viewers coming to the film in 1932, or today, would probably be surprised that this first film feels rather like a sequel to some earlier film that was never made. Tarzan has no past at MGM. He is just a white man who lives with apes in Africa.

In the source novels by Edgar Rice Burroughs, this "Ape Man" is John Clayton, child of English nobility, who, after his parents' deaths in Africa is raised by "great apes." The first Tarzan book, *Tarzan of the Apes*, was first serialized in 1912 and then followed by dozens of sequels by Burroughs and others, as well as adaptations for radio, comic books, the stage, and of course films. So perhaps MGM felt that most viewers in 1932 would buy their tickets already knowing who Tarzan was.

At the time, the studio was hamstrung from making direct adaptations of any of Burroughs's Tarzan novels, even the first one, by their contract with the author, who was busy selling various rights to the character to various media and had ambitions to make his own Tarzan films. So MGM only acquired the rights to the character, to that single character. And they changed that character from the articulate, erudite intellectual in the novels to, as the title promised, a Pidgin English–speaking "ape man." Other characters from the books were ignored or, due to that contract, had their names tinkered with slightly. American-born Jane Porter in the books, for example, became the properly British Jane Parker at MGM.

In 1932 neither MGM nor (especially) Burroughs could have known that it would be the MGM version rather than Burroughs's template that would become the definitive one. So when Burroughs did make his own film in 1935—the independently produced serial *The New Adventures of Tarzan*, which, yes, was truer to the books—it felt like he had gotten his own character all wrong.

MGM had originally bought those rights, as limited as they were, to burn off some of the stock footage that W. S. "Woody" Van Dyke, the studio's globe-trotting specialist in exotic locals, had taken in Africa for the production of *Trader Horn* (1931). Van Dyke himself would be recycled as the director for *Tarzan* as well, although this time the production would be kept almost entirely at the studio.

Johnny Weissmuller, then the most famous and medaled Olympic swimmer in history, was a natural, even obvious choice to play Tarzan, although the studio considered Clark Gable, Joel McCrea, George O'Brien, and even another Olympic champion swimmer, Buster Crabbe, for the role (Crabbe would get his chance in 1933's *Tarzan the Fearless*). Beautiful Maureen O'Sullivan was cast as Jane, with venerable British character actor C. Aubrey Smith as her brush-beating explorer father.

In other casting news, Asian elephants were recruited to portray African elephants, apparently because Asian elephants were more readily available in the United States and because they are easier to train. Unfortunately, Asian

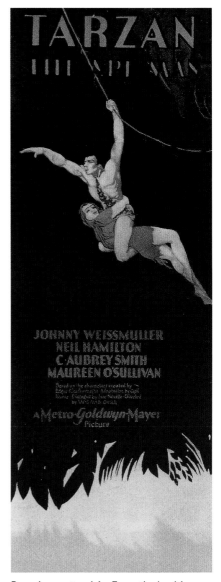

Pre-release artwork for *Tarzan the Ape Man* (1932) featured vine-swinging renditions of Tarzan and Jane, neither of whom here much resembles either Johnny Weissmuller or Maureen O'Sullivan. *Author's collection*

elephants are also less bulky than their African cousins and possess smaller ears. To remedy this, the studio went to the trouble of attaching ear extensions to their elephant actors to try to hide the substitutions. Rather remarkable this, since there was no attempt at geographical or anatomical accuracy on the set in any other way. For example, costumed actors played both pygmies and gorillas, and a South American jaguar stood in for a leopard. The Van Dyke stock footage was also spliced in rather haphazardly or back-projected, rather unconvincingly, behind the actors, which the location-wary MGM often tended to do during this era, even more so than other studios.

Audiences didn't care, and the film was a sensation. Weissmuller's romanticized, none-too-bright jungle man was exactly what Depression-era audiences were craving. The idea of living self-sufficiently in a dangerous but Depression-proof jungle was immeasurably appealing to these audiences in 1932, especially to economically emasculated male audiences. Obviously, a sequel was called for.

Unfortunately, Burroughs was still busy licensing Tarzan rights all over town. MGM realized they would have to make their sequel bigger than those other productions to prove that theirs was the "real" Tarzan. *Tarzan and His Mate* (1934) succeeded, picking up right where the original left off and, perhaps trying to appeal to the series' male fans, including a startling amount of pre-code nudity and violence in the process.

Weissmuller played Tarzan until 1941 at MGM, when the series, still with Weissmuller but without O'Sullivan, moved over to RKO. Sol Lesser, who had produced *Tarzan the Fearless*, continued the series, eventually with other actors, for years.

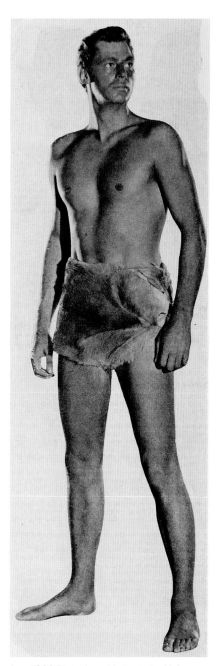

June 1932 *Photoplay* publicity study of Johnny Weissmuller as Tarzan, although the hair, wardrobe, and wedding ring he sports here did not appear in the film. *Author's collection*

Tarzan movies are still being made. Among fictional characters, perhaps only Dracula and Sherlock Holmes have been so consistently durable on the screen. MGM itself remade the original property twice, *Tarzan the Ape Man* (1959) and *Tarzan the Ape Man* (1981). Both were terrible.

And what of the original, the one that started it all? Well, this *Tarzan the Ape Man* is most certainly *not* terrible. The action is constant, even when unconvincing. Suave matinee idol Ivor Novello is credited with writing some of the dialogue, which is interesting since all that most people remember about that dialogue is the decidedly not-so-suave Pidgin English banter between Tarzan and Jane.

Speaking of which, there is real animal chemistry here between this Tarzan and Jane, or rather between Weissmuller and O'Sullivan. Weissmuller, as others have remarked, would have been a great silent star; his body movements are as focused as those of a jungle animal. Note, for example, the way he paws at O'Sullivan in those famous "Me Tarzan, you Jane" scenes—words he never actually says. Here Weissmuller holds his hand with his knuckles turned in, like a primate.

In fact, in some ways this scene, with Tarzan poking and grabbing at Jane, anticipates the later *King Kong* (1933). Maureen O'Sullivan even balls her hands up when she covers her face, just like Fay Wray would a year later. And the elephant stampede through the village in the climax is startlingly similar to Kong's rampage through a native village in the later classic. Actually, that *Kong* scene was similar to an even earlier elephant stampede in an even earlier film, *Chang* (1927), which was created by some of the people behind *King Kong*, so, there you have it.

Tarzan fans point to the pre-code *Tarzan and His Mate* as the highlight of the entire series. But *Tarzan the Ape Man* has some of the same attitudes about jungle sex and violence. One particularly odd sequence has O'Sullivan improbably stripping off her clothes in front of her long-absent father—who gets weirdly agitated by it. A few minutes later she teasingly remarks to him, "You think I'm a child, don't you?" To which he justifiably shoots back, "No. I have ample proof that you're not."

Johnny Weissmuller is one of those one-role actors who are destined to be forever famous for one thing. But unlike other typecast-for-life performers, Weissmuller never even tried, at least not publicly, to break away from Tarzan. And when the actor got too beefy to wear his loincloth, he traded it in for khakis and continued his tropical adventures as a character named Jungle Jim.

Of course, for the rest of his life, everywhere he went, Weissmuller would be requested to "do the Tarzan yell"—that odd scream-yodel-howl that originated here and which the character would forever after be identified with. This ape man is so proficient at that

Tarzan seems to take inventory of Jane's toes in this hand-colored lobby card art for *Tarzan the Ape Man*. *Author's collection*

yell that he is able to produce the sound even while fighting wild animals or swimming underwater! In their 1981 remake, MGM substituted the Tarzan yell for Leo the Lion's roar in their logo. But in real life, it was Weissmuller who epitomized the call.

For the rest of her days, Maureen O'Sullivan maintained that Johnny himself had originated the yell, and that it was he doing it on-screen every time, although others have sworn that it was created by Douglas Shearer's sound technicians. If this is the case, then over the years, Weissmuller got very good at reproducing it. In his last decades, Johnny performed a pretty good approximation of the yell for a bemused Groucho Marx on *You Bet Your Life* and again on *The Mike Douglas Show*, for example.

One time the yell might have even saved his life. According to Weissmuller's son, Johnny Jr., his dad was playing golf in Havana during the Cuban Revolution when, as he tells it, his "golf cart was suddenly surrounded by rebel soldiers. Weissmuller was unable to communicate who he was until he got out of the cart and attempted the trademark Tarzan yell. The soldiers then recognized him and shouted. '¡*Es Tarzán!* ¡*Es Tarzán de la Jungla!*' Johnny and his companions were not only *not* kidnapped, and not murdered, but the guerillas gave him an escort to his hotel."[1]

10

Grand Hotel (1932)

"Grand Hotel. Always the same. People come. People go. Nothing ever happens."

Grand Hotel began its eventful life as a 1929 novel by German expat Vicki Baum, who in her youth had worked as a chambermaid in a Berlin hotel. Irving Thalberg purchased the novel, *Menschen im Hotel* ("People at a Hotel"), and then developed it, not into a screenplay but for Broadway, where it was a major success in 1930. So when the property was finally adapted into a film, it already sported a successful pedigree.

Much has been made of the studio system's keeping dozens of stars under contract who could then be utilized at will. This was true. But in the early 1930s, more than two big stars were seldom assigned to the same film, as this was thought to be a waste of the studio's assets, not to mention a minefield of internal billing and ego issues for the front office to contend with. Occasional musicals like *The Hollywood Review* (1929) did feature multiple stars, but they were kept apart from one another in their own, largely unrelated, specialty sequences.

But Thalberg wondered if perhaps, just maybe, multiple stars in the same setting, interacting with one another on an equal footing, might be able to somehow accomplish the very desirable trick of combining, rather than canceling out, each star's built-in audience. And since *Grand Hotel*, just like those stars, had been developed and nurtured in-house, he felt that he had the perfect vehicle in hand to accommodate his grand experiment.

And so it was that Greta Garbo, John Barrymore, Joan Crawford, Wallace Beery, and Lionel Barrymore, as well as Lewis Stone and Jean Hersholt—and in that very carefully worked out billing order—were brought together by director Edmund Goulding amidst Cedric Gibbons' beautiful, if not very Germanic, Moderne settings.

Probably to the disappointment of many a studio publicist, all the prize animals in Thalberg's menagerie were apparently on very good behavior during production of *Grand Hotel*. Brothers John and Lionel Barrymore had worked together before, of course, and would again, later that year, in *Rasputin and the Empress*. But to everyone's surprise, John also got along well with Greta Garbo, who newly ascendant star Joan Crawford was careful to keep an awestruck distance from.

Contrary to what is assumed about Garbo's famous "I want to be alone" line (which in *Grand Hotel* she utters, in variations, three times), it did not originate in this film. By 1932, studio publicists had already attributed it to her. Maybe she actually said it to one of them. On camera, Garbo also had already danced around the sentence

As expected, *Grand Hotel*'s (1932) key poster art, by William Galbraith Crawford, emphasized the film's many stars. *Author's collection*

several times. In *The Single Standard* (1929), for example, she says (in a subtitle), "I want to *walk* alone." And in *Mati Hari* (1931) she remarks, "I shall probably be quite alone." It's also interesting to note that the versions of the line as she says it in *Grand Hotel* can also be found in Baum's original novel. Regardless, decades later Garbo herself was (mis)quoted as telling "a friend" that "I never said, 'I want to be alone; I only said, 'I want to be *let* alone!' There is all the difference."[1]

It is Lionel Barrymore, as a timid and exploited factory worker, who arguably delivers the best performance in the film. Even so, he's still overshadowed by everyone else in the cast! After all, the older Barrymore brother's fine character-actor work here just doesn't stand a chance against the monochromatic charisma and outright glamour of

Except for some of the signage, *Grand Hotel*'s grandly Art Deco lobby set, although magnificent, was not particularly Germanic. *Photofest*

his many scene-stealing costars—all of whom are working at the peak of their powers and supported by the vast creative might of a studio apparatus then at the very height of its power as well. Against such odds, talent alone isn't enough.

Lewis Stone, as the cynical Doctor Otternschlag, who wearily delivers the "nothing ever happens" line that opens the film, is also a bit of an anomaly among this entourage. Half his face is disfigured—burned perhaps—and although he never overtly alludes to it, Otternschlag is apparently a casualty of World War I. Considering the film's time frame and its Germanic setting, it is interesting that this is the only place within the Grand Hotel that the ghosts of a past war and the specter of a looming war are ever addressed.

None of this was on anyone's mind, of course, in September when *Grand Hotel* was released and became an outstanding success, the most popular film of the year in fact and eventually the winner of a Best Picture Oscar, the studio's second win in four years. Regarding the Oscars, however, the star-heavy cast apparently did cancel one another out—the picture received no acting nominations for any of its many headliners.

Grand Hotel's success led to other all-star casts—most immediately, *Dinner at Eight*, which came out the following year and successfully repeated *Grand Hotel*'s formula, as well as its popular and financial success.

The same lobby set during production. Director Edmund Goulding is seated far left. *Photofest*

MGM would later remake *Grand Hotel* as *Weekend at the Waldorf* (1945). This time the setting was Americanized to New York's Waldorf Astoria hotel. A little-seen third remake, this one a German production, appeared in 1959.

In the 1970s MGM tried, several times, to launch yet another version of the story, this one to be set at their (original) MGM Grand Hotel in Las Vegas—the use of which company executives undoubtably hoped would somehow synergize its Hollywood and hotel operations. Possibly those company executives remembered, or possibly they didn't, that the MGM Grand, then the largest hotel in the world, had been partially designed in 1973 to resemble the set for the 1932 film. Hollywood A-listers Sydney Pollack, Norman Jewison, and Mike Nichols were all attached to the project at different times, but like many MGM projects of this vintage, this particular iteration of *Grand Hotel* failed to materialize.

In 1958 actor Paul Muni tried to revise the property as a stage musical, *At the Grand*, although nothing came of it. In 1989, however, *Grand Hotel* did return to Broadway, again with music. This production won five Tonys and ultimately would run for more than a thousand performances.

Grand Hotel has also returned, after a fashion, in the form of those many later film and television projects where a limited location, a hotel for example, could be utilized as an excuse to bring multiple subplots and multiple stars together, some of whom would never need to interact with the others, so those disparate sequences could be shot separately or concurrently, as needed.

MGM and *Grand Hotel* created the model. But that model has been used by other studios, like Warner Bros. for *Hotel* (1967) and Universal for *Airport* (1970). The too-many-to-name disaster films of the 1970s certainly took advantage of that recipe too. Television also has found that formula (or is it now its own genre?) particularly useful in guest-star powered series like *The Love Boat* (1977–1987), *Fantasy Island* (1977–1984), and of course the tellingly titled *Hotel* (1983–1988).

"Grand Hotel. Always the same. People come. People go. Nothing ever happens . . ."

11

Dancing Lady (1933)

Dancing Lady certainly seems like a routine studio musical. The plot is so basic, and has been used so many times, that it is almost impossible to believe it was based on a book by very respected author James Warner Bellah. Let's see: Joan Crawford is an ambitious dancer who is being courted by rich socialite Franchot Tone but falls in love with Clark Gable, who is also the director of her first Broadway show. That's it.

What makes the film interesting, outside any ornate appeal such material contains, is that *Dancing Lady* is also a near-textbook example of the MGM machinery at work, and the unusual number of personalities, fore and aft of the camera, who ultimately would benefit greatly from that machinery.

The producer of *Dancing Lady* was the very ambitious David O. Selznick. Selznick had recently proven his worth at the studio with the successful *Dinner at Eight* (1933) but wanted another hit to prove that he was more than Mayer's son-in-law.

Star Joan Crawford had recently come off the flop *Today We Live* (1933). So she also wanted to ensure a hit by wrangling her frequent leading man, Clark Gable, into the company as her costar. Problem was, Gable actively disliked Selznick and actively disliked the role. At Crawford's urging and, less successfully, at Selznick's, Gable eventually, reluctantly, acquiesced. Illness would keep Gable off the set for much of the production, however, and when he returned, his underweight post-sickness appearance forced director Robert Z. Leonard to do retakes to flatter his male star.

One of the most head-scratchingly memorable aspects of *Dancing Lady* is its supporting cast. So varied and odd are the disparate personalities collected under the arc lights

1933 half-sheet poster for *Dancing Lady*. *Photofest*

here that critic Ty Burr most memorably described the ensemble as "all the levels of early '30s Hollywood stardom collapsing into one ground-floor pig-pile."[1] In fact, the film marked the debut, or nearly so, of several future stars, many of whom would often work on future MGM projects. Nelson Eddy ultimately got only one number in *Dancing Lady*, "Rhythm of the Day," yet he so impressed the studio brass, and the public, that he subsequently became a major studio asset. Likewise, Fred Astaire, already signed with RKO but not yet on their payroll, made his debut playing himself here, although the dapper dancer is unfortunately referred to on-screen by Gable as "Freddy"!

Further down the cast list, and unlike Astaire and Eddy, Robert Benchley, May Robson, Winnie Lightner, Grant Mitchell, and Sterling Holloway might have already been familiar to 1933 movie audiences. But Eve Arden, who is unbilled, was only making her second appearance on film (she has one line), so she is memorable only in hindsight. Lastly, and most memorably, the Three Stooges—yes, the Three Stooges—make an early appearance. The strange thing is, they are billed in the cast list as "Ted Healy and his Stooges," although all three are listed again in those same credits separately. Healy and Stooge Larry Fine have more business to do on-screen than their cohorts, Moe and Curly Howard, although the boys' rough-and-tumble personas are already completely in line with their future, post-Healy stardom.

Dancing Lady is also a showcase for legendary designer Adrian's crazy, sexy gowns and art director Merrill Pye's glassy, Moderne set designs. Pye's work represented one of the comparatively few MGM titles of the era where Art Department head Cedric Gibbons would *not* be credited in that regard.

Upon its release in November 1933, *Dancing Lady* proved to be everything the studio, and the talent mentioned above, wanted it to be. It gave the ambitious Selznick and Crawford the hit films they desired. It also gave Mayer a template for the assorted elements a successful film needed to contain and how to produce and sell that film for maximum impact. According to Ron Haver in his book *David O. Selznick's Hollywood*, for the next fifteen years (!), the Loews sales department held up *Dancing Lady* as a perfectly marketed picture, a picture that succeeded 100 percent in reaching its entire potential audience.

As a film, however, *Dancing Lady*, as noted above, is almost painfully derivative of earlier backstage musicals, in particular Warner Bros.' recent blockbuster from the same year, *42nd Street*, which had brought musicals back into prominence in a big way. According to Haver, Selznick believed that *42nd Street* lacked "glamour," which was the whole point of that film, as the Depression was well used in that film as an ironic contrast to Busby Berkeley's "happy" musical numbers.

But *Dancing Lady*, in contrast to *42nd Street*'s grubby, realistic milieu, tries to have it both ways. The prospect of the show's closing and the dancers being tossed onto New York's mean streets is always at hand, just as it had been at Warner Bros. Yet because of the much bigger budget, in *Dancing Lady* those mean streets are shown more and are better lit. For example, in a *Dancing Lady* apartment set, grotesquely flashing neon signs outside a window almost anticipate 1940s film noir.

Yet the Selznick, and MGM, reliance on making everything bigger is ultimately counterproductive. The sleazy burlesque house in which Franchot Tone discovers Crawford bumping and grinding in the opening scene, for example, looks bigger, and again better lit, than a legitimate theater uptown on Broadway. A little later, in Mr. Tone's pool house, a table (or is it a piano?) rises out of the floor at his bidding. And a trip to Cuba that Mr. Tone later takes Miss Crawford on becomes a gargantuan production number that Berkeley, who at Warner Bros. was careful to keep his didactic dance routines well away from the real world, never would have engaged in.

Dancing Lady bravely teamed Clark Gable with The Three Stooges. Ted Healy is also pictured here to keep them all in line. *Author's collection*

Director Leonard, another in an endless stable of efficient craftsmen the studio kept busy for decades, keeps the action—and his camera—moving. His bag of tricks here includes an innovative zip pan effect where he whips the camera horizontally, or even vertically, out of one scene and into the next, well mirroring the stories rat-a-tat-tat Broadway vibe. Very cool. Yet the very point of MGM, the reason MGM matters, if you will, is that the producer (née the studio) and not the director was the author (or *auteur*, as the French would later put it) of a movie. So, is this effect to be credited to Robert Z. Leonard, then, or to Selznick/MGM?

Publicity ballyhoo for *Dancing Lady* included Joan Crawford personally inviting her lucky fans on a Hollywood vacation. *Author's collection*

Clark Gable, who as mentioned, was both ill and ill-tempered during the production, hated this film. It's easy to see why. His character is a more charismatic copy of *42nd Street*'s Warner Baxter, who, after all, wasn't required to be an impresario *and* a leading man at the same time. Like Baxter, Gable has to yell most of his dialogue in order to whip the company into shape. The role is only redeemed, lazily if effectively, by the fact that it is indeed Clark Gable playing the part. It is Gable's star power rather than any quality in the script or affectation by Leonard that eventually brings the character around for audiences. It's a good thing, because the script, by a small army of staff writers, does little to reinforce the character's likability. For example, the first time Gable does soften a bit toward Crawford, meaning that he stops yelling at her for five seconds, he slaps her on the butt! This might have been considered sassy in pre-code Hollywood, but it completely fails as an attempt to endear his prickly character to modern audiences.

By the way, those musical numbers that Clark Gable ultimately opens on Broadway are so damned crazy that one might well think they were an opium-fueled fever dream of some mad, avant-garde genius rather than the average-Joe that Gable gives us. This portion of *Dancing Lady* is derivative—big surprise—of something Busby Berkeley would have created as well, although there is only a single "Berkeley-influenced" overhead crane shot included. As with Berkeley, that sequence also incorporates many an effect that would never have been possible on a real stage. Did we mention there's a flying carpet?

Joan Crawford, who after all, does play the title role, has oft been criticized in this sequence and for sequences earlier in the movie, as well as for her other musicals, for her dancing. Actually, Crawford was already a dancer of sorts, although many a critic has remarked that her skills, as such, seemed to begin and end with the Charleston. And yes, just like it was still 1928 (in 1933), Crawford bugs out her eyes, stomps her pretty legs up and down, and flails her arms manically about on the stage every time she is given the opportunity.

Let's agree, then, that Crawford had, let's say, limitations, as a dancer. All right; but inarguably, the lady has no such shortcomings as a star. This is what MGM knew how to exploit and play to. And as with Clark Gable, she is downright impossible to ignore—even while she is "dancing." Crawford also had a palpable sexual chemistry with the otherwise here ill-used Gable—who knew a thing or two about being a star as well.

In the film's climax, Crawford gets to dance with "Freddy" Astaire. As was the case with the Stooges, Mr. Astaire already has his persona—and his top hat and tails—firmly in place here. And like he would do with all his partners for all the decades he was active, he makes Crawford look to be a better dancer than she is, merely by being in his presence.

MGM knew how to play to a star's strengths. MGM also knew how to obscure or minimalize that same star's weakness. *Dancing Lady* itself has plenty of strengths and weaknesses. Yet it still does more than just get the job done. It represents, if never quite transcends, efficient factory filmmaking of its era. And inside of that magical era, that's not a bad thing.

12

The Good Earth (1937)

In 1937 *The Good Earth* was one of the outstanding productions of its time, the winner of sterling reviews, good box office, and Academy Awards. *The Good Earth* was also considered a fitting and appropriate tribute to its late producer, Irving Thalberg, who sadly had died that year at the age of thirty-seven. Eighty years later, the same film is derided and mocked, on the very rare occasions when anyone is brave enough to revive it at all, for its "offensive" racial stereotyping and, worse yet, for sporting a cast full of Caucasian actors impersonating Asians.

The Good Earth is, however, at least name-checked in the recent (2020) TV series *Hollywood*, which dramatized Chinese-American actress Anna May Wong's unsuccessful attempt to secure its leading role. *Hollywood* also showed us Luise Rainer, the actress who did play that leading role, giving her Oscar-night acceptance speech while, according to the series at least, the sidelined Wong looked on bitterly.

As *Hollywood* takes very politically correct pains to show us, *The Good Earth* is an easy target to deride when looking back across the ravine from our more "enlightened" time. The series doesn't bother to tell us that Wong could not *legally* have been cast in the film anyway. The role she coveted was that of the wife of *The Good Earth*'s leading man, Paul Muni, and due to Hays Code regulations prohibiting miscegenation on-screen, a White man and an Asian woman (although the word used at the time would have been "oriental") could not play man and wife—even if the "offending" couple were represented on-screen as being of the same race.

The Good Earth was considered a prestigious effort for the studio in 1937, less so today. *Author's collection*

As horrible as this sounds and, yes, as horrible as it was, Thalberg, to his credit, had sincerely wanted to cast Chinese actors in the film. But he also understood that the film's extravagant budget demanded stars in order to make it commercially viable. The popular Anna May Wong might have worked out box office wise, but sadly there was no comparable male Chinese-American star for her to appear opposite. The casting decision that has damned *The Good Earth*, then, was, to be fair, not so much racist in 1937 as it was financial.

Actually, there were Chinese people in supporting roles and as extras in *The Good Earth*. Chinese-American actor Keye Luke, for example, played the couple's oldest son. There were probably Japanese, Koreans, and Filipinos involved as well, although MGM didn't admit this publicly because, although China reportedly didn't object to Caucasians as the leads, it threatened to boycott the film if Japanese were involved. But most of the roles, as dictated by the casting of the leads, were filled by Caucasians.

Luise Rainer and Paul Muni, trying hard. *Photofest*

For example, Jewish-American star Paul Muni's second wife was played by Jewish-Austrian dancer Tilly Losch, who had played, or would play, similar exotics in *The Garden of Allah* (1936) and *Duel in the Sun* (1947).

It has been printed, and reported online, that Thalberg, perhaps as a consolation prize, offered Anna May Wong the role Tilly Losch eventually played and that Wong, perhaps seeing the part as just another of the oriental temptresses she had long been enacting, turned him down. It's impossible to trace the origin of this story, as there seems to be no internal written correspondence to verify it. But if it is true, the same miscegenation clause in the Hays Code could again have been evoked, and again could have kept Wong, who in 2022 would have her face imprinted upon US quarters, out of the movie in 1937. So, the story is probably fictional.

Paul Muni was one of the most acclaimed actors of his era. And in spite of the perceived black mark of *The Good Earth,* his reputation as an actor's actor is still largely intact today. It should be noted that Muni admirably does his best to make his character, Wang Lung, *not* a stereotype. Yet by refusing to talk with an "oriental" accent or to offensively protrude his teeth or bug out his eyes according to the then-popular stereotype, Muni comes across as what he is: a very good actor who, in trying to avoid cliché, looks and sounds like a regular guy, completely at odds and completely at war with his yellowface makeup and taped-back eyes. Keye Luke, as Wang Lung's son, wisely plays his part the same way Muni does, but because he really *is* Chinese, it works beautifully, proving both the rightness of Muni's interpretation and how wrongheaded his casting is.

Paul Muni had not been above ethnic characterizations in the past; his unforgettably vivid, and very Italian, gangster in *Scarface* (1932) stands out. But when offered the lead in *The Good Earth*, Muni reportedly told Thalberg, "I'm about as Chinese as Herbert Hoover."[1] Yet he took the role and, to his credit if not the ultimate benefit of the movie, brings to it as much dignity as he can.

His costar, Luise Rainer, was German-American, and although her Teutonic accent is occasionally noticeable, her genuinely affecting performance makes that accent and her Chinese makeup somehow less overtly offensive than Muni's. Rainer, who won back-to-back Oscars—here and for the previous year's *The Great Ziegfeld*—uses her body and her expressive eyes to make even planting a peach pit on her wedding day an unforgettable cinematic moment. Rainer had been something of a star on the stage in Europe under the tutelage of legendary director Max Reinhardt, although she is so subtly expressive that one wonders how effective she could have been on stage, without a camera, her quiet emotions seemingly perceptible only to that camera.

The expansive Chinese village built on the backlot for *The Good Earth* is reused here for *They Met in Bombay* (1941).
Marc Wanamaker/Bison Archives

This film, and that camera, is directed by Sidney Franklin, although several other (uncredited) directors were reportedly involved, as was the studio house style at the time. So it is probably Thalberg, and not Franklin or any screenwriter, who we should credit for many of *The Good Earth*'s most affecting moments, moments both tall and tiny. For example, the scene mentioned above with the peach pit pays off poignantly decades later when Rainer's character dies near the (now grown) tree that has sprung from that seed.

Moments like this make it a shame that very few, especially those who see how *The Good Earth* is derided in the *Hollywood* series, will bother to seek out the actual film and then, perhaps, try to get past its admittedly dubious casting choices. Because the actual film remains one of the studio's, and the industry's, crowning achievements.

Novelist Pearl S. Buck, a daughter of missionaries in China, had published *The Good Earth* as a book in 1931, and its Pulitzer Prize–winning success had created a brief vogue in the West for "exotic" Eastern cultures. The resultant movie—which, like the book, charted several decades in the life of a Chinese peasant and his family—was personally produced by MGM and a then-ailing Thalberg on a mammoth $2.8 million budget. Acres of Chinese landscapes were meticulously reproduced on the lot and in the San Fernando Valley. A subplot involving a plague of locusts descending upon the farmers' fields, designed by pioneering montagist Slavko Vorkapich, remains one of the great action scenes in cinema. The special effects here compare favorably with similar sequences created decades later for other marauding insect films like *The Naked Jungle* (1954) and *The Swarm* (1978).

Another highlight of *The Good Earth* is the exodus by the starving farmers to the city. Here the script in some ways anticipates the studio's much later *Doctor Zhivago*. Both films even contain memorable sequences involving an escape from a blighted landscape aboard a train. So it is perhaps worth noting that both stories are Americanized looks at a tempestuous, revolutionary time in an exotic, far off (to Western filmmakers) land. Both stories are also seen through the eyes of a relatively non-politicized individual who, again in both stories, becomes infatuated with two very different women.

The Good Earth also anticipates *Gone with the Wind* in some of the sequences mentioned above and in both films' characters' oft-stated love for the land. Should we go there then? Should we mention that no one has ever criticized the *Doctor Zhivago* cast for not being Russian enough or *Gone with the Wind* for casting three of its four leads with British actors? Although in the latter case, Southerners, in 1939 at least, were reportedly happy that Scarlett O'Hara would not be played by a Yankee.

Time has not treated *The Good Earth* nearly so kindly.

The studio's (short-term, as it turned out) acclaim for *The Good Earth* led it to repeat the formula, for *Dragon Seed* in 1944. This time it was Katharine Hepburn leading a large cast of Western actors under taped-back eyes and yellow makeup enacting a Pearl S. Buck–penned saga. Unfortunately, despite the film's World War II–era pro-Chinese (and anti-Japanese) angle, the result was much less successful then and, even more than *The Good Earth*, is an embarrassing, non-PC pariah today.

And, of course, *The Good Earth* would also be the last film, or at least one of the last films, for its prolific legendary producer, Irving Thalberg. Thalberg never lived to see *The Good Earth* and so never lived to see the card that opens the film, which represents the first time he would ever be credited by his real name on-screen. It says: "To the memory of Irving Grant Thalberg, we dedicate this picture, his last great achievement."

13

Love Finds Andy Hardy (1938)

Forget about Tarzan. Forget about James Bond. The most popular series of films in MGM history, dollar spent for dollar returned, were about a diminutive small-town teenager and his family.

The long-running *Andy Hardy* series began inauspiciously in 1937 with *A Family Affair*, which had been adapted from *Skidding*, a play by Aurania Rouverol. Rouverol was an author-playwright who had already written, sporadically, for the studio and so was probably all too happy to have that studio adapt an original work. Incidentally, the author's daughter, writer Jean Rouverol, would join the Communist party in 1943 and be subsequently blacklisted. For *Skidding*, an actor named Charles Eaton had created the role of Andy "Dutch" Hardy in the New York production. But for the film, in-house contract player Mickey Rooney was cast opposite Lionel Barrymore as his father, James Hardy, a judge presiding over the bucolic small town of Carvel, USA. (In the play Carvel had been specifically placed in Idaho, although this was contradicted numerous times in the films as the series progressed.)

Judge Hardy was clearly the central character in this film, as he had been on stage. And when audiences responded well to the story's drama and (to a lesser degree this time) its comedy, another "episode" was demanded, *You're Only Young Once*, which came out the same year.

A Family Affair had, make no mistake, been a B movie. But it had a Broadway pedigree, had the prestige of the Barrymore name attached to its shirttails, and was similar in tone (and cast) to the recent, and similarly prestigious, *Ah Wilderness!*

(1935). But *You're Only Young Once* could boast of no such pretentions. Consequently, some of the cast, specifically Barrymore, was replaced or declined to participate. (Actually, Lionel was in London at the time of the sequel's production shooting *A Yank at Oxford.*) Therefore, stern, gray-haired Lewis Stone, a long way from his pseudo–Lon Chaney role in *Grand Hotel,* became the new Judge Hardy.

The new, pared-down cast (Andy lost one older sister in the transition) actually helped perpetuate the franchise in that the emphasis shifted subtly (at first) to the antics of Mickey Rooney. In spite of a thread of sentimentality on display in this and all future episodes (an MGM-Mayer trademark), the "dumbing down" of the property also created the template for what would become known as the situation comedy, with rampant misunderstandings and complications ensuing involving Andy's home problems, money problems, and girl problems.

"Now comes the fourth and the best," claimed the ad art for *Love Finds Andy Hardy* (1938). *Author's collection*

Especially his girl problems. The next chapter, *Judge Hardy's Children* (1938), mixed Andy up with an ambassador's daughter (Jacqueline Laurent). Stone was still billed first, but Rooney, now a title character of sorts, stole ample scenes and screen time.

The quintessential Andy Hardy film, *Love Finds Andy Hardy* came out the same year. Many fans consider this to be the best of the series, and subsequent films would seldom deviate from the template established most fully here. Financially, *Love Finds Andy Hardy* was also the most successful of the sixteen episodes eventually produced. In fact, this little programmer—budgeted, as each entry would be, at less than $300,000—would pull in a remarkable $2.25 million at the box office.

Consequently, the golden-egg formula utilized by the series seldom varied much. For example, in *Love Finds Andy Hardy*, Andy's long-suffering girlfriend, Polly Benedict (Ann Rutherford), is going out of town. In her absence, he agrees to escort an out-of-town friend's girl to keep her from getting lonesome. He does this as a favor— and because he's being paid to do so. Either way, it's not at all surprising that his friend is worried, because this abandoned lass is played by Lana Turner. Andy, meanwhile, also makes friends with next-door neighbor Betsy Booth (Judy Garland), an aspiring singer who has a crush on Andy, which he fails to notice because he thinks of her as "just a kid." Complications ensue.

In Carvel, complications always ensue. There is also a subplot about Andy trying to get money to buy his first car; there is a big country club dance coming up too. Of course there is. The most surprising thing about *Love Finds Andy Hardy* is not that, somehow, all these elements are smoothly steamrolled together but that it happens so amusingly. Only, a more serious digression regarding Andy's mother (Fay Holden), who is called out of town when her (unseen) mother gets sick, feels like one subplot too many.

At this point, though, the formula was still relatively fresh and the cast still seemed to be having fun, which is infectious, so it's easy to see how this modest series became so astonishingly popular. The following year, 1939, Rooney and company would make *three more* Hardy films. MGM's total profits that year were $9.3 million, of which $4 million was directly attributable to Andy Hardy and his family. Mickey Rooney, not surprisingly, would be voted the most popular star in the world that year by movie exhibitors. This would happen again in 1940. And again in 1941.

The series was largely a Louis B. Mayer creation. Perhaps "creation" is the wrong word, but the mogul certainly nurtured the environment at the studio where a series such as this could flourish. And he sincerely seemed to believe that the Hardy series represented all that was right and good about the United States and its people. Of course, it didn't hurt that Mayer's feelings were so well validated financially. In 1942 MGM would receive a special Academy Award "for its achievement in representing the American way of life in the production of the Andy Hardy series of films." Probably no honor in his career ever pleased Mayer quite as much.

The series was so successful, and for so long, that Mayer, without anyone noticing at the time, cannily repeated the formula in a second film series about a young doctor and an older doctor, working at the same hospital, who develop a father-son-type rapport with each other. *Young Dr. Kildare* (1938) was the first of a long-running series with Lew Ayres and, interestingly, Lionel Barrymore. And just as Andy Hardy created the

The Hardy family (and some good friends and neighbors) gather for a formal portrait. From left: Cecilia Parker, Sarah Haden, Ann Rutherford, Lewis Stone, Judy Garland, Gene Reynolds, Fay Holden, Lana Turner, and Mickey Rooney. Only Haden, who usually played Aunt Milly, would not appear in *Love Finds Andy Hardy* (1938).

Scott Brogan (www.thejudyroom.com.)

template for an entire genre of American situation comedies, Dr. Kildare too was later revived as a successful (1961–1966) dramatic TV series.

As the above synopsis may begin to illustrate, however, if the Hardys were the typical all-American family, and if Andy was the typical all-American teenager, then typical American fathers in 1938 should perhaps have considered locking up their daughters. True, young Hardy doesn't seem to know how to do anything beyond kiss all these girls, but kiss them he does—again, and again. And afterward he whoops and pistons his teenage limbs up and down like a ribald wolf in a Tex Avery cartoon. When his girlfriend is out of town, Andy also kisses his friend's girl—after promising, and actually being paid cold cash, not to do so. The only girl he doesn't put his moves on is Garland's appealing young Betsy, who apparently would like nothing better.

Andy is not so wholesome as one might think in other ways either. He fights incessantly with his sister, Marian (Cecilia Parker), lies to his father about his intentions to buy a car, and is so callow that he spends more time worrying about who he is taking to the dance than about his own grandmother's ongoing life-and-death struggle.

The rest of the family is no better. The righteous Judge Hardy actually reduces the sentence of a juvenile delinquent because the kid does him a personal favor. While sitting on the bench, he also poaches a cook for his family from under the very nose of a defendant who is at his mercy. Daughter Marion later tries to fire that same cook because, get this, that badly-used-by-all-parties domestic has the audacity to try to throw out some cold coffee! And as for Mom, well, maybe she can be excused for not representing the American way of life so "positively" as other family members because the lady might not even be an American. When Mrs. Hardy goes away to tend her sick mother, her trip is to . . . Canada! Has anyone ever thought to check this suspicious woman's green card? Maybe fellow closet-Canadian L. B. Mayer was responsible.

George B. Seitz is the director here, as he was on ten other series entries. He died in 1944, after *Andy Hardy's Blonde Trouble*, or he probably would have continued with the series, although by that time, the series was finally starting to sputter out. The box office take, still impressive, was finally tailing off, if slightly, and production delays necessitated by Rooney's military stint necessitated a similar period in uniform for Andy (apparently dodging the draft was not among young Mr. Hardy's sins).

Love Laughs at Andy Hardy (1946) would be the last audiences would see of the family for twelve years. That same year, a darker look at postwar American families, *The Best Years of Our Lives*, swept the Oscars, making it seem frivolous and even insensitive to have Andy Hardy depicted as coming back from war, moving into his old bedroom, and resuming his life as a carefree, but now overage, teenager. Although that is exactly what the film tried to have him do.

But audiences had changed, even if Andy hadn't. The cynicism and postwar hang-over those audiences were feeling at the time made these antics in ever-quaint Carvel seem almost instantly dated, although the alternative—a bitter and war-traumatized Andy—wouldn't have worked either.

Twelve years later, however, after television sitcoms had mined and pillaged the series' tropes so extensively, and after postwar angst had been largely wallpapered over, it was felt that the time might be ripe for a reunion with Andy and the gang. Mickey Rooney's career had slumped badly after the war, so his agent easily talked him into taking a Hardy-centric spec script back to his old studio. MGM was interested, if only because, again, the venture could be mounted cheaply. Fortunately, the Carvel sets, like Rooney himself, were still largely intact on the backlot after all those years. The resultant film, *Andy Hardy Comes Home* (1958), was to be a literal homecoming for Mickey Rooney as well.

Sadly, what could be said about Mickey, and about those sets, could not be said about the rest of the original cast. Lewis Stone had passed away in 1953.

The part obviously could not be recast again, so Judge Hardy was given the same fate in the script. In Stone's absence, Rooney basically assumed the role of the father character, now dispensing sage advice to his own son, Andy Jr., played by his own son, Teddy Rooney. Ann Rutherford, who had been playing Polly Benedict since 1937, refused to return as Mrs. Andy Hardy, however, allegedly telling Mickey that "Andy never would have married his high school sweetheart." Maybe that's why the Mick didn't then try to contact Judy Garland.

In spite of its nostalgia value and undoubted good intentions, *Andy Hardy Comes Home* was not a success. Ultimately, the series, although unquestionably a vast influence on popular culture, actual families, American social engineer-

Ann Rutherford and Lana Turner make a fuss over Mickey Rooney while Judy Garland hovers. *Photofest*

ing, and situation comedies, just had not aged very well. In 1958 Americans were fleeing small towns like Carvel for the suburbs, and rock and roll was now the music of choice for a new generation of angrier Andys. This new escapade, updated but outdated, could not help but come across as trite and even somewhat condescending. This was material that, after all, was already antique in 1946. By 1958, a Hardy homecoming was as quaint as the car Mickey had once driven and the songs he and Judy had boogied to so long ago.

14

The Wizard of Oz (1939)

Back in 1981, critic Danny Peary remarked that "it has often been joked that every film made since 1939 includes some reference to *Wizard*." Peary continues by stating, "I'm not sure this isn't true: because almost every title one scrutinizes, from 'A'—*Alice Doesn't Live Here Anymore* (1974)—to 'Z'—the revealingly titled *Zardoz* (1974)—does indeed pay tribute to *Wizard*."[1]

Stories about *The Wizard of Oz* are, as can be imagined, as omnipotent as the movie itself and references to it. There is, of course, the tale of the little person actor who hung himself during production, on camera yet. There is the urban legend that Pink Floyd's *Dark Side of the Moon* album was synced to comment on the film's action. There are the tales of the munchkin actors' debaucheries at the Culver Hotel. There are Judy Garland's complaints about being upstaged by her taller, older costars. There are the stories that *The Wizard of Oz*'s sets, specifically the yellow brick road, somehow still survive at the former MGM lot. There are rumors that the song "Over the Rainbow" is about the Holocaust. There are a hundred more. Tall tales about *The Wizard of Oz* seem to hang about the film like ornaments on a Christmas tree. Most, including all those mentioned above, are patently false.

But the fact that such stories exist only reaffirms *The Wizard of Oz*'s place in the American mythos, even if such myths no longer resonate as such for many of us. More's the pity.

Sadly, we are now, to a degree unimaginable in the twentieth century, largely living in a post-*Wizard* world. Something like 40 percent of today's children have

This banner ad for *The Wizard of Oz* (1939) represents one of many advertising and publicity campaigns the studio used to try to sell their expensive production to the public. *Photofest*

reportedly never seen the film. And many of those modern children, when exposed to the movie for the first time, are no longer able to suspend their disbelief—blaming the film's "primitive" special effects and languid pace for their disinterest. Modern children, and even many adults, are also put off by the film's "corny" tone and sentimentality. The very theme of the movie—stated on-screen and much beloved by Louis B. Mayer—that there is "no place like home" could itself now be considered somewhat off-putting in a society where home, as critics like Peary have remarked, is sadly not always the best place to be, and where most of the population now lives in urban areas as opposed to farms.

Criticism of *The Wizard of Oz* is not new, of course. Fans of the film may be surprised that in 1939, critics generally deemed the film inferior to Walt Disney's *Snow White and the Seven Dwarves* (1937). *The New Republic*'s Otis Ferguson, for example, dismissed the film as "Cecil B. DeMille and the Seven Thousand Dwarves,"[2] and Russell Maloney in *The New Yorker* likewise carped: "I sat cringing before M-G-M's Technicolor production of 'The Wizard of Oz,' which displays no trace of imagination, good taste, or ingenuity."[3] But generally the 1939 reviews were positive, if by no means ecstatic, although a critic then could not realistically be expected to anticipate the effect the film would have on future generations.

Commercially, *The Wizard of Oz* was a success in 1939. But it should be noted that the production cost to the studio had been almost $3 million—only slightly less than the same year's *Gone with the Wind* (although that film was twice as long)—but

Stage 27 dressed as Muchkinland for *The Wizard of Oz* Photofest

still, these massive production costs made it nearly impossible for *Wizard* to generate a profit that year. And it didn't, not until a 1949 rerelease finally pushed the film into the black. Subsequent reissues and, in particular, television broadcasts starting in 1956, have of course made *The Wizard of Oz* an evergreen financial heavy lifter.

It's hard not to think about all those 1956 children, in one-piece pajamas or wearing Davy Crockett coonskin caps, who were encouraged by their parents to sit down in front of their televisions—black and white, but surely glowing blue across living rooms all over the country that year—who were so captivated by *The Wizard of Oz* that they watched it again and again, year after year, and then showed it to their children, who then showed it to *their* children. The film became the cinematic equivalent of a folk song or a beloved storybook that could be enjoyed again and again, if only once a year. So in this case, it wasn't MGM but rather television, initially CBS and later NBC, that created the *Wizard of Oz* cult.

The little people playing the Munchkins discover that the roads outside the studio gates are not paved with yellow brick.
Photofest

These television screenings, which were annual for generations, once made *The Wizard of Oz* the most watched, and most referenced, movie in history. The impact of these yearly trips over the rainbow cannot be underestimated. "Remember that there were only three national networks then," filmmaker Les Perkins reminds us. "So half of America would watch! An *Oz* screening was a major TV event. Kids talked about it in school the following days."[4]

That first Saturday, November 3, 1956, the TV broadcast was hosted by Bert Lahr, the film's Cowardly Lion. This set a precedent in that the film was often aired as a "special" or with a special host. For example, in 1970, for the first telecast after the death of Judy Garland, Gregory Peck introduced the film and of course paid tribute to the film's late leading lady. In 1990 Angela Lansbury was the hostess, in material later used in home video releases. But during all of its network transmissions, the film's annual airing was treated as something unique. As such, *The Wizard of Oz* was often broadcast during Easter/Passover or between Thanksgiving and Christmas. And most of the country tended to tune in too, year after year. It's not at all surprising, then, that the Library of Congress long ago declared *Oz* the most-watched film in history.

The last network airing (again, on CBS) of *The Wizard of Oz* was in 1998. By then the film belonged to TV mogul Ted Turner, who subsequently broadcast it on cable television—repeatedly, constantly, and incessantly—which, along with home-video versions, made viewing *The Wizard of Oz* less of an event and much more like binging on any other old movie. Today *The Wizard of Oz* is the *only* old movie—brilliantly restored for television, Blu-ray, or streaming platforms as it is—that is actually *diminished* by being readily available any time one cares to partake of its pleasures.

To quote Perkins again: "My movie-buff friend Rob Ray pointed out that both *The Ten Commandments* and *The Sound of Music* still have annual network airings. The same could be done for *The Wizard of Oz*. It should again be run on only one network, and only once a year. That network could bring back the tradition of celebrity hosts, and could air it *complete*, as *Oz* began being cut in the 1970s to fit more commercials into a two-hour time slot. With its innocent joys and its universal truths, *The Wizard of Oz* really deserves just such a platform. Especially amid so much dark, angry media today."[5]

15

Gone with the Wind (1939)

Who was that wise, or acidly sarcastic, critic who once told us that there are only two American movies: *Gone with the Wind* . . . and all the rest?

There are movies, and there are *movies*. Regardless of what you, or I, might think about it as a work of popular art or history, as a barometer of popular culture, or even as cinema, *Gone with the Wind* is still the greatest *movie* ever made.

Note that no one today is calling *Gone with the Wind* the greatest *film* ever made. *Gone with the Wind* is instead the John Wayne of motion pictures: adored, despised, revered, fetishized, marginalized, worshiped, politicized, mocked, objectified, parodied. And yet, like—let's just say it—its curiously unsympathetic heroine, *Gone with the Wind* just refuses to lie down and die. Like it or not, *Gone with the Wind* is still very much with us.

Gone with the Wind has been a very important movie, perhaps the most important movie ever, to countless millions of people for generations. This is not only true in the South, where the film was set, but also around the world. For example, released in Japan after World War II, the film, which after all depicts a culture destroyed by outsiders, is still one of the most successful pictures ever released there.

Gone with the Wind has also been a consistent, reliable, decade-after-decade cash cow for MGM. The studio reissued the film in 1942, 1947, 1954, 1961, 1967, 1971, 1974, and 1979. Each of these releases, which, remember, foisted an increasingly aged picture on an increasingly younger and presumably more enlightened audience, still managed to consistently make countless millions of dollars at the box office. Even today, in inflation-adjusted dollars, the thing is unquestionably the most successful piece of popular art ever made. Further theatrical and home rereleases have subsequently feathered the nests of others after MGM foolishly let *Gone with the Wind* get away from them.

There's more. When *Gone with the Wind* was broadcast on network television for the first time in 1976, a remarkable thirty-seven years (!) after its first release, it still managed to amass the highest viewership ratings ever attained on broadcast television for a theatrical film. In all, some 47.5 percent of all households in the United States owning televisions tuned in to at least part of that first historic broadcast. This is a worldwide milestone that even today has not been surpassed, never even been approached. And in this era of infinite television choices, services, and channels, it almost certainly never will.

And there is still more. There have probably been more books written about *Gone with the Wind*, and about the writing of or making of *Gone with the Wind*, than any other comparable human endeavor ever attempted. Novels have also been written about the story's creation and genesis, even continuing the adventures of its fictional characters. There have also been movies and documentaries made and plays produced on the stage about the saga's epic production. What's more, serious critics and literary authors still generate thousands of words annually discussing the film's influences and impact upon the world—often derisively.

The point is that these writers—fans and foes, critics and literary lions—whatever wise or inane things they come up with in regard to *Gone with the Wind*, still won't stop talking about it!

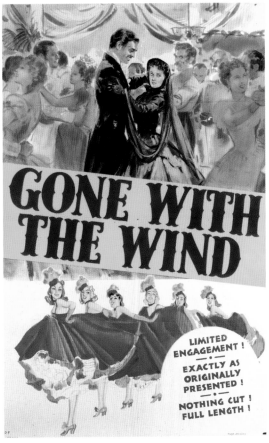

In 1947, for its first major theatrical reissue, MGM commissioned new artwork for *Gone with the Wind* (1939). Audiences again responded to the film, which proceeded to gross an additional, and astonishing, $9 million. *Photofest*

And this is still going on, although, like the film's heroine, many now see *Gone with the Wind* as problematic, racist, and flawed. In 1977 the American Film Institute chose the film, to absolutely no one's surprise, as the greatest of all American films. But in their 1998 survey, it was number four; in 2007 it was number six. The ever-idiosyncratic IMDB poll currently places the film at an inglorious number 165, although a 2014 Harris poll of audiences still placed it at number one.

One might expect Liberal or Black audiences to react negatively to a film that, after all, deals with the relationship between White and Black Americans before, during, and after the Civil War. Director Spike Lee, for example, has, and with some justification, condemned the film, although he does concede to its qualities as cinema. In 2017 *Gone with the Wind*, which had run annually at the Orpheum Theatre in Memphis for a record-setting thirty-four years, was pulled from the schedule because of its perceived racial insensitivities.

Yes, it's true that *Gone with the Wind*'s Black characters are presented as cringewor-thily subservient. But it should be noted that these same characters are also the most honorable people in the film. Hattie McDaniel's Oscar-winning Mammy, for example, is an all-knowing moral compass for the Whites, and for the entire saga.

Surely, in the twenty-first century most audiences of any color could be expected to realize that *Gone with the Wind* presents a point of view, like all art does, and in this case that point of view, correct or not, unpleasant or not, is an antebellum one. This is, after all, a movie about people who *own* people. None of the film's detractors ever bother to recall a scene in which Ashley Wilkes (Leslie Howard) admits that he had planned on freeing his slaves had the war not done it for him—a very liberal stance, if one cares to consider it, for a nineteenth-century White plantation owner.

Interestingly, a 2014 *Economist* poll noted that 73 percent of Black Americans felt that the film was "one of the best" or "very good"—a number not that much behind the number (87 percent) of White Americans who felt the same way, suggesting per-haps that it is political correctness rather than genuine racial outrage that has made *Gone with the Wind* problematic today.

Mercifully, it's not the purpose of this volume to create a bibliography of the fervor and emotions the film has stirred up, and which continue to simmer even today. But the very fact that a movie made in 1939 can still be at the center of so much emotion—derision as well as love—is important, and makes the film important in any reckoning of MGM.

It's also ironic that the film was not originally an MGM production at all. "Forget it, Louis, no Civil War film ever made a nickel," Thalberg is supposed to have told Mayer—a conversation that probably didn't happen. Surely they both would have

Clark Gable and Vivien Leigh attempt to relax during production. The famous duo's off-screen relationship was reportedly adversarial, which perhaps contributed to their fiery on-screen chemistry. *Photofest*

heard of a picture called *Birth of a Nation*? Mayer, in fact, had made his first fortune playing that very film circa 1915.

Instead, the Margaret Mitchell bestseller was purchased by Mayer's son-in-law/former employee, independent producer David O. Selznick, who then had to give Mayer distribution rights in exchange for the services of Clark Gable.

It was Selznick who spent an unprecedented $4 million to create a film that, by design, was intended to be the Hollywood spectacle of spectacles. He fought for the perfect cast and the perfect production and the perfect score. Perhaps, in hindsight, his biggest gamble was his own conviction that he would know that perfection when he found it.

Fortunately, the material warranted his obsession. The Pulitzer Prize–winning book was effectively a Civil War love story with an unforgettable setting, a setting author Pat Conroy has memorably described as a "backwater Camelot."[1] And Selznick inarguably, compellingly, then told that story through the eyes of truly unforgettable characters.

Today people forget that the heroine, Scarlett O'Hara (Vivien Leigh, of course), actually represents not the antebellum South of slavery at all but rather the new South, and the new Southern belle. Mitchell herself was an Atlanta journalist and jazz-age

On the eve of production on the biggest film in history, producer David O. Selznick tries hard to look contemplative while exploring some of its expensive sets on the Pathé backlot. *Photofest*

flapper, after all. Every other character in the story, even the cynical realist Rhett Butler (Gable, of course), by the end retreats into nostalgia. But the final strength of the novel, the film, and its heroine is that none of them are sentimental. A world may collapse in the wind today, but tomorrow, as they all tell us repeatedly, is another day.

Like Rhett Butler, David O. Selznick eventually retreated into his own past as well. He spent the rest of his life trying to impossibly "top" *Gone with the Wind*. And although his opus was, as noted, rereleased to tremendous success throughout his lifetime (he died in 1965), Selznick himself was unable to share in that windfall. Stupidly, in 1943 financer Jock Whitney, who had bought out Selznick's interests in the picture, sold those rights to MGM, giving the company, almost inadvertently, the most commercially successful film in history.

At least until 1986. That was the year that, to MGM's detriment and as yet another testament to the film's evergreen appeal, media mogul Ted Turner purchased MGM — the entire studio, lock, stock, and library — at a cost of some $1.6 billion.

He did this, reportedly, because he wanted to own *Gone with the Wind*.

Ted Turner's obsession with *Gone with the Wind*, like *Citizen Kane*'s love for his lost sled, has been very well documented. Born in Ohio, Turner has repeatedly said that he only found himself as a person when he moved to the South with his family. Eventually, and tellingly, he ended up in Scarlett O'Hara's own Atlanta. Ted Turner also looks a bit like Clark Gable, a resemblance he plays to by sporting a small mustache. Subordinates and business associates have often noted that the best way to please Turner is to remark on the resemblance.

Among his several homes is the so called (by Turner) Avalon Plantation in Florida—the name of which evokes yet another lost era of Cavaliers. Inside the house could long be found the original portrait of Scarlett O'Hara as seen in the film. In a 2004 article in *Architectural Digest*, ostensibly about the home, Turner and his friends were both quoted. The mogul in particular was flippant but also unintentionally frank in discussing the portrait, and its hold over him at the time:

> "When I bought MGM with its great library and owned *Gone with the Wind*, I toyed with the idea of opening a *Gone with the Wind* Museum in Atlanta, and I was looking for memorabilia to buy to put in it," Turner recounts. "This painting turned up, and when the museum didn't happen, I hung it in my house. It's when Scarlett tells Rhett she's not going to have sex with him anymore 'cause she doesn't want any more kids. She says, 'I'm going to lock my door at night,' and he tells her that if he wanted to get in, no lock would keep him out. Later, he's in his bedroom down the hall, where he has this picture of her hanging, and he takes a big swig of whiskey or something and then hurls his glass at it—you can see the mark where it hit." A frequent guest at Avalon confides, "Ted's men friends always point at the painting and say to their wives, 'Frankly, my dear, I don't give a damn!' None of Ted's wives or girlfriends have ever been able to stand that picture, by the way; it's just too much competition—it makes Scarlett the lady of the house." Turner readily admits to "identifying" with Scarlett every bit as much as Rhett. "She liked the land; she liked her plantation—that's where she was going when everything fell apart."[2]

Eventually, a *Gone with the Wind* Museum *was* established in Atlanta and, true to his word, Turner has allowed the portrait, painted for the film by artist Helen Carlton, to be displayed there.

If Turner really did buy the studio to obtain one film, a certain type of person with romantic sensibilities might well speculate whether anywhere else in the world can be found another single item, epoch, or individual one man has paid so much for in order to attain. If so, then in addition to meaning a lot of things to a lot of people, *Gone with the Wind* was also, for Ted Turner anyway, the modern age Helen of Troy.

16

Puss Gets the Boot (1940)

As the Tiffany's of the entertainment industry, MGM studio brass in the 1930s were frustrated by their failure to create a cartoon franchise that could compete with the output of independent producer Walt Disney. During that decade Disney's product was distributed by Columbia Pictures, then United Artists, and finally by RKO, bringing popular and critical success, and one Academy Award after another to those rival studios. Another rival studio, Warner Bros., whose animated product was created by Leon Schlesinger Productions during this period, spent much less money on their cartoons than Disney, but their product was also, at least in the opinion of that MGM brass, frustratingly popular with audiences.

MGM already had its own in-house cartoon studio, founded in 1937 and headed by Fred Quimby, which in the 1930s consistently failed to garner either audiences or awards. Their "Captain and the Kids" series, for example, although based on a successful and of course expensively acquired comic strip, resoundingly failed to catch on with either audiences or exhibiters, and "Count Screwloose," another seemingly can't-lose import from the funny pages, immediately followed exactly the same dismal pattern.

Surely gun-shy after two expensive failures, the "Barney Bear" shorts, the fledgling unit's third time at bat was developed completely in-house. In fact, Barney's grumpy mannerisms were largely based on the studio's also in-house, resident live-action curmudgeon, Wallace Beery. Both Buddy and Beery would subsequently rattle about the studio for several more years, with some success. But "some success" was not then the MGM business model.

M·G·M CARTOONS

PUSS GETS THE BOOT...

SINCE EVE evolved from Adam's rib, cats have waged constant war against mice. Now comes a one-mouse revolution brought on by a cat, that ends in victory for the mouse.

This story, as told in Rudolf Ising's latest M-G-M Cartoon, "Puss Gets the Boot," relates how this one small mouse, taking advantage of one large cat's shortcoming, subdues the larger warrior in a battle of wits and with the aid, of course, of circumstances.

Ising's cat feels particularly wicked, this day. Before putting an end to the mouse of his choice, he decides to toy with it. As the mouse pokes his head out of his hole, friend cat grabs him with his tail, flips him in the air, and lets him fall to the floor senseless. The cat then dips his paw into some ink and draws a false hole in the wall for the mouse. As soon as he awakens, the mouse makes a dash for his hole, runs into the solid wall and is knocked unconscious again. This time, when he awakens, he is angry. With great courage he strolls up to the cat and punches him right in the eye.

Furious, the cat runs after the mouse, and dashes right into a pillar that supports a beautiful vase. The vase falls to the floor, crashes into a thousand pieces, and the cat, Jasper, by name, is in for it. Immediately, the housekeeper chases after Jasper with a broom, beats him, and warns him that if anything else is broken in the house, he will be thrown into the street forever.

Now, the mouse, named Pee-Wee, knows how to handle Jasper. If Jasper tries to hurt him again, he'll break something and blame it on the cat. The next time Jasper chases Pee-Wee, the mouse runs to the edge of a table, grabs one of a set of cocktail glasses, and defiantly shouts that he will drop the glass if the cat comes any closer. With each of Jasper's lunges, Pee-Wee threatens to drop the glass. Finally, just to be ornery, Pee-Wee does drop the glass which Jasper catches, before it breaks, by the skin of his teeth. Another glass and still another come hurtling down with Jasper catching each one before it hits the floor. Now Jasper gets wise and places soft cushions all over so that even if Pee-Wee does drop the glasses, they won't break.

Jasper moves toward Pee-Wee, who threatens to drop another glass. Jasper laughs, the mouse drops the glass and it falls on the pillows and doesn't break. Immediately, Pee-Wee is in Jasper's tail, being tossed up and down like a ball of wool. But Jasper flips Pee-Wee a bit too high. The mouse catches on the ledge of a mantel on which there are many valuable plates. Immediately he starts throwing them to the floor. The cat dashes around madly, catching each dish until his arms are full.

Calmly, Pee-Wee comes down from the mantel, and kicks Jasper right into next week. Up in the air goes every dish, and down they come. The housekeeper catches the cat and banishes him from the house forever.

Calmly, and with great confidence, Pee-Wee strolls back to his hole, sighing, "Home, Sweet Home."

Pre-release publicity for *Puss Gets the Boot* (1940), such as this exhibitor's synopsis, did not treat the little film as anything special. Note, for example, that future feline superstar Tom the Cat is still named Jasper; and Jerry the Mouse, in spite of being christened Jinx during production, is here referred to as Pee-Wee. *Author's collection*

Things got better when, in 1939, the department's expensive animated short *Peace on Earth* was nominated for an Academy Award. But that film's grim subject matter—a world of animals after people have killed one another off—precluded its becoming either a series or a stand-alone moneymaker.

All this was about to change, though, when Joseph Barbera and William Hanna, both of whom were part of the department already, teamed officially for the first time to create a short called *Puss Gets the Boot* (1940). Unlike the moralizing *Peace on Earth*, however, this was intended from the start to be the inauguration of a (hopefully) long-running series. The stars of this short were a housecat named Jasper and a troublesome mouse, unidentified on-screen but referred to by Hanna and Barbera, and by producer Rudolf Ising, as Jinx.

Puss Gets the Boot was, as Hanna and Barbera, and Isling and Quimby had hoped, a big success. In fact, it was nominated for an Academy Award, which it lost to *The Milky Way*, which, indicative of the Cartoon Department's sudden winning streak, was also an MGM short. Even better, this unexpected and fortuitous one-two punch by the department represented the first time since the Best Animated Short category had been created (in 1931) that Walt Disney had not won in that category!

The Milky Way got the glory, but it was *Puss Gets the Boot* that instigated, as had been intended, the series. But it was not intended, not even hoped for surely, that the series would then become one of the most successful series, animated or not, and by whatever definition of the word "series" one cares to apply, of all time.

Certainly, audiences in 1940 had never seen anything quite like the (quickly renamed) Tom and Jerry. Eighty-plus years on, it's impossible to describe just how fresh a tale of a cat chasing a mouse could then be. In contrast to the Warner cartoons, which were topical, talky, and gag-driven, and Disney's "Silly Symphonies," which strove to be lyrical and poetic, the adventures of that cat and little mouse were entirely new, as well as fast paced, crude, rude, and violent.

And very successful. Hanna and Barbera produced 113 more Tom and Jerry cartoons in the initial series, winning seven Academy Awards in the process. The duo also appeared in the live-action features *Anchors Aweigh* (1945), where Jerry dances with Gene Kelly, and *Dangerous When Wet* (1953), in which they both swim with Esther Williams. The series trumpeted violently on until 1958, when MGM closed its Cartoon Department for the first time.

But even that didn't keep that mouse and cat out of the limelight. In 1962 the studio released a compilation feature called *Tom and Jerry Festival of Fun*, which combined scant new footage with clips from their early exploits. The unexpected success of this project caused MGM to then contract with assorted outside, and occasionally inside, producers to create new and original cartoons starring the duo. These shorts were often produced overseas and/or on tight budgets, but despite the obvious drop in quality that resulted, the pair's rewarmed adventures continued to be successful with audiences. Those shorts, under different titles and by different people, continued to run intermittently until 1982, long after there was no market for any other theatrical cartoon shorts. Even today, Warner Bros., the current owner of the franchise, continues to put the cat and mouse through their (now less-violent) paces intermittently in both big-screen and television or direct-to-video productions, most recently with 2021's predictably titled feature *Tom & Jerry*, which largely placed the animated duo in a live-action setting.

The future Tom and Jerry, in their debut, were less anthropomorphized than they would later become, although, unlike assorted mice and rabbits infesting rival studios, they would largely retain their identities as animals. *Author's collection*

But what about where it all began? What about *Puss Gets the Boot*?

Well, for starters, this little cartoon, along with *Steamboat Willie* (1928), which introduced Mickey Mouse, and *The Wild Hare* (1940), the official debut of Bugs Bunny, is probably the most influential seven minutes of animation ever made. And Mickey and Bugs, it should be mentioned, have to date only "won" a single competitive Oscar each, and that the mouse and the rabbit have always been supported by a stable of other popular cartoon characters. But the cat and mouse seldom needed to team up with anyone. Tom and Jerry were the whole show.

One way that Disney, and to a lesser extent even Warner Bros., did consistently outmaneuver MGM was in the world of character-based merchandise and what would become known as consumer products. In particular, Mickey Mouse, since his debut, has been consistently and aggressively marketed as a moneymaking product. MGM, by contrast, has always been terrible at marketing anything other than their movies. Even so, even allowing for the astounding shortsightedness of MGM executives during these decades, it's hard to ignore the sheer volume, the thousands of Tom and Jerry–related ephemera—comic books, toys, commercials, video games, parodies, and even dubious food products—that have featured the contentious duo over the years. Try to imagine, if you can, the unforgettable—and bone-snappingly violent—theme park

Future cartoon legends William Barbera and Joseph Hanna at work on an early (1940) Tom and Jerry short. *Marc Wanamaker/Bison Archives*

the duo might have presided over had MGM management ever been inclined to create such a place.

This penchant for vigorous comic violence running through the series has become a Tom and Jerry trademark of sorts, so much so that *The Simpsons* TV series has long parodied the duo's remarkable bloodthirstiness as *The Itchy & Scratchy Show*. But in their first appearance, the cat and the mouse, in comparison to what would come later, are actually rather . . . subdued. Most of the comedy involves Jerry trying to get Tom (it's impossible, after all these years of branding, to call them Jinx and Jasper) thrown out of the house by the unfortunately named "Mammy Two-shoes." Unless you count some furniture falling onto Tom and Jerry getting his tail pulled, the only violence in this first short is perpetuated against some innocent martini glasses and dishes, lots and lots of dishes.

The duo also looks a little different here than they would in later exploits. Their hair is scruffier, and Tom's face and paws are more realistically feline than they would become later. In 1940 all this in itself was innovative. Animal characters in other studios' cartoons were heavily anthropomorphized. Mickey Mouse was, and is, basically an eleven-year-old boy in short pants who we only accept as a mouse because of his name. Bugs Bunny, who showed up at about the same time as Tom and Jerry, at least looks like a rabbit, or at least a wiseass Warner Bros. cartoonist's conception of a rabbit, but personality-wise he was really much more like Groucho Marx, here sarcastically wagging a carrot instead of a cigar.

Tom and Jerry, however, *this* mouse and *this* cat, even after long decades of tinkering and dubious "improvements" by artists far less talented than Hanna or Barbera, still remain, stubbornly, *only* a mouse and *only* a cat. They didn't (usually) speak. They didn't (usually) wear clothes. They didn't (usually) drive their own cars, have jobs, or buy little pink houses in the suburbs. Tom was a cat (a *tom*cat). Jerry was a little gray mouse. And all these years on, they still are.

Which is sorta nice.

17

Mrs. Miniver (1942)

On March 4, 1943, Greer Garson won an Academy Award for her performance in *Mrs. Miniver*. Accepting the award from fellow British expat Joan Fontaine, Garson then proceeded to give the longest acceptance speech in Academy history. Her remarks, unsurprisingly, have not been preserved in their entirety, but some in attendance have claimed that Garson held forth on the stage of the Ambassador Hotel that night for thirty minutes or more, although her biographer insists she actually delivered a comparatively brisk and breathless five-and-a-half-minute oration. Her remarks apparently only *felt* like they ran on for half an hour to those unfortunates in the audience.

Even more unfortunately, Garson's long-winded thank-you to the Academy, and to everyone she had ever encountered, is the only thing anyone who still remembers *Mrs. Miniver* chooses to recall about that film today.

This was not always the case. In its time, *Mrs. Miniver* was controversial, even revolutionary, and to an extent that was beyond the gratitude all too well expressed by the lady who so well-embodied her.

It should be noted that when L. B. Mayer read the *Mrs. Miniver* screenplay in August, 1941, the United States was not yet at war with Germany. At the time, MGM was still trying to hang on to its European markets, even while Hitler was trampling those markets.

However, director William Wyler, himself a Jewish refugee from Europe, had originally been attracted to the material specifically because of its inflammatory, pro-Allies nature. The script, based on a 1939 book, profiles the fortunes of the very British, but relatable to Americans, Miniver family. Because the material had been published mostly before the war, it took four MGM screenwriters to update the material, which

It might not have been the "greatest movie ever made," but *Mrs. Miniver* (1942) was undoubtably the perfect film for, and of, its era. *Photofest*

by the time of production now included up-to-the-minute German bombings and even the Dunkirk evacuation.

MGM has always been considered the most fawningly Anglocentric of the Hollywood studios. Their fat roster of contract employees included many venerated veterans of Hollywood's so-called British Colony, and the sort of product the studio tended to favor in the 1930s veered toward English classics by the likes of Dickens, Stevenson, Shakespeare, and Austen. Yet in 1936, Mayer canceled production of an anti-fascist movie to be called *It Can't Happen Here*, apparently at the behest of Georg Gyssling, the German consul. That same year, the studio actually invested in German armaments, although presumably as a tactic in order to get blocked currency out of the country. Even as late as mid-1940, MGM, along with Paramount and 20th Century Fox, was still maintaining offices in Berlin. So films like *The Mortal Storm* (released in June 1940) and *Mrs. Miniver* represented a surprisingly rapid about-face on the part of the studio, which, with the rest of Hollywood, thereafter wrapped itself in the flag and the creation of unwaveringly pro-Allies propaganda.

Although the Miniver family is British, they are presented as being identical, except for some charmingly British idiosyncrasies, to their American counterparts. The film opens with Mr. Miniver (Walter Pidgeon) buying a car that he is afraid to tell his wife about, while Mrs. Miniver is buying a hat that she is afraid to show her husband—a situation comedy contrivance that would not have been out of place in an Andy Hardy film. In some ways *Mrs. Miniver* also anticipates *Meet Me in St. Louis* by some three years in its idealized depiction of a very relatable and likable nuclear family unit. Both films, for example, include a charming, and similarly named, seven-year-old. Things rapidly get more serious, however. And the bombings and air raids and shortages the Minivers are subjected to probably forced American families in American cities like St. Louis to wonder if, under similar circumstances, they would persevere as admirably as their British counterparts are shown doing.

It worked. The film was still in production when the United States entered the war in December 1941. *Mrs. Miniver*, then, was one of the very first films to illustrate to American families, in a relatable way, why they were sending their husbands and sons to fight in far-off lands. Franklin Roosevelt and Winston Churchill both praised the film by name, Churchill going so far as saying it had done more for the war effort than a flotilla of destroyers. Another, more unlikely fan was Joseph Goebbels, the Nazi minister of propaganda, who admitted that he wished Germany had been able to make something similar!

A speech about the sacrifices made by families like the Minivers, delivered in the film by a vicar from inside his war-damaged church, was reprinted in magazines, read from actual pulpits, and even dropped from airplanes over German lines. It surely did more to convince the public at large of the evils of fascism than even Charlie Chaplin's pacifistic, prewar address in *The Great Dictator* (1940) had.

Being the right film at the right moment, *Mrs. Miniver*, also and not insignificantly, made a lot of money for MGM. The most successful film in the world for 1942, the picture also, and unsurprisingly, dominated the Academy Awards that year. In addition to Garson's win, even allowing for her acceptance speech, there was still time to hand the film six other Oscars, including statuettes for best picture, supporting actress (Teresa Wright, who played Mrs. Miniver's doomed daughter-in-law), director Wyler, and awards for the small army of screenwriters who had collectively written it. *Mrs. Miniver*'s success even led to a sequel, *The Miniver Story* (1950), which, unlike the original, could actually be shot in England. The follow-up, however, now set in a world

Greer Garson greets a war-weary Walter Pidgeon on the British homefront, and the MGM backlot. *Marc Wanamaker/ Bison Archives*

that no longer needed its Mrs. Minivers, would not duplicate the success or impact of the original.

But even during the war, not *quite* everybody on the Allied side loved *Mrs. Miniver*. Playwright Lillian Hellman, who had worked with Wyler on *These Three* (1936), reportedly saw the film at an advance screening and came out crying. Wyler approached to console her and was instead told that the tears were "because it's such a piece of junk, Willie. It's so far beneath you."[1]

Junk it may be, but *Mrs. Miniver* is, nonetheless, junk of the very highest order. Wellman's direction is self-assured and efficient. Although he is afforded few chances to evidence any sort of personal style, when he is given the opportunity to show us his talents, he more than rises to the occasion. For example, the tense sequence in which Garson, after being pinned down in a car during a bombing, believes that she and Wright have both survived the attack—until she looks up and sees light coming through bullet holes in the roof—is so brutal, brutal yet strangely beautiful, that the result would not have embarrassed even Alfred Hitchcock, the screen's master of artful mayhem.

Equally suspenseful is the extended sequence in which a downed German airman holds Mrs. Miniver at gunpoint in her kitchen. The soldier is played by Helmut Dantine, who would later marry the daughter of Nicholas Schenck, and who briefly became something of a matinee idol. Mrs. Miniver behaves so kindly to the wounded

The 1940 evacuation of Allied soldiers from France, largely executed by British civilians, was dramatized in *Mrs. Miniver*. The same story would be told again, in a less timely fashion, in the film *Dunkirk* (2017). *Photofest*

German that one rather expects that he will eventually reciprocate sympathetically. So it is shocking when the rather handsome Hun doesn't—and, in fact, even tries to kill her—although in this case, Wyler's subversion of our expectations may be more due to the film's propaganda quotient needing to be met than to the skills of its director.

The cast works up, or down, to the level of the material. Greer Garson, for example, suffers admirably. However, the dynamic between her and her oldest son, played by Richard Ney, is rendered inadvertently creepy when one learns that the two actors, actually only ten years apart in age, would marry in 1943.

It should be mentioned that the film's legendary closing speech—the one later reprinted and dropped from airplanes—is delivered by Cecil B. DeMille–regular Henry Wilcoxon, who rewrote and reworked the material, along with Wyler, right up until the moment it was actually filmed.

Mrs. Miniver wisely does not try to top this speech. The oration and the film both conclude with the camera panning up past Wilcoxon's words and looking out through the church's bombed-out roof, where British planes are seen flying bravely across the English Channel—the pilots of those planes having been called to duty, no doubt, by speeches like this, and by movies like *Mrs. Miniver*.

18

Song of Russia (1944)

From any critical standpoint, *Song of Russia* is an adequate but undistinguished movie. But in terms of the trouble it would later cause its studio, its makers, and the industry it was a product of, its song was cataclysmic.

It's hard to trace exactly why *Song of Russia* happened, and how it happened at MGM. Louis B. Mayer later testified, literally under oath, that one of his producers, Joe Pasternak, had wanted to "make a picture with Tchaikovsky's music and it would have to be laid in Russia."[1] This may be the truth, or at least part of it. Backing up this statement, when he was asked about Mayer's attitude about the picture, one of its screenwriters, Richard Collins, is known to have laughed bitterly and said about Mayer that, "He wanted to make a musical."[2] Although, seemingly contradicting this, Mayer also mentioned at the same time that his studio had specifically been asked, presumably by mysterious and lurking government forces, forces even more powerful and omnipotent than his own, to make a movie glorifying the Soviet Union and its contribution to the Allied cause.

"Asked?" But by whom? Who were these government forces? The most likely suspect was the mysterious Office of War Information (OWI), which during the World War II years launched a far-reaching propaganda campaign designed to paint America's allies, including the Soviet Union, in the best possible light for the American public. In 1947, when L. B. gave his testimony before the House Un-American Activities Committee, the idea that mighty MGM could be made to do anything, even by Uncle Sam, seemed to make Mayer alternately happy to be asked to perform such a duty for his homeland and hesitant about saying if he had been ordered to perform that duty at all. Consequently, the mogul flipflopped uncomfortably between his two favorite

Despite its title and pro-Soviet bias, MGM's poster art for *Song of Russia* (1944), although most curiously executed largely in red, still tried very hard to assure prospective audiences that this was the "love story of an American."

Author's collection

roles, patriot and patriarch, perhaps realizing, too late, that for the first time the audience he was performing in front of, the United States government, was one he could neither intimidate nor manipulate.

The "Tchaikovsky musical" Mayer presumably already wanted to make, maybe, was also deemed ideal for the propaganda purposes the OWI needed to see fulfilled. According to their own records, the OWI was given access to the various drafts of *Song of Russia* (then titled *Scorched Earth*) throughout its preproduction and was even able to make suggestions accordingly. At least one draft was reportedly even shared with the Soviet embassy! It is perhaps to the studio's dubious credit that these suggestions were not always carried out.

Robert Taylor was eventually cast as an American composer on tour in the Soviet Union. Susan Peters played Nadya, the Russian girl he falls in love with. The imperious Russian Gregory Ratoff, known on the set as "Gregory the Great," was—perhaps randomly, perhaps not so much—assigned to direct them.

Song of Russia opened in January 1944. No one took much exception in the centralist press to the propagandistic elements of the screenplay, and the public was more interested in Taylor and Peters's on-screen plight than in the movie's efforts to make our Soviet allies look like just regular folk. Members of that public, if not the press, seemed to like the film well enough. *Song of Russia* was well attended and successful. So when its run was completed, everyone involved assumed that the movie would go onto a shelf in a vault in Culver City, and that would be the last anyone would hear of it.

It was only after the war that the film's rather insidious half-life would become apparent, and that Mayer's innocent seeming "glorious romance set to Tchaikovsky's loveliest melodies" (that's what one of the ads had said) proved itself to be a ticking timebomb.

The explosion came in 1947 at the infamous House Committee on Un-American Activities (HUAC), which concerned itself with Communist infiltration in the entertainment industry. Suddenly the Soviets were no longer America's bosom allies but instead were deemed to be sinister enemies of the American way of life. And movies like *Song of Russia*, as well as Goldwyn's *North Star* (1943) and Warner Bros.' *Mission to Moscow* (1943), which seemingly glorified that insidious threat, suddenly seemed very dangerous. It didn't matter that these movies were made at the behest of the very government the subjects of these films presumably wanted to overthrow.

The rather apolitical (but Republican) Mayer, as well as Robert Taylor (also Republican) were both subpoenaed. Mayer's rather ineffectual testimony was contrasted with Taylor's, who at first stated outright that the film contained Communist propaganda and that he was "forced" to make it, even implying that his upcoming

"The grand love story of a Yank in Moscow." That's what MGM told audiences they were getting with *Song of Russia*, but it was more than that. *Author's collection*

commission with the US Naval Air Corps would be in danger if he refused. But then Taylor confoundingly backtracked on that statement by saying that "nobody can force you to make any picture."[3] Presumably "nobody" here referred to both Mayer and Uncle Sam. More damagingly, Taylor gave the name of fellow actor Howard Da Silva as being "disruptive" at Screen Actors Guild meetings. The word "disruptive" apparently was code for "Communist," and that word, perhaps unwittingly, led to Da Silva's subsequent backlisting. Decades later, Da Silva would play Louis B. Mayer in *Mommie Dearest* (1981). Author Ayn Rand also made an appearance at the hearing to testify about how falsely *Song of Russia* depicted the lives of Russian peasants.

Mayer, Taylor, and Rand succeeded better than they knew in getting others in trouble on the witness stand. After all, they didn't have anything personally to hide themselves, so little was at stake—for them. More insidious was what happened to the film's vast credit scrawl of screenwriters, all of whom, at the studio's instructions, took a shot at *Song of Russia* during its development. And all of whom would pay dearly for doing so.

Those writers, Paul Jarrico, Richard Collins, Leo Mittler, Victor Trivas, and Guy Endore, all really *were* Communists, had associated with Communists, or had at least attended a party meeting in in the 1930s. The truth was, every concerned, politicized screenwriter during this era, when capitalism seemed to be failing, had probably done the same thing. But this particular group were all, to a man, subsequently blacklisted or gray-listed for their activism and also subsequently had to work in Europe, under other names, or fronted by other writers in order to pay the bills for the next decade and a half.

Author Robert Mayhew once interviewed Collins, who emphasized that he and his left-leaning cowriters did not seek out the project. For all of them, it was just another assignment, which later turned out to be toxic. He did say, "I guess as good communists we felt wonderful and thought this was a good opportunity,"[4] but the party itself apparently took no specific interest in the film, never tried to guide its direction, and probably thought the end result as silly as their polar political opposite, Ayn Rand, eventually did.

The movie that caused so much agony is a trifle that, far from trying to influence anybody politically, instead contorts itself into pretzels to show us that Russians are just like us. And it succeeds so well that never for a moment does *Song of Russia* ever feel like the story is supposedly taking place in another country. This is in spite of a lot of Soviet-supplied stock footage and the appearance of a well-appointed and expensive backlot Russian village. Except for the Nazis, who none too soon goosestep in to menace our heroes, the title might as well be *Song of South Dakota*. At one point, Taylor, excitedly watching the dancing, well-fed peasants, remarks in his best American drawl how "everyone seems to be having a good time. I always thought Russians were sad," apparently saying this to remind the audience exactly what country is being depicted.

Despite his little mustache and a widow's peak even more defined than Bela Lugosi's, Robert Taylor's forte was always playing regular guys. So while he is convincing enough when he's enthusiastically inspecting crops with Nadya's family, he is way out of his depth as the brilliant virtuoso conductor he tries to essay here. It always seemed that one of MGM's goals was to try to make composers, scientists, and opera singers into just regular folk, however, so in that regard Taylor is suitable, and he was certainly a better choice than Van Heflin or Walter Pidgeon, who the studio also briefly considered for the role.

Susan Peters was a relatively unknown entity in 1944, although she had recently received an Oscar nomination for her smallish role in the studio's *Random Harvest* (1942). *Song of Russia* was to be her big chance as a top-billed leading lady. Unfortunately, she is also an unknown entity to most audiences today, as her career would be cut short in 1945 by a hunting accident. The tragic actress died in 1952.

The role of Nadya was supposedly designed with Greta Garbo in mind. The Swedish Garbo had successfully played a Russian in *Ninotchka* (1939) but had not appeared on-screen since 1941, so this would-be casting coup was probably only wishful thinking on the studio's part, or more likely a chance at some free publicity

Director (and sometimes actor) Gregory Ratoff, "Gregory the Great," on the set with Robert Taylor, who perhaps hopes to appear even more all-American here by wearing cowboy boots. *Photofest*

using the still-magical Garbo name. Ingrid Bergman was also considered, but David O. Selznick, who controlled her contract, disliked the hot-potato pro-Soviet angle of whatever script he read and wisely refused to loan her.

It's a shame Peters' career was so relatively short, because she is spirited and occasionally even funny within the confines of her role. Or at least she makes lines like "It is a privilege to drive a tractor" sound like they *should* be funny. At the beginning, the audience knows she is supposed to be a Russian woman because she is seen wearing an unfashionable hat no American girl would be caught dead in, and in the climax she bravely volunteers to fight for Mother Russia—as a pianist! Peters is at least a good sport throughout.

Song of Russia is a timid, mediocre movie. Its politics and propaganda quotient is both diluted and at the same time blatant. It tries to show uninformed Westerners the "real" Russia, but is altogether too weak-kneed to ever even mention the word "communist."

Unfortunately, that word has hovered over the movie ever since.

19

Meet Me in St. Louis (1944)

In art, there are accidental masterpieces. The elements just happen to fall into place, in just the right order and in just the right amount. The magic happens haphazardly, almost inadvertently.

In cinema, however, there are also masterpieces by design, where the best elements, the greatest amount of talent, and the most money—far above and beyond what is lavished on the usual assembly-line product—is aspired to as well. Although if the alchemy isn't there anyway, no amount of tinkering, recasting, and reshoots or additional line items in a budget are going to fix the problem.

MGM's entire business model was based on the concept that a level of proficiency could be consistently reached for, and obtained, by using the same methods and the same people repeatedly, without variation, indefinitely. Yet even at MGM it was realized, almost from the start, that room on the assembly line also had to be made to accommodate the two types of projects described above. Because the first would occasionally, hopefully, happen anyway, and because the second could, should, be *made*, again occasionally, to happen as well. The concept was that these occasional "special" projects were necessary and important, and would bring prestige to the company if they succeeded. And that if they failed, if the alchemy didn't happen, then these losses could be absorbed by the surrounding successes.

Meet Me in St. Louis was not originally designed to be a thoroughbred. But it developed into one of those special projects very quickly because of the persuasive powers of one man, producer Arthur Freed.

Director Vincente Minnelli, though, not Freed, is popularly considered to be the "author" of *Meet Me in St. Louis*. And his direction of the film certainly cannot be faulted. Minnelli is also undoubtably responsible for coaching an unforgettable performance from his star, Judy Garland, whom he then married. But Minnelli came into the project relatively late in its gestation. So, as was the MGM way, it was producer Freed who instigated the purchase of the rights to Sally Benson's so-called "Kensington" short stories and then commissioned at least half a dozen writers to write at least half a dozen screenplays, none of which he was initially satisfied with.

The problem with those stories, which had originally appeared in *The New Yorker* and then, supplemented with new chapters, as a novel, was that there was no particular through line, no story. These nostalgic little vignettes instead consisted of almost unconnected anecdotes by Benson regarding

Colorful poster art for *Meet Me in St. Louis* (1944). Note how the film's breakout star, Margaret O'Brien, has been crudely pasted into the action after the fact—and in black and white! *Photofest*

her early twentieth-century childhood on Kensington Avenue in, yes, St. Louis.

What attracted Freed to this material is unknown, as the producer, although born in South Carolina, had left home for New York and an eventual vaudeville career at a young age, and his Jewish background, boarding school education, and youth spent performing in honky-tonks and piano bars hardly seemed simpatico to the gentle wisp (and WASP) of nostalgia that permeated the stories, all set in a time when the worst thing possible in life would be to miss out on the World's Fair.

But that very nostalgia, that yearning for an earlier time, even if one had never actually experienced that time firsthand, was common among men of Freed's age (he was in his late forties) during this period. His nostalgia for a life he had never lived is

Meet Me in St. Louis rather brilliantly used these Currier and Ives–inspired "slides" on-screen to dramatize the passage of time. *Photofest*

borne out by his unsuccessful attempt during this period to make a musical from the Broadway play *Life with Father*, which was set during the same era. (Leon Ames, who played the patriarch in *Meet Me in St. Louis*, did, however, later play the title character in a television version of *Life with Father*.)

The year 1944 was of course also the darkest days of World War II, and with so many far away from home and fighting enemies in far-off lands, home and hearth and a period before not only that second world war but also the first, probably held an appeal as well, even if Freed's army of writers were initially unable to distill that appeal into a compelling screenplay.

The answer to these script problems, it finally occurred to Freed, was almost too obvious. The answer was that the story wasn't a story; the story was the *setting*. There are occasional hints of a plot circling about the edge of this setting, of course—the elder daughters' boy problems, assorted mischiefs perpetuated by the youngest daughter (Tootie, who would be played by Margaret O'Brien and who Benson based on herself), and, foremost, the upcoming 1904 World's Fair, which the family is much anticipating attending. Lastly, there is a looming move by that family from their beloved St. Louis

Those beautiful sets from *Meet Me in St. Louis* continued to be used by other projects for decades. Notice the Baldwin Hills oil derricks in the background in this candid study. *Marc Wanamaker/Bison Archives*

to New York City before the fair opens. This last detail would be particularly, and falsely, remembered by viewers as an important story obstacle, although it doesn't rear its head until the movie is half over.

Freed developed the property as a musical, and three of the most beloved of all American songs originated within the film: "The Trolley Song," "The Boy Next Door," and, of course, "Have Yourself a Merry Little Christmas." *Meet Me in St. Louis* is often regarded as one of the first musicals in which the songs were written to advance the plot. But again, what plot? The first two songs comment on ground the script or visuals have already well covered: "The Trolley Song," after all, takes place *on* a trolley. And the third song actually *contradicts* the story, because at the time that song appears, the story is busy concerning itself with anything *but* a merry little Christmas—although the song's music and lyrics are anything but upbeat.

People also tend to forget that these three songs represent the *only* musical numbers to be found in this mostly diegetic "musical." There are other songs, of course, but they all represent actual music of the era, and they are performed, mostly only in fragments, not as musical numbers but rather as how those characters would have sung or danced to those ditties in the real world. There isn't even a performance of the title song; although several characters start to sing "Meet Me in St. Louis" more than once, no one ever finishes it. "Have Yourself a Merry Little Christmas" is presented "naturally" as well, although some of the musical instruments heard behind the lyrics do not have an on-screen source. *Meet Me in St. Louis* anticipates, sometimes by more than a quarter century, later "realistic" musicals like *Cabaret* (1972) and *Fame* (1980).

The film's production ultimately changed the physical look of the studio as well. Company bean counters wanted Freed and Minnelli to redress the studio's backlot New England Street, well known at the time for the Andy Hardy series, to represent 1904 St. Louis, but Freed and Minnelli insisted instead that an entirely new set be constructed—at a cost of $200,000! The resultant "St. Louis Street" continued to stand on the backlot until 1970 and was eventually utilized in hundreds of other projects.

Arthur Freed's hand is all over the completed movie. For the song Leon Ames sings at the piano, it is actually Freed's voice we hear. But as costs mounted (the final budget was approximately $1,700,000) and the production schedule stretched out to an eventual seventy days, the producer clashed with Mayer over those mounting costs, Minnelli's meticulous dithering, and all the time-consuming innovations required by the lush but expensive Technicolor photography.

But in the end, all of Arthur Freed's efforts were validated when *Meet Me in St. Louis* premiered in, yes, St. Louis in November 1944 and then opened in early 1945 to ecstatic reviews and to entertainment-starved wartime audiences, who eventually made the film the second highest grossing motion picture in the studio's history (behind only *Gone with the Wind*). In the decades since, *Meet Me in St. Louis* and, particularly, "Have Yourself a Merry Little Christmas" have continued to be embraced by millions who, like Freed, apparently felt a longing for an era, for a life, for a lifestyle they had never experienced.

This love for this era, which *Meet Me in St. Louis* was among the first to tap into, continued long after that film had completed its long run, long after the war had ended, long after the people who remembered that war had themselves grown old. It continues today, because of the movie.

Seeing a movie, of course, can never be the same as actually living through that movie's period. But thank you Arthur Freed, thank you Vincente Minnelli, thank you MGM, and thank you *Meet Me in St. Louis*; in this case the movie version is undoubtably, infinitely better.

If you don't believe that the illusion is finer than the reality, that movies are better than life, then look no further than to Sally Benson, the original Tootie. In reality, and contradicting what happened in the movie, her real family did in fact, in 1903, forsake their beloved St. Louis for New York City.

She missed out on the World's Fair.

20

The Postman Always Rings Twice (1946)

As with horror movies, comedies, and Westerns, the popular assumption is that MGM was the wrong studio for film noir. Maybe so, but the truth, like the genre itself, is much more convoluted and shadowy.

Yet if the genre was not popular at the studio, it was still relatively prolific there. According to *Film Noir, An Encyclopedic Reference to the American Style*, MGM produced thirty examples of the genre between 1936 and 1974. In contrast, RKO, the company most associated with that type of film, contributed forty-two, only thirteen more. The list of thirty MGM movies the authors cite as MGM noirs, however, inexplicably does not include arguably their most famous one, *The Postman Always Rings Twice*, although the film is still discussed favorably in the body of the text. Nor does that same list include, although not the authors' fault this time, other titles in the genre released after that book's publication, most notably for our purposes, the 1981 remake, which MGM this time coproduced.

All this confusion well tabs the point that as a genre, film noir has always been notoriously slippery to categorize. Part of the difficulty comes from the factor that, quite unlike Westerns or horror movies, film noir was not recognized as a genre at all until long after World War II, and then at first only by the Europeans, who had been noticing that a lot of American-made films were characterized by low-lit criminality and cynicism. But a great many films, including a great many of MGM's, could fit within those criteria. So the genre, because of its loose parameters and seemingly suspicious, outside-Hollywood origins, has long, and years after the fact, been manipulated to include almost any gangster picture, like the studio's *The Beast of the City* (1932), or detective films like the MGM mainstay *Thin Man* series. Interestingly, one of the first commonly regarded film noirs ever made was at MGM, Fritz Lang's *Fury* (1936).

What is certain is that it's preposterous to think that anyone at any studio during this era ever said, "Let's make a film noir," or, in Louis B. Mayer's case, dictated that his studio would *not* make one. It's exceedingly unlikely that Mayer ever heard the phrase, or that he would have known what in hell it meant if he had. And if he had used the term, or an equivalent, in a derogatory way, those thirty-odd examples indicate that no one was listening to him anyway.

What is true is that Mayer was not personally attracted to such material. According to biographer Scott Eyman, he hated *The Postman Always Rings Twice* specifically. But Mayer was also adroit enough as a businessman, even in his later

The Postman Always Rings Twice (1946)—MGM done black.
Author's collection

years when his grasp of popular taste was less certain, to understand that some audiences, especially after the war, would respond to such material. And so his studio, in turn, acted accordingly.

For many, the ultimate MGM noir would be *The Asphalt Jungle* (1950), which does possess the ultimate film noir title. And the film in possession of that title is in every way a thoroughbred, as well as a defining example of its genre, if such a thing is possible. But it's also a film that could have been made at any studio during this era, provided that studio had director John Huston working for them when they did so. The point is that, ultimately, *The Asphalt Jungle* is much more a John Huston film than an MGM one.

The Postman Always Rings Twice, however, is very much a product of its particular studio. It includes more location work than most MGM films, and the leading man,

Lana Turner, the duplicitous "Cora" in *The Postman Always Rings Twice*, sizes up James M. Cain, author of the source novel. *Photofest*

John Garfield, was borrowed from Warner Bros. But in every other significant way, the film was very much an MGM production, done black by director Tay Garnett, who, unlike the idiosyncratic Huston, was in every way a company man.

MGM, and by extension, Mayer's faith in the material, is given credence by their purchase of the source novel in 1934, a full twelve years before they would use those rights—and after Columbia, RKO, and Warner Bros. had rejected the property outright as too hot for the movies. Metro even allowed it, or more likely looked the other way, when French and Italian versions of the novel opened up, in 1939 and 1943, respectively, because they knew that very few Americans would ever see those films or even be aware of their existence.

By the mid-1940s, however, Mayer perhaps believed that audiences and presumably even the Breen (censorship) office were ready for such frank material. And ultimately, in spite of some Hays Code objections and a few state-by-state censorship problems, he turned out to be correct. So the film was fed into the studio assembly line, and Lana Turner, whose frank sexuality had made it hard for the studio to find suitable roles

In 1946 New York's Loews State Theater featured both live vaudeville and *The Postman Always Rings Twice* on its huge stage. *Photofest*

for her, was cast as Cora, a bored waitress married to the owner of a roadside diner, played by Cecil Kellaway. Kellaway is named "Smith" here, although in the book he would carry the more ethnic moniker of "Papadakis." Garfield would be the drifter who comes between them. In the book the two's romantic relationship was rather explicitly raw and masochistic. All of that had to go for the movie, of course, except for Garfield's line to Turner, "Give me a big kiss before I sock ya," and his threat, or maybe it's a come-on, that he's going to "sock you in the jaw, maybe."

The Postman Always Rings Twice was, in some ways, a remake of sorts of Paramount's *Double Indemnity* (1944). Both films shared a common author for their source material: James M. Cain. They both dealt with an unhappy wife and her lover's attempts to murder her husband. Most oddly, in both versions the couple is first befriended and then pursued by a third party. In *Double Indemnity* that outsider is named Keyes and is played by Edward G. Robinson. In *The Postman Always Rings Twice*, the equivalent character is now called Keats, this time played by Hume Cronyn.

Both stories end unhappily too, with multiple betrayals and murders and executions before their respectively ironic fade-outs.

Of the two films, *Double Indemnity* is better regarded today, perhaps because Billy Wilder is better regarded than Tay Garnett. Part of the reason is probably because *Double Indemnity* was directed by the suitable-for-canonization Wilder, so it can boast of a single author to attribute its brilliance to. *The Postman Always Rings Twice*, to its detriment, is rather regarded as just the "product" of a studio. Garnett, by the way, was later described by Turner as a "roaring, mean, furniture-smashing drunk,"[1] so whatever his demons, he perhaps deserves our sympathy more than our adoration.

To modern eyes, and in comparison to *Double Indemnity*, *The Postman Always Rings Twice* might also feel just a little bit flabby. Things keep happening—like the first, near-murder of Kellaway, or Garfield's leaving the diner behind and then returning; and then later, like a postman ringing twice, these same things happen again. *Postman* also features a blackmailer who menaces the couple but is disposed of just a little too easily, seemingly adding little to the momentum of the story. Also taking us nowhere, presumably, is the excessive amount of screen time given to a nosy district attorney (Leon Ames).

All these sequences appear to contribute little. But stick with it. *The Postman Always Rings Twice* only seems to be biding its time. The endlessly random turn of seemingly un-orchestrated events, the subplots and red herrings and backtracking in the plot, all do have a reason, and the payoff involving the duplicitous lovebirds' fates is as well-orchestrated, ironic, and nasty as any ending in any film.

In a way, in his version of the material, Billy Wilder took the easy path in building to his climax. Nothing in his script (written with Raymond Chandler) is random. He ties his plot into a neat, airless bundle of bodies. But in their version, Garnett or his studio make *everything* random.

Here it is fate or God or the devil who decides to deliver a sucker punch, and just for the hell of it too. This streak of icy fatalism, which *Postman* has and *Indemnity* doesn't, is one of the great and oft-used film noir tropes, and it was never used better than here.

This sense of hopeless nihilism, of sad fatalism if you will, that shadows *The Postman Always Rings Twice* and its entire doom-ridden genre is perhaps why the meaning of that title, not made overtly clear in the book, or in the 1981 remake, is explained so explicitly here. Having gotten away with a premeditated murder, Turner is then killed in a random accident. And so Garfield ends up facing the hangman, not for the crime he is guilty of but for the one he isn't.

Fate, like the postman, can apparently be delayed, but it always comes back to ring again.

21

On the Town (1949)

In 1949 the war was over and the economy was booming. Except perhaps in Hollywood, where the studios had just lost their decade-long battle to keep the federal government from forcing them to divest themselves of their theater chains. What's more, business in those theaters, overall, was static.

During its silver jubilee year, as they proudly referred to their twenty-fifth anniversary, MGM still had a few things to celebrate, however. The company's profits for that year were almost $7 million, which is not so impressive when one considers that in 1946, just three years earlier, that number had topped $18 million. Still, a profit was a profit. Several other studios, like Universal, were anxiously running in the red.

The highlight of the year for MGM at the all-important box office was *On the Town*, which posted a worldwide box office take of $4,440,000—more than twice that film's hefty $2,111,250 budget. Those pleasing numbers ultimately ensured the film's producer, Arthur Freed, autonomy on the lot to continue to do pretty much as he pleased. A privilege he would continue to enjoy until the early 1960s, when he and many other longtime studio insiders found it increasingly harder to get inside the front office to pitch their projects.

None of this was a problem in 1949, however, although Mayer did object to Freed's insistence on shooting *On the Town* on location. The film, after all, was about three sailors on leave in New York City, so why not film their adventures in New York City? Mayer resisted because there were acres of hyperrealistic New York sets standing on the backlot, just a few blocks from that front office.

How this discussion actually proceeded has, sadly, not been recorded. But Freed probably pointed out that real sailors, as well as real soldiers and pilots, had recently returned from a real war after seeing the real world. Backlot re-creations of New York and of the rest of the world, which might have been convincing to audiences ten years earlier, would no longer work after those audiences had seen the real thing. In the end, Freed won. But Mayer won too. He allowed the unit a location trip, although it was only to be a very brief one, about a week. The rest of the movie would have to be shot on the backlot.

Freed's director was Stanley Donen, a choreographer who had never helmed a feature film but who had apparently, and without credit, "codirected," much of the recent hit *Take Me Out to the Ball Game* (1949). *Ball Game*'s official director had been legendary director-choreographer

MGM went *On the Town* in 1949. That town was New York City. *Author's collection*

Busby Berkeley, although neither Donen nor that film's star, Gene Kelly, had come out of that project with much respect for its aging director—or at least not for the fading, alcoholic Busby Berkeley of 1949. Costar Betty Garrett, in a documentary on Kelly, remembered that Berkeley loved riding on the camera crane and kept telling his crew to move it "back, farther back." "Yeah, back to 1930," Kelly had mumbled under his breath.[1]

Kelly and Donen did come into that project, and out of it, with a mutual respect for each other—and a mutual desire to direct. For *On the Town*, Kelly and Donen announced that they wanted to officially helm the film together, with Kelly starring as well, of course. In spite of the unorthodox nature of this collaboration, Freed, and presumably Mayer, ultimately signed off on it. Frank Sinatra, still at the height of his teenybopper fame, and Jules Munshin, both of whom had also been in *Ball Game*, and both of whom also got along well with Donen and Kelly, quickly were cast as the other two rambunctious sailors.

The whirlwind location trip to New York for *On the Town* was almost as difficult and arduous as the location trip to the South Seas had been for *White Shadows in the South Seas* twenty years earlier. New York City in 1949, much like the South Pacific in 1928, had very little to offer the production in the way of technicians, equipment, or skilled manpower. So almost everything, and everyone, had to be expensively brought out from California. Once there, technical problems were exacerbated by the large Technicolor cameras the unit was using and the additional lighting equipment these cameras required. Inconsistent and often rainy weather was also a constant liability, as was the studio-based crew's almost complete inexperience working in actual, practical locations.

What's more, when Frank Sinatra's New York fans found out their heartthrob would be filming in their city, they followed the crew wherever that crew went, shrieking and fainting and drowning out the playback equipment for the (prerecorded) songs, pushing over barricades, and waving and throwing kisses to the camera, ultimately making many shots unusable. Donen and Kelly finally had to find places to shoot where they could keep those crowds away, like behind the fences of the Brooklyn Navy Yard and against a wall at Rockefeller Center, although even in these scenes, you can occasionally see the crowds at the top of the frame, waving at their hero.

It was worth it. *On the Town* is a delight. Is there anything on-screen more joyous than the opening "New York, New York" number, for example? It's one of the few songs that was retained from the film's Broadway source, although the lyrics, which originally included the word "hell," had to be censored and rewritten.

The musical numbers, even without that word, still sparkle today. Decades later, critic Elvis Mitchell cannily remarked that *On the Town*'s pulse-quickening, ebullient routines literally "kicked the wall down."[2] And the fact that, for the first time, that wall, at least occasionally, was a real wall in a real place many in the audience might even have visited made the numbers feel more real, more intimate than ever before. Music on-screen would never be the same again.

That said, when seen today, especially in comparison with later, more-audacious Freed Unit musicals, some of the delights associated with the genre, although present, don't gel here as fully or as well as they would elsewhere.

Some of this can be blamed on the clunky—even by musical theater standards—mechanics of the plot. Whatever one has to say about Freed's later *Show Boat* (1951), for example, that film, also adapted from a Broadway musical, came ready packaged with a solid if, to contemporary eyes, eventually watered-down screenplay and plot upon which to hang the production numbers. *On the Town* came with three sailors on leave.

Betty Garrett, Frank Sinatra, Ann Miller, Jules Munshin, Vera-Ellen, and Gene Kelly really are in New York here. Note the chipped paint and garbage. *Photofest*

There are also some questionable choices served up by Donen-Freed-Kelly, even within the musical numbers, which is where all three of them would most be expected to shine. For example, in light of Frank Sinatra's star power and popularity at the time, it's a curious decision on the part of this film not to give the legendary crooner a single song to croon. Sinatra has some places to shine in the ensemble numbers, to be sure, but no solos. Charlton Heston, of all people, once cannily said about Sinatra that "every song this gentleman sings is a four-minute movie."[3] But none of those songs are to be found in *this* movie.

It's also interesting, if perhaps only in hindsight, that Gene Kelly is romantically and musically teamed up with Vera-Ellen instead of that tap-dancing marvel Ann Miller. Audiences were thus denied what would ultimately be their only chance to see those two hoofers dancing solo together on-screen.

There are some interesting curiosities to be found in the rest of the cast too. Jules Munshin, as the third sailor, has as much screen time as Kelly and Sinatra do. And it is he who is paired, unlikely as it sounds, with Ann Miller. And yet he is billed *fifth* in the credits. Munshin needed a better agent.

Then there are Betty Garrett and Alice Pearce, who are paired with, respectively, Sinatra and Kelly. Both ladies are terrific. Garrett was briefly a fixture at MGM as a tart-tongued second lead before becoming ensnared in the early 1950s communist scare. Fortunately she resurfaced decades later as a welcome fixture on the television sitcoms *All in the Family* and *Laverne and Shirley*. Alice Pearce was the only holdover from the Broadway production of *On the Town* that this movie was adapted from; she too would become a TV personality as nosy neighbor Gladys Kravitz in the *Bewitched* TV series. Bea Benaderet, later the voice of Betty Rubble in *The Flintstones*, and TV mainstay Hans Conried also appear, uncredited. Maybe the two of them shared an agent with Jules Munshin.

It's been noted before elsewhere how often MGM would reference itself in its own movies. This practice tended to flicker out in later decades, after Mayer and Mayer's era of long-term contracts and smug self-promotion had dissipated. But the practice was certainly still in evidence at the time of *On the Town*. Clark Gable, Mickey Rooney, Ava Gardner, and *Goodbye Mr. Chips* (produced in 1939!) were all MGM properties, and were all referenced by name here. Go team!

On the Town's big "serious" dance number is the "A Day in New York" set piece, which gives codirector Kelly a truly sublime chance to shine. The song, an instrumental, is presented as a dream sequence, a way for Kelly's character to express his frustrations when things are at their worst. Specialty pieces like this were already a mainstay in Freed musicals (Vincente Minnelli's *The Pirate* being an early example). But these sometimes satiric, sometimes surreal, sometimes pretentious sidebar numbers would quickly become particularly associated with Gene Kelly, with the working-class characters Kelly played, and with those characters' and, by extension, the audience's yearnings and aspirations.

That's certainly fair enough, and artistically valid too. But in a way, these numbers also represent lazy storytelling at its most self-serving. Think about it. "A Day in New York" exists only to give *On the Town* a somewhat side-handed way to step out of and then comment on itself. And to do so without bothering to integrate these self-serving asides into the actual story.

Here, for example, the segment repeats, only in dance this time, what the audience already knows. After all the main plot is, well, about a day in New York, isn't it? Fortunately, as is certainly the case here, these numbers in these Freed films are usually also so dynamic, so colorful, and the talent on display so self-assured and spirited that it is hard, usually, to object to their inclusion. Especially since it is usually these very same numbers that are pulled out and put under glass as prime examples of the

Frank Sinatra, Betty Garrett, Jules Munshin, Ann Miller, Gene Kelly, and Vera-Ellen really are in Hollywood here. Note how clean the streets are. *Photofest*

"artistry" of MGM's musicals. This cut-and-paste can be done surgically, and easily, because these numbers serve to encapsulate the plot of a movie for people who will never bother to see the rest of the film. CliffsNotes for MGM musicals, if you wish. And in an era when fewer people are watching older movies, reading literary works, or listening to music composed by earlier generations, I suppose that any way to get people to enjoy *On the Town*, or at least some of it, is worthwhile.

Lastly, let's point out one more time that *On the Town* contains very little actual New York footage, unsurprisingly considering how hard it was to get that footage. Although, upon seeing the film, generations of native-born New Yorkers would probably swear otherwise. And almost all of what little is on display is burned off in the first portion of the film, much of it in that ebullient "New York, New York" number. Most of *On the Town*'s very tangible New York "atmosphere" comes in fact from scenes taken later on the backlot, probably to the great relief of the crew, under the studio's tried-and-true assembly-line conditions.

As was the studio's policy at the time, the very last thing seen on the screen at the very end of *On the Town* are the words "Made in Hollywood, USA."

22 and 23

Battleground (1949) and *The Red Badge of Courage* (1951)

In 1948 the Loews corporate office selected Dore Schary, formerly a boss at RKO, as vice president in charge of production at MGM. This approximation of Irving Thalberg's old title was a blatant slap in the face to Louis B. Mayer on the part of Mayer's longtime enemy in the corporate office, Nicholas Schenck, who not so subtly seemed to be announcing to the world that L. B. needed "another Thalberg." Even worse, to his horror Mayer found that he was now expected to defer even routine decisions to Schenck or, even more humiliatingly, to the much younger Dore Schary.

During this chaotic period, the production of two very idiosyncratic war movies, both of which were ultimately produced over Mayer's objections, became the basis of many contentious arguments between Mayer and Schary, arguments that often led to Schenck supporting Schary. The arguments regarding these two similar and yet very different films ultimately contributed to Mayer's final dramatic downfall.

The tale of the first of these films begins during Schary's days as head of production at RKO. He had long been interested in a film about World War II's dramatic Battle of the Bulge. To this end, in 1947 he commissioned screenwriter Robert Pirosh, who had participated in the actual conflict as an infantryman, to return to the site on a research trip. Schary liked the script Pirosh submitted upon returning home so much that when he moved to MGM in 1948, Schary negotiated with RKO's new owner, Howard Hughes, for the rights to take Pirosh, the script, and three other films he was developing along with him.

Lobby cards for *Battleground* (1949) and *The Red Badge of Courage* (1951), two films about two wars, which together changed the destiny of their studio. *Author's collection (both)*

William A. "Wild Bill" Wellman consults his *Battleground* script with actor John Hodiak.
Photofest

Next up, in February 1949, Schary signed William A. "Wild Bill" Wellman as his director; the project, titled *Battleground*, commenced shooting in April. The film was shot entirely on soundstages at the studio, in the Pacific Northwest, and on the backlot at RKO's nearby "40 Acres," where a war-ruined village, recently used by Wellman in *The Story of G.I. Joe* (1948), conveniently still stood.

Battleground, released at the end of 1949, was the highest grossing movie of the year for its studio, and the second-highest grossing film in the United States for that year overall. The reviews, also overall, were exemplary. At the Academy Awards, Paul Vogel's black-and-white cinematography and Pirosh's screenplay both captured

Cinematographer Paul Vogel (seated, left) and director William Wellman (pointing) line up a low-angle shot for one of *Battleground*'s rare actual exteriors. Vogel later estimated that 90 percent of the film was shot on MGM's Stage 15, then the largest soundstage in the world. *Author's collection*

Oscars. The film offered Americans a sort of delayed catharsis for the recent war and to the experiences of its veterans. And most veterans found the picture's stark, unglamorous depiction of those experiences more realistic than other Hollywood versions of their tale.

In short, everyone liked *Battleground*. Everyone except Louis B. Mayer.

Mayer had endured Schary and *Battleground* both being brought over from RKO over his objections. With Schenck as a champion, there wasn't much Mayer could do about Schary. But he had outright vetoed *Battleground*, claiming that having just endured a real war, people were tired of war films. This was the same objection Mayer had voiced regarding Thalberg's *The Big Parade* in 1925.

Dore Schary of course had a trump card to veto Mayer's veto of *Battleground*. He went over Mayer's head all the way to Schenck, who, not surprisingly, sided with his "new Thalberg" instead of his aging studio head. So when *Battleground* went on to both popular success and Academy Awards, the rift between Mayer, who felt that he had been betrayed by a subordinate, and the ambitious Schary, who was chafing under Mayer's rule, deepened even more.

Today, even in light of more recent, more graphic war films like *The Deer Hunter* (1978) and *Saving Private Ryan* (1998), *Battleground* remains one of the genre's benchmarks. The real-life World War II adventures of Pirosh and others involved, as well as the real-life (World War I) battle experiences of Wellman, infused the story with a tangible, terrifying realism that films made during the conflict had often avoided so as not to disturb the families of those actually fighting the war.

Like many war films, *Battleground* is an ensemble piece, although top-billed Van Johnson is a bit more prominent than the rest of his large, capable cast of costars. Consequently, the film is about the collective rather than about the individual, although, as with most war films, this concept is carried, probably inadvertently, too far. It is often hard to tell who is who. Because the soldiers all dress alike, have similar haircuts, and look equally weary and disheveled, the audience is forced to engage with the men of the 101st Airborne Division, whose story the movie tells, largely as a group.

Fortunately, the members of that group, at least generally, do not appear to be too old for infantry service, which had often been a problem during the actual war, when many leading men were fighting on the battlefield rather than on the backlot, leading to many a geriatric movie battle/fantasy.

Even today, it's hard to believe that most of the snow scenes were shot on a large soundstage in front of a hand-painted backdrop, but it's true. The only time this amazing indoor set fails to convince is during the opening credits when, briefly before the film's title flashes on the screen, one can see how forced perspective is being used to create the illusion of having a bigger space available than there really was. But everything after that opening shot largely convinces.

Also adding to the sense of reality is that Wellman, at least until the last twenty minutes, largely avoids using scratchy stock shots from the actual battle, which unfailingly drains one's suspension of disbelief regarding the re-created sequences involving the actors surrounding these shots.

It's also hard to blame Wellman, or MGM, for the omission of those actors' icy breath, as would have happened in a snowy French forest but would not have occurred inside the heated soundstage where those actors were actually working. This was always a problem in winter sequences in classic-era Hollywood films. Sometimes this anomaly was remedied by shooting inside a refrigerated vault or a meat locker; now, of

Director John Huston consults with his star, Audie Murphy, on the contentious set of *The Red Badge of Courage*. *Photofest*

course, it is easily fixed using CGI. But in *Battleground*, most audiences, caught up in the story, fail to notice that the location is never as uncomfortably frigid as the actors are pretending it is.

The second war film to emerge from the wars at MGM was *The Red Badge of Courage*, based on Stephen Crane's 1895 novel about a Civil War deserter who then returns to the battlefield. *Red Badge*, like *Battleground*, is an admirable MGM movie by anyone's standards. But once again, its very existence, the very act of its going into production at all, nearly tore its own studio apart. Ultimately, it was *The Red Badge of Courage* that deepened the fissures *Battleground* had exposed and led to Mayer's departure and Schary's ascendance, forever changing the course of that studio from that point on.

The Red Badge of Courage was also, arguably, the first film ever made that concurrently, or subsequently, led to publication of a "making of" book. Today of course, the equivalent of such a volume—on paper, in the popular press, or online—accompanies every big studio release and many an independent as well, but at the time, the publication of *Picture* (yes, even the name noted its singularity) by noted journalist Lillian Ross denoted, and early on, that *The Red Badge of Courage* truly was something different.

Dore Schary again championed the picture. Mayer hated the idea of making a movie about a coward but finally acquiesced, although he memorably, if anachronistically, snorted, "I wouldn't make that picture with Sam Goldwyn's money."[1]

Throughout the production of *The Red Badge of Courage,* the studio gamely tried to emphasize the film's entertainment qualities over its grim subject matter. But it was much discussed on the lot that director John Huston and company were on thin ice, especially since Mayer refused to even see the film until it was finished, which was never a good sign. When Huston went over schedule (if initially by only three days), it didn't help either. Initially, the film came in at $1,548,755—only about $50,000 over budget.

True to his word, Mayer didn't actually see the film until it was previewed with an audience at the Pickwick Theater, outside Beverly Hills. Thirty-two people were recorded as having walked out before the end credits. Mayer at least sat, stone-faced, until the end and then exited without talking to anyone.

Perhaps wisely, John Huston, as was his way, immediately left town for Africa to start his next film, *The African Queen.* So it was Schary who was left to deal with the film—and with Mayer, who was finally quoted by Ross as saying, somewhat incoherently, "*Red Badge of Courage*, all that violence? No story? Dore Schary wanted it. Is it good entertainment? I didn't think so. Maybe I'm wrong. But I don't think I'm wrong. I know what the audience wants. Andy Hardy! Sentimentality! What's wrong with it? Love! Good old-fashioned romance."[2]

Schary, much frustrated by Mayer, and by that audience reaction, then sat down and dictated some new narration to be layered into *The Red Badge of Courage* as it was cut and reshaped, again and again, in an attempt to make it more palatable to audiences, as well as to the head of the studio that had made it. It is not known if any sycophants in the front office ever suggested turning the film into an Andy Hardy vehicle to placate Mayer, however. Maybe all of Mayer's yes-men had crossed over to the Schary camp by this point.

Interestingly, that opening narration explicitly mentions that Stephen Crane's 1895 novel had long been *accepted* by critics and the public alike as a classic story of war, as if Dore Schary was here telling whatever critics he had left in the Thalberg Building,

M-G-M, the company that released "GONE WITH THE WIND", presents a new drama of the War Between the States

STEPHEN CRANE'S immortal classic

THE

RED BADGE OF COURAGE

"*Pictorially breathtaking! The performers all first-rate!*"
—LIFE

starring

AUDIE MURPHY · BILL MAULDIN

A JOHN HUSTON PRODUCTION · Screen Play by JOHN HUSTON
Adaptation by ALBERT BAND

Directed by JOHN HUSTON
Produced by GOTTFRIED REINHARDT

N. Y. PREMIERE   TRANS-LUX
THURSDAY · 52nd on LEXINGTON
PL. 3-7434
LAST 4 DAYS! "KIND LADY"   IT'S MOVIETIME, U.S.A.

Unfortunately, even evoking the ghost of *Gone with the Wind* did little to attract audiences to *The Red Badge of Courage*. *Author's collection*

and one critic in particular, that he had literary right on his side and was now drawing the battle lines over a story about battle lines.

It didn't matter, of course. The final, final budget of *Red Badge of Courage*, after all the postproduction tinkering, was now $1,642,017.33. Unsurprisingly, *The Red Badge of Courage*, however it was cut and reshaped, still remained undigestible to Mayer and, ultimately, to audiences—certainly to audiences of Mayer's generation.

On June 23, 1951, Louie B. Mayer resigned from MGM. "After all those years on the throne," an unidentified executive told producer Gottfried Reinhardt, "what's going to happen to him now in this lousy, fake town."[3]

Upon release, three months after Mayer's departure, Schary's truncated, now a little over an hour-long *Red Badge of Courage* was met with as much indifference by audiences as *Battleground* had garnered enthusiasm. Critics were kinder than the public, praising the film's acting, mood, and cinematography, but most moviegoers stayed away, and those who saw the film—usually pathetically slotted into the bottom half of a double feature—found it to be uninvolving and ponderous.

Schary, to his credit, wrote a letter to Huston in Africa, apologizing for the film's extensive recutting. And Huston, to his credit, wrote back. "I said I had seen the picture. I told him I approved of everything he had done." He later admitted, "I lied to Dore."[4]

The truth is, as a film, what's left of *The Red Badge of Courage* is an exhilarating cinematic experience that holds up today as one of the best antiwar movies. What's more, its ironically ever-battling themes—that any sane human would resist a war, yet still summon, against all reason, the cathartic savagery required to win that war—possesses a keen catch-22 duality that today makes the film weirdly acceptable to both doves or hawks who happen to see it. No mean feat.

James Whitmore, who had costarred in *Battleground* (1950), narrates soulfully—although without knowing about the machinations behind the scenes, one really can't help but wish that Huston himself, in his sardonic tones, had been able to provide that benediction. "He had performed his mistakes in the dark, so he was still a man," Whitmore intones after star Audie Murphy's frightened flight from the battlefield—a line that comes right out of the book, if not right out of John Huston.

The Red Badge of Courage also benefits from Harold Rosson's oft-diffused black-and-white cinematography, which combines stark Mathew Brady–style nineteenth-century stoicism with odd filtered lighting and surreal compositions, such as sunlight dappled through a flag.

The acting is extraordinary down to the last man (a literal statement, as there are no women in the film). Casting Murphy, World War II's most decorated hero, as a soldier who initially runs from battle was a risky move on Huston's part, and on the part of the studio. But it pays off, for Huston anyway; Murphy here contributes the best work of his career, at least off the actual battlefield.

Elsewhere, familiar character actors Royal Dano, Arthur Hunnicutt, and Andy Devine are also superb, perhaps as fine as they would ever be in anything. Although their respective roles were all truncated to one sad degree or another during the film's torturous postproduction, Dano in particular believed he had lost out on a potential Oscar nomination due to excessive postproduction tinkering.

It should be noted that Bill Mauldin, another World War II veteran and a much-beloved cartoonist, also memorably appears as Murphy's buddy. This is relevant because the film's narrator, James Whitmore, had also been in *Battleground*, where he had based his weary infantryman on the "Willie and Joe" cartoon characters created by, yes, Bill Mauldin.

Of course, finally, it is John Huston who deserves most of the praise for *The Red Badge of Courage.* Huston, yet another World War II veteran who had walked away from the conflict but never really escaped the war, well understood the chaos, exhilaration, and wastes of battle. His haunting, haunted film is full of wise, sad little touches—like the soldier who dutifully stops dying long enough to put on his wire-rim spectacles.

The Red Badge of Courage is a bookend of sorts to other studio war films, going all the way back to *The Big Parade.* Although unlike in that film, we don't see Murphy's "Youth" (the character's name is Henry, although it is only used in passing) before the war. Because we learn so little about him, he becomes an everyman and, by extension, a surrogate for the audience in a way that entitled rich boy John Gilbert in the earlier film could never be.

Battleground had also dropped its characters into the middle of a war with no big-picture context, and reasonably had presented them as considering running from that war. But director Wellman had kept *Battleground*'s point of view fluid, with multiple characters representing a bigger picture and thus keeping paranoia at bay. *Battleground* celebrates the collective as surely as *The Red Badge of Courage* explores an individual response to war. We are now given no other point of view, so Henry's flop-sweat terrors become our own. The Youth is separate, disconnected from his comrades. He is a ghost in his own skin.

An odd comparison, the only other Civil War film that internalizes its content to such a degree is the short film *An Occurrence at Owl Creek Bridge* (1961), also based on a nineteenth-century tale, but which instead of chronicling a hero's journey, shatteringly becomes an ironic horror tale. Author Peter Straub once described the book *The Red Badge of Courage* as a "ghost story in which the ghost never appears."[5] John Huston's filmization of that book doesn't shy away from showing us that ghost. And he is us.

Unlike *The Red Badge of Courage*, Metro Goldwyn Mayer has had a long afterlife, although after the win-lose, one-two punch of *Battleground/Red Badge*, things would change. In 1952 the studio announced that it would be known thenceforward by its already oft-abbreviated name, MGM, presumably since Goldwyn and now Mayer were no longer there, and because no one remembered what (or who?) Metro was anymore.

24

Singin' in the Rain (1952)

In the early 1950s there was a venerated and prestigious MGM musical that was also a financial blockbuster, charmed every audience member and critic who encountered it, and won the Academy Award for the best picture of its year.

That film was *An American in Paris*, not *Singin' in the Rain*.

Today it is impossible to talk about musicals for more than a few seconds without mentioning *Singin' in the Rain*. Its status as the greatest MGM musical ever made, and as the greatest musical ever made by anyone, is very nearly inarguable. And don't forget that *Singin' in the Rain* has also routinely, dependably, consistently landed somewhere in top-ten lists overall as one of the greatest *films* ever produced.

That said, *Singin' in the Rain*, remarkably, did not have a particularly significant impact on the studio that made it, either financially or critically. At least it didn't when it first came out.

An American in Paris, by contrast, had a vast impact on its studio and on audiences and critics during that era. In a way these two films, which were almost sister productions and shared many of the same creators, are also flipsides of many of the same issues, ideas, and themes. One of them became a critical darling and a blockbuster. The other became beloved by the world as very few films have ever been.

Arthur Freed, of course, produced them both. *An American in Paris* was designed to be the innovator, to push the American musical to new levels of excellence and expression. *Singin' in the Rain*, by contrast, was a way to reuse some old songs the studio already owned.

This poster art for *Singin' in the Rain* (1952) well evokes the music and exuberance, if not the humor, of the actual film. *Photofest*

The story of both films goes back to 1929, the era one of them is set in, when George Gershwin wrote an orchestral composition called "An American in Paris." Freed had long thought the piece might work well on film as a musical backdrop for a Gene Kelly specialty dance. He also realized that the prestige of staging such a well-regarded "classical" piece would reflect well upon him and the studio. A deal was worked out with Gershwin's brother Ira, who was no stranger to composing lyrics for music written by his late brother.

The Gershwin music, it was decided, would be innovatively combined with expressionistic artwork, surely another nod to the intellectuals, and justified somewhat in the script by making Kelly a bohemian American artist, struggling to be discovered in Paris. With Vincente Minnelli in the director's chair and almost-nineteen-year-old Leslie Caron making her film debut as Kelly's costar, the production, with Paris re-created entirely by art director E. Preston Ames on the backlot, went, not at all surprisingly, significantly over budget and over schedule. The seventeen-minute ballet at the end, with all its wild, expressionistic sets built on Stage 27, alone cost the studio half a million dollars.

It was worth it. When *An American in Paris* was released in November 1951, it was an immediate, unqualified triumph. The film was catnip for the critics, who rhapsodized about how Minnelli, Freed, and Kelly had brought a new sophistication and intelligence to the American musical. Produced at a final budget of $2.7 million, the film made back more than double its production costs. *An American in Paris* also brought the studio countless millions of dollars' worth of prestige and awards, Oscar and otherwise, acolytes, and acclaim.

Singin' in the Rain, by contrast, was almost an afterthought. Freed had long wanted to reuse many of his old songs, written with Nacio Herb Brown, in a new musical. But by the atomic-era 1950s, many of these songs were dated—charmingly so, but still dated. One of the first decisions made, then, was to set the film in period, in the late 1920s. Since many of these songs already had a show business sensibility, the next obvious decision was to utilize show business, specifically Hollywood, as a backdrop. Gene Kelly at the time was still very much involved in *American in Paris*, but Freed knew that he and Stanley Donen would be perfect for the material. He continued to develop that material while *Paris* was in production.

Eventually, this still unnamed "Freed project" worked its way up, as all MGM projects still did, to the Thalberg Building where L. B. Mayer approved the project as one of his last acts at MGM. In her autobiography, Debbie Reynolds remembered meeting Gene Kelly in Mayer's office and telling him she couldn't dance, which Mayer and Kelly both refused to accept (she danced).

Mayer would be replaced on the film's third day of production. He would die in 1957, although in some ways, the day he left MGM could have been the date they carved on his headstone.

The songs continued to dictate the direction of the story. Eventually, the already oft used in other films "Singin' in the Rain" became the title of the film. Surprisingly, considering how popular the song, composed in the late 1920s, already was, no other

Colossal, memorable, and a bit extraneous, *Singin' in the Rain*'s "Broadway Melody" number utilized every dancer, chorus member, choreographer, musician, arranger, vocalist, and neon sign the studio had at their disposal. *Author's collection*

musical had used the number as its title. Although it was eventually performed three times in the film, "Singin' in the Rain" as a number was never intended to be an artistic equivalent to the *American in Paris* ballet finale.

The iconic version of that song, with Kelly joyfully splashing about in a downpour, actually comes in the middle of the film. It involves no other dancers besides Kelly, and utilized only one (pre-standing) set on the backlot. It did involve a lot of rain, though. Shot over two days, July 17 and 18, 1951, the top of the set was tarped off to simulate darkness, and piping with showerheads provided the deluge. Someone did have to knock some holes into the street in order to give Kelly deeper puddles to dance in, but by the standards of MGM, the number was almost a throwaway.

The same thing was true of Donald O'Connor's legendary "Make 'em Laugh" number. Although this time written specifically for the film, it again involved a single, simple set and only one performer. Decades later, in 2009 Joseph Gordon-Levitt bravely re-created this number on *Saturday Night Live*. He introduced his version to the show's young audience by saying, "If you haven't seen that movie, don't worry; your grandma has."

Much more lavish than "Make 'em Laugh" was the "Broadway Ballet" number, which rather redundantly charted the rise and fall of a dancer. Cyd Charisse was brought in for this sequence to dance with Kelly. There is an odd jump cut in the middle of their tryst, which some have speculated resulted from some cut frames that revealed a little more of Charisse than the censors were then comfortable with.

Many old-timers at the studio still remembered the transition to sound during that era and how difficult it had been. This material eventually took up much of the plot. *Singin' in the Rain* cheats a bit in this regard, though, as it depicts silent movies as already being made on "sound" stages, and a boom mike is featured on a set before they were invented—even though elsewhere, hilariously, microphones are depicted as being hidden inside costumes and bushes, which those old-timers remembered as how it really had happened.

In their quest for perfection, taskmasters Kelly and Donen spent almost as much money on *Singin' in the Rain* as had been lavished on *American in Paris*. *Singin' in the Rain*'s original budget had been set at approximately $1.7 million, but because of the film's presumed success, the studio stood by while the budget increased, eventually to $2.5 million. One wonders if that would have happened had Mayer still been in charge.

Singin' in the Rain's March 27, 1952, premiere was not held in Hollywood at Grauman's Chinese Theatre, as it should have been, but in New York. The reviews and box office were both ultimately respectable, but after the triumphant, art form–advancing innovations of *An American in Paris*, the goofy nostalgia of *Singin' in the Rain* seemed a bit of an artistic backstep. Looser, funnier, and seemingly unambitious, *Singin' in the Rain*, to 1952 audiences, did not appear to be the high-toned work of art its predecessor had been.

Another reason audiences were lukewarm to *Singin' in the Rain* was that both it and *An American in Paris* seemed to those audiences to share more than just a lot of the same names in their credits. It could not have escaped notice at the time that in each, Gene Kelly plays an aspiring artist, a painter in one and an actor in the other. In both he has a loyal friend-confidant and falls hopelessly in love with a girl who, because of complications, he is then denied. There is also a secondary leading lady lurking about who is financially and physically attractive but whose love he is unable to return. Our hero is, also both times, prone to express his joys and his sorrows through song and dance. Yes, these are plot elements of both *An American in Paris* and *Singin' in the Rain*. But they are also plot elements of *most* musicals. And these elements are also

MGM's regiment of still photographers routinely documented every production on the lot, constantly in search of a new way to publicize that production or its stars. Here, for example, Jeanne Coyne; her former husband, Stanley Donen; her future husband, Gene Kelly; assistant dance director Carol Haney; and Donald O'Connor pretend to be interested in an umbrella full of cheap giveaways. *Photofest*

probably why *Singin' in the Rain*, following in the Oscar-bait wake of *An American in Paris*, might have seemed in 1952 to be a bit of a retread.

It would take more than a decade for audiences, and then critics, to realize just how wonderful *Singin' in the Rain* really is. How life-affirming and magical and funny it is. And how every number and every performance seemingly could not have been improved upon by anyone, anywhere else, ever.

Today, even those who don't respond to musicals, and don't respond well to *An American in Paris*, are usually still charmed by *Singin' in the Rain*.

25

The Blackboard Jungle (1955)

In the 1950s, under Dore Schary's leadership, MGM made a concerted effort to remain relevant by producing many topical, hard-hitting dramas detailing the issues then affecting modern life. *It's a Big Country* (1951) used vignettes as a plea for tolerance; *Bright Road* (1953) boasted of a (nearly) all Black cast; *Scandal at Scourie* (1953) dealt with religious politics, *Bad Day at Black Rock* (1954) grappled with the effects of Japanese-American internment during World War II. And perhaps most overtly of all, Schary's *The Next Voice You Hear* (1950) featured God delivering a sermon—over the radio, yet.

One of the best, and certainly the most influential, of Schary's "message movies" was 1955's *The Blackboard Jungle*, a no-punches-pulled indictment of America's schools, here presented as ineffectual breeding grounds for street gangs and juvenile delinquents.

Unfortunately, *Blackboard Jungle*'s box-office success did little to improve America's school system; instead, the film probably made the situation worse. It was discovered that actual would-be juvenile delinquents who saw the movie were in fact influenced by its depictions of cool, leather jacket–wearing thugs, and that those teenagers then tried to imitate those thugs' speech patterns, clothes, and criminal activities. For that reason, the film was restricted from viewing by children in some cities and in the United Kingdom—which, of course, only made teenagers even more determined to see it.

Where *The Blackboard Jungle* really left its mark on the world, however, was in its soundtrack. That soundtrack first introduced an all new and emergent musical genre, rock and roll, to audiences, the film being the first time "that music" had ever been used in a mainstream movie.

Bill Haley & His Comets' "Rock Around the Clock" had been released as a single in 1954, on the B-side of a platter (something called "Thirteen Women" was on the other side of the disc) and had failed to chart. The film included the number almost as an accident. And it was possibly used at all only to show how debased and vulgar teen music had become since, for example, the days of Mickey Rooney and Judy Garland. If this is true, the movie cynically seemed to want to have it both ways, because the song is played under the opening credits and continues into the first scenes, which depict not the students but rather adult star Glenn

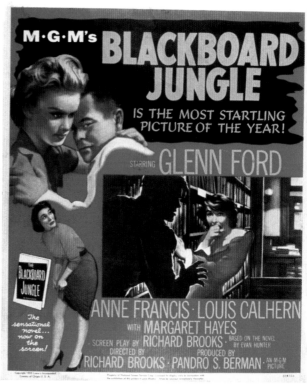

The poster art for *The Blackboard Jungle* (1955) was not at all subtle in emphasizing the lurid nature of the material. *Photofest*

Ford. The number shows up again at the end, also featuring Ford, and even as an instrumental at the midpoint. So it appears that the adult filmmakers indeed wanted the song to be a hit, and wanted it to be associated not only with the film's juvenile delinquent characters either. In fact, Glenn Ford was partially responsible for the song's appearance in the film. He found the single among his son Peter's records and apparently liked it enough personally to play it for director Richard Brooks, leading to its historic inclusion.

Peter Ford may have been among the first fans of "Rock Around the Clock," but there would soon be many more kids adding it to their record collections. The film came out in March 1955, and by July the song had reached number one on the *Billboard* charts, the first time a rock and roll number had ever done so. Unfortunately, MGM had failed to buy the tune outright, so instead it was Decca, the original label, that owned the recording. Decca couldn't press new copies of the song fast enough to meet demand, so teenagers, unable to otherwise experience it, instead bought a ticket or snuck into theaters where the movie was playing and then stayed all day to be able to rock around the clock again and again.

Reportedly, these young audiences also got out of their seats while the number was playing and danced along in the theater aisles as well. To combat these spontaneous sock hops, some crabby theater owners took to turning off the sound under the opening credits.

While the movie's soundtrack was championing, or at least conceding, the existence of rock and roll, less heralded is the rest of *The Blackboard Jungle*'s score, which includes jazz recordings by Stan Kenton and Bix Beiderbecke. (Interestingly, before the advent of rock and roll, it was jazz that had been considered a corruptive influence on the youth of America.) In one scene a teacher, played by Richard Kiley, has his precious jazz records mocked and then destroyed by his students, signifying that the earlier beatnik-jazz era had ended and a new generation with its own rituals and rhythms had now arisen. White suburban audiences who had never "got" musicians like Kenton and Beiderbecke must have been horrified to see that their children now considered even jazz to be old-people's music.

Director Richard Brooks, an independent, no-nonsense ex-Marine, seemed to enjoy ratcheting up his film's generation-gap tensions too. The adults are all presented as being either ineffectual or unwilling to accept the new ways of the world. Most of the teachers are portrayed as too cynical, too tired, or just afraid of disciplining their students. Even Ford's idealistic young teacher admits at first to being unable to relate to the younger generation.

This gulf between teens and their parents or educators was very much evident in the news and on cinema screens in the 1950s. Although *The Blackboard Jungle*, like most juvenile delinquent films, does itself no favors by placing such elderly-looking "teenagers" in its classrooms. Sidney Poitier was twenty-eight in 1955, Vic Morrow was twenty-six, and Dan Terranova and future film director Paul Mazursky were both twenty-five—the same age as Anne Francis, who played Ford's pregnant wife.

That is not to say that Brooks doesn't get fine performances out of his actors. Glenn Ford's good work here rightfully pleased the studio so much that he was given a lucrative contract that would keep him on the lot for most of the next decade. Ford, Morrow, and Poitier probably got the most out of their appearances in the film. Vic Morrow would soon spend four years at the studio on the *Combat!* TV series. As for Poitier, his innate decency, showcased so effectively here, would soon make him a major star. It has been pointed out by others, but is worth mentioning here, that the African American Poitier plays the "good" student in *The Blackboard Jungle* and the

Among the future notables posed against what looks suspiciously like a soundstage wall are Jamie Farr (with glasses), Vic Morrow (with money), Paul Mazursky (with ladder), and Sidney Poitier. *Photofest*

blond, good-looking Morrow turns out to be the bad kid—still somewhat shocking at the time. Elsewhere in the cast, Louis Calhern (in one of his last performances), Margaret Hayes, Kiley, and Francis all acquit themselves well as the put-upon grown-ups. Two more future TV fixtures, Richard Deacon and Jamie Farr (billed as Jameel Farah), also make notable early appearances.

Some of the film's very 1950's attitudes and assumptions date it a bit today. As mentioned, Anne Francis is effective in her role as Ford's wife, although that role consists entirely of her staying home, worrying about her husband, and trying not to suffer a miscarriage.

A modern viewer could also well ask why this completely integrated public high school has no female students, yet, unwisely as it turns out, hires female teachers? And how are those teachers supposed to teach when the classes seem to be only about six

Glenn Ford follows behind Anne Francis, who follows behind *The Blackboard Jungle*'s camera crew. *Marc Wanamaker/ Bison Archives*

minutes long? One also has to forgive the scene where Ford goes back to his own old school—a model of social harmony and effective teacher-student interactions—a scene that is obviously only there to show that not all American schools are as bad as the snake pit where he now has the misfortune of teaching.

It's probably impossible to imagine the lightning in a bottle that *The Blackboard Jungle* was in 1955, coming out a few months before Warner Bros.' *Rebel Without a Cause*, which also dealt with juvenile delinquency, but this time told from the juveniles' point of view. It is difficult today to imagine what it must have been like that year for teenagers to finally get to see films reflecting their problems and using their music to dramatize those problems. Today of course, when most movies are about, or for, teenagers, and when even rock and roll itself is becoming "old-people's music," one can only imagine how exciting it must have been in 1955 when the houselights dimmed and first Leo and then Bill Haley & His Comets roared from the speakers.

Forbidden Planet (1956)

Forbidden Planet was one of the first big-budget science fiction films ever made by a Hollywood studio, one of the first color or widescreen science fiction films ever made by anyone, and the first original science fiction film ever produced by MGM (1929's *The Mysterious Island* having been loosely based on a Jules Verne novel). It was also an acknowledged influence on *Star Trek*, the techno-thriller genre, and probably *Star Wars*, as well. So the film still casts a very long shadow over its genre, and its studio.

Originally the project was intended to be a second-tier, very low-budget (by MGM standards) potboiler, instigated by Schary when he, or someone at the studio, noticed that the world was in the midst of a "flying saucer" craze. This fad had been instigated in 1947 when pilot Kenneth Arnold spotted an unidentified flying object that resembled just such a crazy thing in Washington State, and by the mid-1950s this mania still showed no sign of abating.

Low-budget studios like American International Pictures (the library of which MGM would acquire in 1997), as well as majors like 20th Century Fox (1951's *The Day the Earth Stood Still*), RKO (1951's *The Thing from Another World*), Paramount (1953's *War of the Worlds*), Warner Bros. (*Them!* in 1954) were making a great deal of money fanning the flames of this craze, which could not have escaped notice in the carpeted offices of the Thalberg Building.

Apparently, it was rather late in preproduction when the studio, perhaps realizing the inherent potential of the project, beefed the budget up to its own 1950s era, A-level proportions. In some ways, this late infusion of cash from the front office made the resultant film somewhat lopsided. The special effects and music and art direction were astonishing; yet the script and cast were still, by MGM A-picture standards at least, somewhat lacking. Regardless, the very fact that in 1956 MGM created a science fiction film at all, good or bad, determined *Forbidden Planet*'s status as a landmark of its new genre.

The final script, by Cyril Hume (whose association with the studio went all the way back to 1924), was allegedly based on Shakespeare's *The Tempest*, which gave the project a certain air of cultural respectability. Shakespeare scholars might have recognized the bones of the play, although the then-popular vogue for psychoanalysis led to the play's "Caliban" character being recast as a "monster from the Id," which menaces a group of space explorers rescuing a reluctant scientist and his daughter who have long been stranded on the titular planet, Altair IV.

What's most amazing about this amazing poster for *Forbidden Planet* (1956) is that nothing like the scene depicted here occurs in the actual film. *Photofest*

Another longtime studio veteran, Walter Pidgeon, played the scientist. He brings the proper gravitas to the role; his stately performance is the best in the film, but one wonders what a true A-lister like James Mason, Laurence Olivier, or even James Cagney could have brought to the same material. Starlet Anne Francis, who the studio for some reason could never quite make into an actual star, is his daughter, who, until the Earth expedition arrives, has never seen another human being aside from her father. She's very good, but the captain of that expedition, and her eventual romantic partner, is played by Leslie Nielsen. Nielsen's years-later fame as a comedian really works against his earnest but wooden performance here.

Forbidden Planet's most memorable character, and the only element in the film many people remember, is Robby the Robot. Robby was actually not a robot at all

A technician, accompanied by the top half of Robby the Robot, secures one of *Forbidden Planet*'s otherworldly sets.
Photofest

but a costume designed by Robert Kinoshita, who was working for Albert Arnold "Buddy" Gillespie, who had been head of the studio's wonderous Special Effects Department since 1936. Robby was executed at a final cost of $125,000, but that expense was quickly offset by his (it's hard to say "its") reuse in an immediate follow-up, *The Invisible Boy* (1957), and in countless later movies and television shows. The original Robby was sold at auction in 2017 for $5,375,000—almost three times the entire original *Forbidden Planet* budget.

The impressive blue-green Altair IV landscapes were painted in the Scenic Arts Department; the flying saucer the Earth crew travels about in was a combination of miniatures, elaborate interior sets, and full-size mockups. The Freudian-inspired monster from Walter Pidgeon's mind, who the script suggests is incestuously protective of his daughter, represented one of the few elements the studio did not create in-house. Rather,

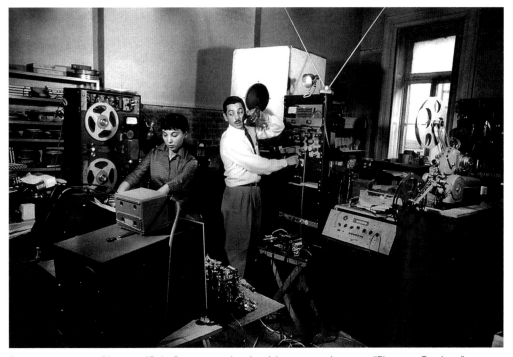

Scientists or sorcerers? Louis and Bebe Barron at work in their laboratory on the unique "Electronic Tonalities" soundtrack heard throughout the film. *Author's collection*

the animated outline of the monster, which looks a bit like Warner Bros.' Tasmanian devil, was outsourced, or rather created for MGM, by artists on loan from Walt Disney.

The music, for the first time in any film, was completely created electronically—on a circuit board yet—by Bebe and Louis Barron, who Schary reportedly had heard one night making those sounds in a Greenwich Village nightclub. This "music" certainly is avant-garde and certainly otherworldly, although it is also, for these same reasons, very hard to relate to and ill-suited for suggesting any sort of emotion or mood to an audience beyond unease. On the liner notes for the film's soundtrack album, which would not be released until 1976, the Barrons remarked that, "We were delighted to hear people tell us that the tonalities in *Forbidden Planet* remind them of what their dreams sound like."

All these elements, even that musical score, give *Forbidden Planet* a scope, professionalism, and prestige rarely seen in science fiction films of this vintage. Some of the ship-in-flight optics compare well with the studio's *2001: A Space Odyssey*, which would not be released for another dozen years. Many *Forbidden Planet* fans, and there are still a great many, first saw the film as children and still consider it among the best its genre has to offer. Among those fans, surely, was Gene Roddenberry, whose first *Star Trek* pilot, "The Cage," also dealt with a military space federation, monsters conjured up from the mind, and a "forbidden" planet, and at least one other *Trek* episode, "Requiem for Methuselah," would borrow ample elements from *Planet* as well.

And yet *Forbidden Planet*, in spite of its scope and influence or its critic-baiting nods to Freud and the Bard, does not seem to enjoy the respect or critical acclaim of some of its science fiction contemporaries. And its fan base seems to be limited to those who saw it as children rather than those who encountered it first, and more critically, as adults. Part of the reason for this relative indifference is, sadly, MGM itself. Unlike Universal, which then already had a growing catalog of science fiction films in their library, and which often sported the same familiar actors and directors, or Paramount, which had the visionary George Pal on the lot in the 1950s, *Forbidden Planet* was a one-off for MGM. It didn't lead to the same team's making more films in that genre, and none of those involved with *Forbidden Planet* had then, or would have in the future, any particular association with the genre.

Forbidden Planet's director was Fred M. Wilcox. Wilcox was yet another in the endless assembly line of reliable hacks MGM faithfully kept on payroll for generations. In 1956 Wilcox was best known on the lot for three successful Lassie films. It's been oft stated here that (usually) the studio and not the director of an MGM movie is that movie's author. But in this case, as neither the studio nor the director of *Forbidden Planet* had a history in science fiction, that just makes this film, which initially ended up losing $210,000 for its studio, even more of an orphan.

What's more, it would be several more years, with *The World, the Flesh and the Devil* (1959), *Village of the Damned* (1960), and George Pal's moving onto the lot, before MGM would consistently venture into the genre's starry skies. Let's put it this way: As was the studio's way at the time, MGM management somehow blindly managed to miss out, almost in total, on the massive science fiction boom of the 1950s. At least until 1960, when that boom was long over.

27

Jailhouse Rock (1957)

The most consistently successful collaboration between an artist and a film studio in the 1960s was of course that of Elvis Presley and MGM.

Yet unlike their successful longtime collaboration with an earlier king, Clark Gable, the studio, as was then the way in Hollywood, never "owned" Elvis outright. At the same time he was minting money for MGM, Elvis was also working successfully for Hal Wallis at Paramount and at United Artists, although starting with *It Happened at the World's Fair* (1963), MGM was his favored-nation home studio, and from then on even movies for those other companies would often be shot at MGM.

Because Elvis Presley unarguably revolutionized both music and popular culture at large, people tend to underestimate his parallel potency as a movie star. Between 1956 and 1972 his thirty-three movies made, when adjusted for inflation, some $2.2 billion at the US box office. Those movies averaged a profit margin of more than three times their individual production costs. And those production costs were miniscule too—those films, in spite of their colorful, sometimes exotic locations, were usually shot on the cheap and on the lot. And those films were often among the very last film credits for many of the venerable sets on the MGM backlot. So a perusal of Elvis vehicles in the 1960s is also a tour of the MGM lot at sunset.

Unfortunately, most of those Elvis vehicles were, as films, pretty terrible. Even the songs in those vehicles were pretty terrible, which would have been unforgivable in a musical by any other artist. But Elvis was so indestructible during this era that his fans didn't care. One has to wonder, if these fans would support their hero singing

bad songs, badly, in bad movies, how big a movie star Elvis
Presley could have been had he,
or his studio, bothered to give a
shit about the final product.

It didn't matter. So sure was
the studio in the 1960s that an
Elvis picture would be money
in the bank that MGM allowed
Sam Katzman—"king of the
quickies," who had been churn-
ing out low-budget monstrosi-
ties since the 1930s, and who earlier would not have been given a
pass to drive through the gates of
MGM—to produce their Elvis
films basically independently,
cherry-picking only the company's production and distribution assets. Katzman, taking
full advantage of this symbiotic
system, and suddenly equipped
with the keys to the biggest studio in the world, could deliver
a new Elvis film, on demand, in
less than three weeks!

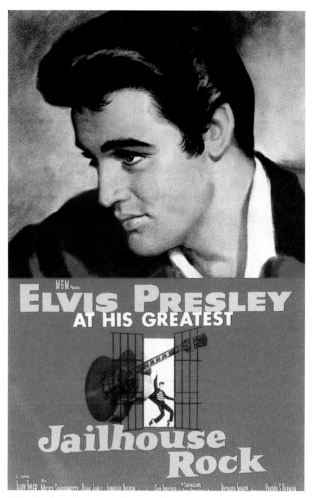

"Elvis Presley at his greatest" snarled the ad art for *Jailhouse Rock* (1957). It was true. *Photofest*

It took a long time, but even-
tually, by the late 1960s, the king's fans did begin to tire of the formula. Audience and
record sales consequently began to falter as well. Elvis, however, was such a big star
that he was insulated from any blowback generated by bad word-of-mouth or declining box office/record figures. MGM continued to pay their star progressively more,
even as his films were making progressively less, although even *The Trouble with Girls*,
his last narrative MGM movie, managed to drag in nearly $20 million (again, inflation
adjusted) at the 1969 box office.

The point here then is that the Elvis phenomenon simply cannot be ignored in any
study of MGM. Elvis Presley arguably has been as important an asset to the studio

overall as Gable or Crawford, Rocky or Andy Hardy or James Bond. This is little commented on, but it's true.

Yet, although even the worst Elvis movies made money—we are looking at you, *Kissin' Cousins* (1964) and you, *Harem Scarem* (1965)—a few of them, like *Viva Las Vegas* (1964) and to a lesser degree *Girl Happy* (1965), against the odds were kind of fun. One of them, *Jailhouse Rock*, financially the most successful film Elvis Presley ever made at the studio, is even considered to be a minor classic of its kind.

It's interesting that MGM, arguably the most conservative, traditional studio in classic Hollywood, is also the company most responsible for introducing rock and roll to mass audiences for the first time. Between the apparently endless Elvis films, *The Blackboard Jungle*, and *High School Confidential* (1958), the studio arguably did more to acclimatize the genre to the world's teenagers than did Dick Clark. American International Pictures made the most rock and roll movies, but MGM, who had Elvis, made the most money. The success of Elvis Presley at the studio also brought other contemporary musicians to Culver City during this era, including Hank Williams Jr. (although years before his later chart-topping success), Robert Goulet, Robert Morse, and Herman's Hermits, however quaint these artists might all seem now.

Elvis Presley, in the mid-1950s still a dangerous and untested commodity, made his movie debut in a supporting role in Fox's *Love Me Tender* (1956), which was a huge success, although the four rock and roll songs grafted into the soundtrack added little to the authenticity of the film's Civil War–era setting. More suited to the singer's emerging style was Paramount's semiautobiographical *Loving You* (1957), which led him to MGM. And then to *Jailhouse Rock*.

Unlike other early rock and roll films, including those mentioned above, *Jailhouse Rock* does not try to sanitize or whitewash the singer's or the music's image to make them safe for teenagers or their parents to welcome into their homes. One has to wonder if MGM realized this, or cared, at the time. But intentional or not, in this film Elvis is insolent, surly, and has a James Dean–style chip on his shoulder. Early in the film his character, Vince Everett, beats a drunk to death and rightly goes to jail for manslaughter. When he gets out and pursues a career as a singer, he actually exploits his outlaw image, anticipating Jimmy Cliff's character in *The Harder They Come* (1972) by more than a decade. At one point, Judy Tyler, who plays Elvis's promoter, wards off his advances by saying, "How dare you think such cheap tactics would work with me." To which Elvis/Everett snarls, "That ain't tactics honey. It's the beast in me." Later on, at a party Elvis is asked by a boorish snob about, of all things, "atonality in jazz music," to

Elvis with his adoring fans—as re-created for the cameras *Photofest*

which he replies, "Lady, I don't know what the hell you're talkin' about." No wonder parents were worried.

And Elvis, at the time, was the perfect person to symbolize everything these parents were worried about. The earliest R&B singers were Black, which unfortunately severely limited their appeal in the largely White suburbs. When Elvis's records first started playing on the radio, local (Tennessee) stations used to specifically mention that he had attended Humes High School in Memphis, which was a White school—a coded way of saying this kid could sing like a Negro but, thank God, wasn't one. There was also the problem that till this point, early rock and roll stars either were too old—Bill Haley was thirty and looked even older when he recorded "Rock Around the Clock"—or were, like Buddy Holly, not physically aligned with what audiences expected them to look like. Elvis, however, who had recently started dyeing his blond-ish pompadour jet black, looked like the sort of kid who might well have bullied the scrawny, bespectacled Holly in high school. The result was a sensation.

Motion Picture Daily carried this catchy trade ad in November 1957. *Author's collection*

The title song should probably be mentioned here. Elvis performs it as part of a musical movie being shot with him, autobiographically, in the lead. He assisted in the choreography of the number as well as the singing and dancing. The electrifying result is arguably the most famous moment of his entire movie career. Ironically, Gene Kelly was on the lot then and even watched some of this scene being shot, and so witnessed this world-forever-changing moment from the shadows of the soundstage. Decades later, this collision of "traditional" music and rock and roll would (ironically? coincidentally?) be weirdly dramatized in Kelly's last original musical, *Xanadu* (1980).

Other than *Jailhouse Rock*'s intrinsic historical interest, the film, while arguably better than any other Elvis musical, still follows a formula—a formula that at least had not yet grown repetitive or been weakened by censorship.

Elvis is at his very best here. *King Creole* (1958) and *Flaming Star* (1960) both offered him more three-dimensional characters, and in both cases he rose to the challenge admirably. But never again would Elvis be more Elvis-like on-screen. Even in his two MGM documentaries—*Elvis: That's the Way It Is* (1970), and *Elvis on Tour* (1972), where he played himself—by this time the king sometimes seemed to be flying on autopilot. But in *Jailhouse Rock* he fully embodies the scary, sexual rock and roll godhead before the army and drugs and middle age had siphoned so much of the magic away.

Jailhouse Rock, in addition to using MGM as the ambiguous (and suggestively named?) Climax Pictures, as was still the studio's way, also name-drops MGM itself, or at least MGM Records, in its dialogue. The studio's ambiguous, point-of-God presence is also represented by the swimming pool Elvis memorably gyrates next to. This pool, a standing and much-beloved backlot set, went back to even before Esther Williams first jumped into it. Incidentally, this same pool would later be used by the king again, in *Spinout* (1966).

Call-outs to Elvis's real life are as prevalent as references to the studio, sometimes unintentionally so. For example, Elvis's much-heralded stint in the army (1958–1960) featured famous footage of him getting his very famous hair cut for bootcamp, which was here anticipated by almost identical scenes of Elvis getting his very famous hair cut for his prison stint. In that prison, his cellmate is a former hillbilly singer who later becomes his much-abused, Col. Tom Parker–style manager. And Mickey Shaughnessy, who plays the role, even looks a bit like Parker.

This subplot is featured in *Jailhouse Rock*'s rather weak climax, which involves a fistfight between master and mentor, and which anticipates a better scene in *The Carpetbaggers* (1964). After the fight, Elvis/Everett, whose vocal cords may have been damaged in the melee, repents of his antisocial, rebel ways. This part, of course, never happened in real life, although Elvis would soon be emasculated himself, and much less dramatically than depicted on-screen.

After this repentant coda, which felt like a sellout in 1957 and today, in hindsight, feels even more like a corner turned, one can't help but wonder if, as we now know would soon happen to the real Elvis, the character he plays here will ever be as raw and honest onstage again.

It is this constant intersection, this jagged waltz between role and performer, that makes seeing *Jailhouse Rock* today such a bittersweet, meta experience. Because, just like Vince Everett presumably does, we know now that Elvis Presley too is about to sell out big time.

28

Cat on a Hot Tin Roof (1958)

Dore Schary lost his job in late 1956, although he probably would have agreed that in the late 1950s, there was no better indication that audiences were ready for more adult material than the crackling success of his old studio's *Cat on a Hot Tin Roof*.

Playwright Tennessee Williams's steamy drama had opened on Broadway in 1955. Even before a film version was announced, every actress in Hollywood seemingly had her eye on the lead role of Maggie, the sexually frustrated wife of a plantation owner's son. Marilyn Monroe, Ava Gardner, Lana Turner, and Grace Kelly were all considered or reportedly desired the role.

Elvis Presley, Montgomery Clift, Don Murray, Robert Mitchum, Ben Gazzara (from the stage production), and even James Dean (although a seeming obstacle was that he had died in 1955) were discussed for the role of Brick, her possibly homosexual husband. Ultimately no one was surprised when the studio's own Elizabeth Taylor and then up-and-comer Paul Newman were selected. Again ultimately, when the film came out, no one, except perhaps for a few of the names above, was disappointed by the sweaty, successful mix of sex and psychology that *Cat on a Hot Tin Roof* offered.

Newman, as noted, was a relative newcomer in 1958 when *Cat* premiered. But Taylor had grown up on camera, and at MGM, starting in 1943, when she was a precocious eleven-year-old. Fortunately, unlike most child performers, Taylor's popularity actually increased with the advent of puberty. Unfortunately, MGM had a hard time finding suitable vehicles for her even as she became their most popular commodity. Most of her best roles and performances in the 1950s came as a result of loan-outs to other studios that were perhaps less overtly bashful about cashing in on her emergent sex appeal.

This would no longer be a problem after *Cat on a Hot Tin Roof*. The carnality of her performance and her chemistry with Newman must have proved to her studio that Elizabeth Taylor could no longer be considered anyone's idea of a girl next door. Three years late she won an Oscar playing a call girl in *BUtterfield 8* (1960), which unfortunately for MGM, also concluded her longtime studio contract. Elizabeth Taylor would work at MGM again, but as a very expensive freelance artist.

Cat on a Hot Tin Roof, even if no one knew it at the time, is another of those end of one era–beginning of another sort of movies. Its use of its glamourous stars, neither of them ever better or more physically attractive, combined with MGM's characteristically lush cinematography, art direction, costuming, and music, all bespeak the studio system at its very best, even if that system was then tearing itself apart. But at the same time that system's standard-bearer, MGM, was now, at least here, proving itself willing to deal with more adult material and in a more adult fashion. It is significant that *Cat on a Hot Tin Roof* was filmed not at the less-moribund Warner Bros., where the previous Williams adaptations *The Glass Menagerie* (1950), *A Streetcar Named Desire* (1951), and *Baby Doll* (1956) had emerged, and not in gritty black and white like those films, but instead in vivid color amid the very epicenter of Hollywood "fantasy," although whether that was a good thing or not in 1958 is debatable.

Audiences in 1958 were more than ready for more-provocative screen material. The poster art for *Cat on a Tin Roof* inferred that Elizabeth Taylor was more than ready to provide it. *Photofest*

Elizabeth Taylor was the last MGM-created superstar. Unfortunately for the studio, in 1958 her long-running contract with them was about to expire. *Author's collection*

As a sort of hybrid of old-school glamour and the new permissiveness of its era, the resultant film does, especially to modern eyes, possess its share of eccentricities. The Pollitt family plantation is rendered, inside and out, entirely through an enormous and complicated soundstage set built just for the film. To be clear, this setting is more realistic than the equivalent location for the stage version would have been. But it is not particularly convincing *here* because, unlike on the stage, the film's otherwise very capable director, Richard Brooks, is obviously not trying for an expressionistic look. The painted backdrops with painted moss hanging from painted trees just do not convince. Nor does the house for a minute look lived in except for its basement, which is (symbolically?) over lit, over cluttered, and full of cobwebs.

Incidentally, late in the film, this same problematic indoor plantation again betrays its origins when Newman grabs a banister and it vibrates because, of course, the rail is not attached to a real staircase. Perhaps this malady is exclusive to re-created Southern

Paul Newman was almost seven years older than Elizabeth Taylor, although in 1958 he was the young, new star and she the veteran. *Author's collection*

settings, though, as the same thing had happened to a porch rail almost twenty years earlier in *Gone with the Wind*.

The relative visual failure of *Cat on a Hot Tin Roof* is particularly unsatisfying because a set very similar to this plantation, literally called, yes, "The Southern Mansion," had already stood on the MGM backlot since 1938—and could easily have been commandeered as a supplement to the indoor setting and blown some real air into the film's claustrophobic milieu.

Sometimes, not often but sometimes, the things that happen on this set fail to convince as well. As a movie and, it must be said, as a play as well, *Cat on a Hot Tin Roof* can sometimes be a little bit blatant in its symbolism. Brick's crutch and the way he ineffectually wields it of course symbolize his impotence, and some of his dialogue is not so subtle in this regard either—his remark that "People like to do what they used to do after they've stopped being able to do it" being a good, and unsubtle, example. Also note how Brick and Maggie's brass marital bed is often literally placed between them in Brooks' surely very much thought-out compositions. Whatever could that mean? Incidentally, there may have been two identical such beds rolling around the studio in 1958. One of them also showed up in *The Unsinkable Molly Brown* (1964), before being sold in the 1970 auction; another, or maybe it was the same one, made for an aptly symbolic running gag in the TV series *Love, American Style* (1969–1974)

Remember that although all of this was bold stuff in 1958, the aging production code still had to be obeyed during this era. The studio's correspondence with the Hays office to get their film a code seal itself constitutes a battlefield of compromises and arguments and lines both pulled from the script and drawn in the sand regarding what could and could not then be depicted on American movie screens. Ultimately, and unsurprisingly, the play's presumed homosexual angle had to be mostly removed. This partial amputation rendered Newman's motivations for not bedding his wife somewhat murky, and reportedly displeased Tennessee Williams to no end. Yet, what is surprising is how little this alteration finally affected the film's narrative. Making the movie "about" repressed homosexuality would have rendered specific the conflicts and lies—the mendacity, as the film repeatedly calls it—of the battling family's dynamic and made it all, perhaps, just a little too pat. In the movie, Brick's issues turn out to be with his father (played, in a thunderous performance, by Burl Ives) and with his general disgust and disappointment with his life, with his family, and with his world—all of which is, arguably, better, if not braver, than a dark and Freudian third-act revelation would have been. The result was that in 1958, the *Cat on a Hot Tin Roof* audiences saw had been compromised, but not yet neutered.

The same thing, come to think of it, could then still be said about MGM.

29 and 30

Ben-Hur: A Tale of the Christ (1925) and Ben-Hur (1959)

MGM's most influential years were bookended by these two colossal productions, both of which were major successes of their eras. Which is fortuitous, because the failure of either costly production would have probably led to the collapse of the studio.

Ben-Hur: A Tale of the Christ started its life as a novel published in 1880. The author was Lew Wallace, a colorful Civil War general and governor of New Mexico Territory during the notorious "Lincoln County War" era that brought Billy the Kid to brief and bloody prominence. The book, his second, was not an immediate bestseller but eventually became a worldwide sensation, arguably the biggest selling novel of the nineteenth century.

The story of the book and both films concerns Judah Ben-Hur, a first-century Jewish prince on a quest to avenge the betrayal of his family and fortune by his former friend Messala, a Roman. Judah's adventures, including a spectacular sea battle and chariot race, happen to run parallel to, and occasionally intertwine with, the life of Jesus Christ.

The story was spectacularly if improbably adapted for Broadway in 1899 and ran successfully in different venues and versions for years. The first filming of the story, produced in New Jersey in 1907, was an undoubtably brisk fifteen minutes long!

The film rights were acquired by Goldwyn before the merger. The sea battle scene was shooting in Italy when Thalberg, in one of his first executive decisions, canceled production there and moved the entire expensive project back to Hollywood where, at a reported cost of $300,000, the Roman-style coliseum was created near the studio for the film's spectacular chariot race. This of course set a precedent for company operations,

For *Ben-Hur: A Tale of the Christ* (1925), the new company shipped out lavishly illustrated promotional volumes for theater owners, from which this is an illustration. *John Stephen*

which would be enforced for the next forty years—namely, that everything, anything, could be shot at the studio under the controlled conditions the studio offered.

Fortunately for the studio, and for Thalberg in particular, his intuition that movies should be made in a factory paid off. Produced at a reported cost of almost $4 million, making it the most expensive film of all time to that point and for many years after, *Ben Hur: A Tale of the Christ* was fortunately a colossal success, a success that ultimately helped define both its era and its studio—although its huge expense ensured that it would not actually make a profit until a 1931 reissue pushed it into the black.

Ben-Hur: A Tale of the Christ still plays well today. The sea battle is even more savage and realistic than it would be in the remake. It's filled with nice touches of cruelty, including a Roman prisoner strapped to a ship's figurehead and then cruelly used as a battering ram, and glass balls filled with venomous snakes fired at the Romans. The film's climax, the chariot race, is justifiably celebrated as well, and is as breathtakingly spectacular as its reputation implies.

It's hard not to notice, however, that amid all this splendor there are few close-ups. In fact, director Fred Niblo's camera rarely gets closer than mid-waist to his actors, which sometimes works to the film's detriment but also contributes to its overall "biblical tableau" ambience. Although Niblo is the only credited director, Charles Brabin, before being replaced, is known to have directed some of the early, Italian-filmed location scenes. Rex Ingram and B. Reeves Eason also worked on the film, either alongside Niblo or as second-unit directors. This plethora of disparate men at the megaphone

In any incarnation, the big chariot race has always been a key element in advertising *Ben-Hur*. *Photofest (both)*

could be taken to constitute an early example of MGM's producer-favoring policy that directors are merely traffic cops, and thus easily interchangeable.

For modern audiences, the welcome pre-code flashes of nudity, as well as the film's explicit scenes of torture and mayhem, keep things lively. Also most lively is the vivid two-strip color process utilized for certain scenes, although it's hard to discern why those particular scenes were chosen and not others. A nice stylistic touch would have been, for example, to save the color for whenever Jesus shows up. And this is done, to a point, like in the elaborate and colorful re-creation of the Last Supper, but other, Jesus-free scenes arbitrarily utilize the color effect as well.

Attention should probably also be paid to the film's floridly overwritten intertitles. This was often the case during this era, but the problem is exacerbated by this film's ancient setting, making the results even more purple sounding than they would have been if the film had been set in a contemporary (1920s) milieu. For example, the Roman slave ships are described as "stately and beautiful. But under beauty, deep-locked in the hold of each ship—a hell of human woe."

Sadly, the acting tends to fall into the same trap. Ramon Novarro is stalwart and likable as Ben-Hur, but regrettably, he sometimes relies on arm-waving and breast-beating to make his point. Rudolph Valentino was reportedly considered for the role, and as perplexing as the idea may now seem, Valentino would have been very apt in the court intrigue scenes after the sea battle and before the chariot race, where Judah vamps, and is vamped by, assorted female foes, and even sports a Valentino-style bolero outfit while doing so.

Actually, both *Ben-Hur* versions suffer in their midsections, between the big action scenes—a structural flaw also found in the source novel. After the unforgettable spectacle of the chariot race, for example, when audiences are reaching for their hats, there is still almost an hour of lepers and crucifixions to go before the actual conclusion comes into view.

The 1925 *Ben Hur*'s conclusion was not really a conclusion at all, of course. Because more than thirty years later, the much-wronged Jewish prince would return.

In 1949 the box office triumph of Cecil B. DeMille's *Samson and Delilah* returned the biblical epic to prominence after more than a decade in eclipse. The genre continued to thrive throughout the 1950s—which, remember, was an era when the threat of nuclear annihilation and fear of potential communists lurking behind every mailbox made the idea of a God who was more than willing to explain to us, in a booming voice, exactly who in the world was good and who was evil—and in widescreen and stereo sound yet—tremendously appealing.

The Roman Circus Maximus set in 1925 and 1959. *Photofest (BW) and author's collection (color)*

MGM's initial contribution to this trend was *Quo Vadis* (1952), which itself was massively successful. For the rest of the decade, though, their epic output consisted largely of medieval- or Napoleonic era–set swashbucklers. At the end of the 1950s, however, after many false starts the studio made up for their lack of faith in the form by returning to the setting of one of their greatest triumphs.

When distinguished director William Wyler was announced as the man who would be in charge of a remake of *Ben-Hur*, many were surprised, as *Wuthering Heights*

(1939) and some Westerns represented the only period offerings evident in his long career. Wyler also was reportedly not initially happy with the script MGM came up with. But he accepted the project as a challenge and because, as he often said later, he wanted to make "a Cecil B. DeMille film." He also undoubtably liked the $350,000 payday (with points) MGM came up with.

In the decades since the studio's first chariot race, Hollywood had changed. Remember that the first film had started shooting in Italy and then was brought home to the studio to save on costs. This time, ironically, the film would be almost entirely Italian made—to save on costs.

Post–World War II American producers had discovered, to their delight, that low-cost production facilities, as well as an abundance of eager-to-please talent, crew, and extras and a most generous dollar-to-lira exchange rate, were now beckoning to them from across the sea. So this time, in contrast to the studio's long-standing policy, only a few days of production, at the very end of the endless production schedule, would happen in Culver City, although the special-effects scenes, including the naval battle miniatures, would be shot on the lot. The postproduction work, optics, and editing would be created stateside as well.

But even with the financial incentives of shooing overseas, a new *Ben-Hur* did not come cheap. Ultimately the budget exceeded $15 million, twice what the studio had originally budgeted and almost four times the cost of the original film. Eventually the chariot race alone would cost a reported $4 million. MGM probably also spent almost as much as the film's budget in marketing after the film was completed. There was a cost in human life too. Producer Sam Zimbalist died in Italy of a heart attack during the production, although stories about other human and horse-related fatalities during production are apparently fictitious.

Fortunately for the studio, the completed film was a triumph, artistically and, much more importantly for that studio, financially. The worldwide box office gross for *Ben-Hur* has been reported as $75,000,000. At the 1959 Academy Awards, the film won eleven of its twelve nominations, a record that stood for almost forty years until it was tied by *Titanic* (1997). Among those double-digit wins was the Best Picture Oscar, making *Ben-Hur*, to date, the last film with the MGM name already on it to win that Oscar.

The film and its predecessor both share a similar visual look as far as art direction. Note specifically the chariot race scene; the look of the coliseum in the 1959 film is not particularly based on history but on the look of the coliseum in the 1925 film. Cedric Gibbons, the legendary MGM art director who, from even before the 1925 *Ben-Hur* until his retirement in 1956, supervised the art direction on effectively every MGM

Legendary director William Wyler (astride camel) and his legendary star Charlton Heston seem to be enjoying themselves on the set of 1959's *Ben-Hur. Photofest*

movie (some fifteen hundred titles) died in 1960. So it's not known if he lived to see so much of his visual mise-en-scène so blatantly recycled.

Also borrowed from the 1925 movie is the gimmick of not showing Jesus to the audience. Instead the Savior is suggested, obscured, or seen from the rear or with his back to the camera. It is effective both times, but it works better here because of Wyler's superior talent for camera placement. In the 1925 version, for example, the memorable Last Supper sequence is blighted to an almost comic effect by the necessity of placing one of the apostles right in the middle of DaVinci's famous composition in order to obscure Christ's features.

The 1959 *Ben-Hur* is certainly a class act all the way. The MGM Camera 65 process utilized in the film encompasses an extremely wide (2.76:1), extremely narrow image, which Wyler fills expertly with massive sets and crowds. If the sea battle is, overall, slightly less effective than in its earlier incarnation, the chariot race now works even better with the addition of that very wide screen, color, sound effects, and music. Messala's chariot this time is outfitted with *Mad Max*–style spikes on its axle, which he is not hesitant to utilize to grind holes in Ben-Hur's chariot. Near the end of the race, there is also a spectacular jump over some wreckage by stuntman Joe Canutt—an accident that was kept in the movie to breathtaking effect.

Charlton Heston. What to say? Director Irvin Kershner once remarked on the actor's effectiveness perfectly, saying, "In *Ben-Hur* they found an incredible, iconic figure in Charlton Heston. He was almost mythic. He was big in your mind. It was difficult to unsettle him. He was very concentrated in his purpose, always, which I think most people would *like* to be."[1]

Unfortunately, other than the iconic Heston's iconic Judah, the cast, although gargantuan, is generally undistinguished. Welsh actor Hugh Griffith won an Oscar as the wily Sheik Ilderim, although he would be much more memorably wily in *Tom Jones*, four years later. Jack Hawkins as Arrius, Ben-Hur's Roman benefactor, is entirely too British to be convincing in his toga. Haya Harareet as Ben-Hur's love interest, Esther, is ethereal and earthy, but also surprisingly passionless (Where, oh where, was Sophia Loren?). Likewise, Stephen Boyd is merely adequate as Messala.

What is surprising is that none of this seems to matter. Perhaps a cast of actors all working at the top of their games would have been a detriment to the overall effect of the film and to the effect of the iconic Heston, which is really all that audiences had come to see anyway.

In 2003, rather remarkably, Heston returned for a final lap around the coliseum in an eighty-minute animated version of the story cheaply produced for children. It was one of his last performances before his death in 2008. There was also a not-well-remembered two-part television version of the story in 2010.

In 2016 MGM itself produced an official big-screen remake of *Ben-Hur*, although they refused to refer to it as such (the questionable phrase "re-adaptation" did come up in publicity, however). It was shot at Cinecittà Studios in Rome, just as the 1959 version had been. Released by Paramount, the nearly $100 million film was a box-office disaster.

31

North by Northwest (1959)

North by Northwest is universally acclaimed as one the greatest and most quintessential Alfred Hitchcock films. It is also the only film the director ever made at MGM. MGM, however, got considerably less out of the film than Hitchcock, his star, Cary Grant, or audiences ever did.

In 1958 Hitchcock owed a film to MGM, if you can call a promise to be paid a quarter million dollars and a net percentage "owing" the studio anything. The Hitchcock-MGM film originally was supposed to be something called *The Wreck of the Mary Deare*, which director Michael Anderson eventually ended up filming when Hitchcock and his writer, Ernest Lehman, lost interest in it. Together Hitchcock and Lehman instead dreamed up a sort of throwback to the director's earlier, lightweight spy-chase thrillers such as *The 39 Steps* (1935) and *Saboteur* (1942). *Saboteur*, for example, had climaxed with a wild scramble across the outside of the Statue of Liberty. For this new film, Hitchcock hoped he could feature something similar, this time with his cast chasing one another across the implacable presidential faces on Mount Rushmore. To that end, the original title of this new film, whimsically and irreverently, was to be *The Man on Lincoln's Nose*.

But as the story got bigger and wilder, so too did the budget. Eventually *North by Northwest* ended up costing the studio some $4.3 million. *Mary Deare*, by contrast, when finally filmed, cost only $2.5 million. Although it must be said again that the studio's *Ben-Hur*, which came out the same year, cost more than $15 million. So, while MGM's indulgence of Hitchcock's whims was indeed expensive, the famous director was not as pricy as Jesus.

James Stewart, a frequent and favorite Hitchcock leading man, was originally attached to the project, but as the character developed into a suave, cocktail-swilling Madison Avenue type, Hitchcock and Lehman, and eventually the studio, realized that another of the director's favorite actors, Cary Grant, would be the caper's perfect, if again expensive, leading man. MGM, hoping to save a few dollars, then suggested one of their resident brunettes, Cyd Charisse, as Grant's leading lady. Hitchcock vetoed this, insisting on his own choice: cool, blonde Eva Marie Saint.

James Mason, who was almost as debonair (and expensive) as Cary Grant, was then cast as the villain.

Hitchcock shot the film on expensive locations across the country, from Culver City to New York City, with the studio dutifully paying for the

North by Northwest's key art seemed to take the film much more seriously than its creators did (1959).
Author's collection

overages and excesses, as per Hitchcock's ironclad contract. He also insisted on shooting all of this in VistaVision, an expensive process the studio had to pay Paramount for permission to use. Likewise, the studio had to pay Grant, who must have had the same lawyer as his director, a $5,000-per-day penalty, on top of his fat salary, when the production start was pushed forward.

The indignities against the studio continued. MGM had hoped to release the final film at a running time of under two hours in order to get in an extra theatrical showing per day. Once again, though, Hitchcock pointed out that his contract gave the director rather than the studio final cut, so his preferred and approved two-hour and sixteen-minute *North by Northwest* is what audiences saw.

Those audiences loved *North by Northwest.* They immediately embraced it as the ultimate Hitchcock chase film: sleek and wicked; scary and romantic. The film also anticipated, and perhaps inspired, the James Bond/spy craze the next decade would usher in. Critics praised *North by Northwest* too, although somewhat condescendingly. Many of those critics noted that Hitchcock's antics here really constituted a sort of director's greatest hits album, with set pieces from earlier in his career revisited and reshaped for a sort of old-man's victory lap.

Hardly true. A variation on a theme, when performed by that theme's original creator, can still be a masterpiece. And the work of a master, two masters if one is inclined to include Cary Grant—here both operating together at the very top of their charming powers—can be impressive indeed, however derivative.

One might even call *North by Northwest* the product of *three*

Director Alfred Hitchcock carves out a spare minute during the production of *North by Northwest* to satisfy his sweet tooth. *Photofest*

masters, the third being its studio. Here, MGM's Art, Special Effects, Sound, Costume, Editorial, Postproduction, and Music Departments all contribute perhaps their all-time-career-best work. Cary Grant even gets to sing a bit of MGM's unofficial theme song, "Singin' in the Rain," while in the shower. How else, and where else, could all of this have happened, and happened so well?

Lehman's deft script moves at a breakneck pace that, arguably, would not be matched by any movie until 1981's *Raiders of the Lost Ark*. Although Cary Grant's suave hero does not so much anticipate Indiana Jones or, as has often been pointed out, James Bond as tap into the actor's other Hitchcock roles (of which this was his fourth) and even into Grant's screwball comedy characters of the 1930s, in which a younger version of the actor was subjected to countless embarrassments, humiliations, and implacable leading ladies like Katharine Hepburn and yet still managed to remain, forever, Cary Grant.

James Mason, Eva Marie Saint, and Cary Grant, like any other visitors to Mount Rushmore, have their picture taken in front of the monument. *Photofest*

Further proof that critics in 1959 who might have thought *North by Northwest* was directed by a nostalgic old man whose best years were already in his rearview mirror were wrong came with Hitchcock's very next film, *Psycho* (1960). *Psycho* proved to be just as innovative and avant-garde as *North by Northwest* was self-nostalgic. It also cost less than $1 million to make, four times less than *North by Northwest*, and went on to make four times more at the box office.

This would have been acceptable at MGM, of course, had *Psycho* been made by MGM. But it wasn't. Instead, it turned out that Hitchcock had used MGM merely as a cash register from which to extract a (large) paycheck while he recharged his creative batteries before returning to another studio (in this case, Paramount) to orchestrate the biggest and most innovative experiment of his career.

Such was the pattern at MGM during this era. Throughout the 1950s, many a legendary filmmaker, after a flop or two elsewhere, would go to MGM to make one movie, at which point that studio, delighted, would open the gates and alert the press. And that director would take advantage of this publicity by leveraging it with another studio, often the studio they had just left, and then take that other studio's now-improved offer and leave MGM behind to lick its wounds.

John Ford, for example, went from making *The Searchers* (1956) at Warner Bros. to the expensive, but less good and less successful *The Wings of Eagles* (1957) at MGM. Then he went back to Warner Bros. In 1960 another legendary director, Michael Curtiz, then mostly sucking the last dregs of stale air from the tank of a distinguished career, made the relatively undistinguished *Adventures of Huckleberry Finn* (1960) at MGM, cashed their fat check with his name on it, and then used the prestige that film gave him to run off to an even fatter deal for *The Comancheros* (1961) at 20th Century Fox.

Alfred Hitchcock behaved no better, and in some ways he was worse. As the only director during that era whose name could be counted on to denote a brand and sell tickets—much as the name "MGM" once had done—Hitch played the game brilliantly. At the time he was smarting from the relative flop of his recent brilliant but underattended *Vertigo* at Paramount. So he fled to MGM to bask in the effect of their still-enormous publicity machine. That department promptly staged amusing pictures of Hitchcock glaring wryly at Leo the Lion and of Leo glaring right back. Hitchcock also allowed his name and macabre persona to be used in an MGM thriller he wasn't even involved with—*The Gazebo* (1959), in which Glenn Ford phones up the master in order to discuss the finer points of murder. Basically, Hitchcock took full advantage of his fame and prestige, and the fame and prestige of MGM, used them both to his personal advantage, and then ungratefully ran off to another studio and his biggest career hit ever!

Although *North by Northwest* was, as noted, a major financial success, and even though it justifiably became an all-time classic for its studio, the truth is that after Hitchcock, Grant, Lehman, and even Paramount/VistaVision had made their demands and taken their cuts, the studio found that there was little left of the pie for them.

At the time, after decades of union demands, departmental raises, and sales taxes and property taxes, MGM studio overhead was so high that it was now difficult for anyone at the studio, except for longtime salaried employees and outside talent utilizing it for

Author's collection

production facilities and distribution, to make any money there. Because the studio was MGM and was still considered the Tiffany's of the industry, every artist or craftsperson entering the gates would automatically raise their standard rates, reasoning that this was MGM and they could afford it.

Consequently, at the end of the day, and after all the work MGM and its staff put into *North by Northwest*, the final adjusted profit for the company, as opposed to the director or the star, turned out to be only $837,000—only $200,000 more than the much cheaper, Hitchcock-inspired *The Gazebo*.

Alfred Hitchcock apparently knew this would happen. Cary Grant apparently knew this would happen. Most of the industry seemed to know this would happen. But in 1959, MGM, with its hundreds of lawyers, accountants, and advisors, seemingly had yet to figure it out.

32

How the West Was Won (1962)

How the West Was Won is never listed as being among the great Hollywood movies—or as one of the great Hollywood Westerns. It never even makes the cut as one of the great MGM movies. For example, the comprehensive documentary *MGM: When the Lion Roars* doesn't mention it at all, not even during its discussion of the too-many overproduced would-be blockbusters the studio detonated in the 1950s and 1960s.

It should be noted up front, however, that *How the West Was Won* was much more than a "would-be" blockbuster. In fact, it stands as the single highest grossing movie of its era. It's also worth mentioning that Columbia Pictures' much better regarded (today) competing spectacle, *Lawrence of Arabia*, was left far behind in the box-office sands at a distant number two for the year they both came out.

How the West Was Won was also generally, and surprisingly, well-reviewed by critics worldwide that year. *Variety*, for example, called it "a magnificent and exciting spectacle,"[1] and at the 1963 Academy Awards, the film picked up three Oscars out of an impressive eight nominations.

Part of the original appeal of the film certainly came from Cinerama, a cumbersome but startlingly effective process that combined an immersive directional stereo soundtrack with three projectors running in sync to provide audiences with a stunning proto-IMAX, quite nearly 3D effect. Early Cinerama projects were travelogues. But a deal between Cinerama and MGM would result in the first, and ultimately only, narrative Cinerama projects ever made: *How the West Was Won* and *The Wonderful World of the Brothers Grimm* (also 1962)

Many who saw those films, or anything in Cinerama, still remember the experience, which partially explains the still thriving *How the West Was Won* cult. But in fact, MGM struck 70mm or grainy pan-and-scan 35mm prints of *How the West Was Won* for those cities and countries unequipped to project true Cinerama, and the film was successful and much praised in those very compromised formats as well.

How the West Was Won has also been shown thousands of times, again badly cropped, on television, and with the join lines between the three images glaringly visible. ABC first televised *How the West Was Won* in October 1971 and continued to schedule it in primetime, usually over two nights, through the 1970s and long after virtually every other vintage movie (aside, it should be noted, from MGM's other heavy-hitters, *Gone with the Wind* and *The Wizard of Oz*, as well as Paramount's *The Ten Commandments*) had been consigned to the late-show graveyard.

The advertising for *How the West Was Won* (1962), almost without exception, emphasized the film's spectacle, its stars, and its wide-screen aspect, even in cities not equipped to project true Cinerama. *Photofest*

For those who couldn't wait for the next rerun, MGM also helpfully supplied a small-screen miniseries version, starring a majestically leathery James Arness, which ran off and on for four years during this period.

How the West Was Won has also appeared in every imaginable home format. A Super 8mm "digest" version, with the film's multigenerational plot whittled down from 164 minutes to a brisk 17(!) was one of MGM's first ever releases of their library titles to the general public. Later the film was made available in VHS, Betamax, LaserDisc, and DVD. In 2008 an expensive six-year restoration by Warner Home Video resulted in a

The Cinerama camera, when encased in its soundproof blimp as it is here, weighed a hefty eight-hundred-plus pounds.
Photofest

best-selling Blu-ray that finally erased, mostly, the join lines linking the three panels and delighted the film's fans.

Even Cinerama, the unwieldy three-panel format the film was shot in, has been brought back in service of the film. Those rare, holy grail–level theatrical screenings of *How the West Was Won* in that format inevitably result in sell-out, line-around-the-block spectacles—now sixty years after the film's original presentation in that format. And if you can't venture to one of the (reported) two theaters in the world equipped to project Cinerama, that's okay; the film runs on the Turner Classic Movies network several dozen times a year. It's probably playing, or available for streaming, on that network or elsewhere right this minute.

How to explain *How the West Was Won*? For one thing, no other movie looks quite like it. A Cinerama camera contained three 27mm lenses, each of which approximated the focal length of a human eye. Which meant there could be no close-ups, not unless the camera, just like a human eye, moved in for one, which didn't work well because the three cameras assigned to get the three images would crisscross if that camera got closer

Unlike many cameo-filled epics of its era, most of the stars cast in *How the West Was Won* played its leading roles. A surprising exception, however, was John Wayne, whose General Sherman is on screen only long enough to inform Ulysses S. Grant (Harry Morgan, right) that "this war's gonna be won in the West!" *Photofest*

than waist level, less than two feet from the subject. The film the image was captured on was a standard reel of 35mm celluloid, or rather three standard reels, but each of the three images on that celluloid was larger than usual—six sprocket holes per frame as opposed to the standard three. And because the (magnetic) soundtrack was on yet another reel of 35mm film, the spot where the optical track would have been could now contain, yes, even more image.

The result of all these mechanizations was a clear, deep, and immersive picture that filled up and overwhelmed a viewer's entire field of vision and its peripheries. Yet even when watched "flat" or on a TV set, the film has a weirdly mesmerizing quality about it. It's like watching the Mississippi River roll by through a porthole on a riverboat. You're missing a lot of the action, to be sure, but it's still damned hard to turn away and risk missing even more.

Luckily, *How the West Was Won* was also made at exactly the right moment, and by exactly the right people. For one thing, Cinerama had only recently evolved technically to the point where it was ready to tackle narrative cinema at all, and its partnership with MGM gave both companies a massive hit just when they needed it. Also, the truly extraordinary, once-in-a-lifetime all-star cast and technical talent, all of whom were still at the peak of their creative talent in the early 1960s, would probably have been an impossibility, say, even five years later.

How the West Was Won's "The Civil War" segment, for example, directed by no less than John Ford, is practically a summation of that director's beloved style, rhythms, and obsessions. Indeed, his segment encapsulates almost everything we associate with that director's work: Western action, gunplay, sentiment, John Wayne, traditional music, people talking to gravestones. If only the Civil War had taken place in Monument Valley! Ford's segment is also, arguably, the last great film the director ever made—virtually a poem on film—and is sometimes shown at film festivals or in film school classrooms as a succinct example of the director's distinctive style.

How the West Was Won is also, for its time, remarkably frank in its depiction of violence. In this regard the film anticipates, to a degree, later sagebrush bloodbaths by Sam Peckinpaugh. For example, at one point the usually genial James Stewart hurls an ax into the middle of an opponent's back, an act of carnage that for years was cut for television. Later, an outlaw is hurled off the top of a moving train—landing face-first into a cactus! Also much remembered by early-1960s audiences was the depiction of an entire creek stained pink with the blood of soldiers after the Battle of Shiloh. "There ain't much glory in looking at a man with his guts hanging out," screenwriter James R. Webb's script grimly comments.

Actually, Webb's Oscar-winning screenplay, which would also become the basis for a best-selling Louis L'Amour novel, is unusually and surprisingly capable, even intimate, especially when contrasted with the empty and impersonal spectacles epic movies before and after would often become. He punctuates his vast Western landscapes and four-generation-spanning narrative with improbably wry dialogue, sentiment, song, and interesting characters, all the while never failing to deliver the expected cannonballs, cornpone, and manifest destiny.

It should be noted that once again, MGM was lucky in this regard. Had that screenplay been written earlier—say, a decade earlier—Western and racial stereotypes would have dated it very quickly, as has happened with Cecil B. DeMille's epic Westerns, which now play as largely ludicrous to modern audiences. And had the story been produced even a few years later, it would have dated in the other direction and instead would have reflected the conventions of the revisionist, spaghetti and acid westerns of the 1960s and therefore lost the timeless, folktale appeal *How the West Was Won* audiences still respond so well to.

How the West Was Won also benefited immensely from its all-star cast, many of whom would not have been available or would have been too old had the film come out at any other subsequent time. And it was only because of the clout and prestige of MGM that many of these stars were recruited to enact quintessential versions of themselves, sometimes for one last victory trot across the Western landscape. Therefore, saddle-sore stars like James Stewart, Gregory Peck, Henry Fonda, John Wayne, Richard Widmark, Karl Malden, Robert Preston, Andy Devine,

Two of *How the West Was Won*'s three credited directors, John Ford and Henry Hathaway, put on a brave front while possibly longing for the easier days of silent cinema. *Photofest*

Dub Taylor, and Walter Brennan could be joined here by younger, sometimes soon-to-be spaghetti western icons like Eli Wallach, Harry Dean Stanton, and Lee Van Cleef, giving the film a somewhat startling, timeless quality it somehow, to a point, manages to retain even today.

Despite its refreshing narrative purity, one should not dismiss *How the West Was Won* as being entirely irony free. The film ends with Alfred Newman's sweeping music thumping away under aerial footage of a modern freeway with hundreds of mid-twentieth-century Studebakers and Chevys choked to a standstill in traffic.

This, the film seems to be telling us, is apparently what we have won.

33

Dr. No (1963)

No. *Dr. No*, the first filmed adventure of secret agent James Bond was not an MGM production. It was made and released by other hands by other people, in other places.

That said, in the twenty-first century, in all probability there would not be an MGM had there not been a movie called *Dr. No* back in 1963. In the nearly one hundred years the studio has been around, no other single property has been so branded to, and so protected by, the gatekeepers of the company as this one. And no other property in MGM history has been so desired by corporate raiders, independent producers, or other studios. One particular lawsuit involving ownership of the franchise was in and out of courtrooms for fifty very litigious years.

It's a complicated story. We'll try, for the purpose of this essay, to keep it focused as much as possible on MGM's part in it, and how they became the guardians of one of the most successful and long-running film series in history.

James Bond first appeared in 1953 in author Ian Fleming's novel *Casino Royale*. Fleming apparently based his suave, blunt spy on several acquaintances he had known, as well as on himself. Its success hastened both a second novel, *Live and Let Die*, and, that same year, a TV version of *Casino Royale*, for which Fleming was reportedly paid only $1,000. Actually an episode of an anthology series called *Climax*, this "Casino Royale" stared all-American Barry Nelson as the very first James "Jimmy" Bond. More memorably, Peter Lorre was also on board as the first Bond villain.

In 1961 English producer Harry Saltzman optioned the rights to film eight of Fleming's (at that time) nine Bond novels, *Casino Royale* having been already taken. The option also included future Fleming works, although initially it would expire in six months.

With reportedly just days to go before losing those rights, Saltzman met American producer Albert R. "Cubby" Broccoli, who had long been interested in the Bond novels himself. When Broccoli could not buy out Saltzman, he partnered with him instead, and Eon Productions, along with a second (holding) company called Danjaq, was created.

The most recent Bond novel at the time, *Thunderball*, was originally planned to be the first one filmed. But two screenwriters, Kevin McClory and Jack Whittingham, who Saltzman and Broccoli had never heard of, promptly slapped Fleming with a lawsuit claiming they had collaborated with the author on an earlier, unsold screenplay, which Fleming had then based his novel on. Not an auspicious start.

Consequently, Eon decided that *Dr. No*, published in 1958, would

The poster art for the first James Bond film already featured the attractive women, phallic firearms, and spies in tuxedos MGM still successfully uses to sell the series today. *Author's collection*

be their first James Bond film. This decision came about in part because their deal with United Artists allowed them only a slightly more than $1 million budget, and because this particular book, largely set in Jamaica, required less expensive globetrotting than some of its sister novels.

The sparsity of cash available for the production also torpedoed Cary Grant's hoped-for participation as Bond, which is what both Saltzman and Broccoli had desired after seeing the actor playing spy games in MGM's 1959 crowd-pleaser *North by Northwest*. Grant, however, had received a salary of $450,000—plus percentage points—for that one. Ultimately, a then relatively unknown Scotsman, Sean Connery, accepted the paltry $20,000 he was offered to play the spy.

When *Dr. No* was released in America, both the reviews and the box office were all right, but not particularly ecstatic. Surprising when one considers how successful the series would soon become.

And it was, of course, intended to be a series. The next film, *From Russia with Love*, opened in 1963 in London but was postponed to 1964 in America reportedly due to the Kennedy assassination, after which many movies depicting political violence ended up being postponed. The late president, incidentally, had reportedly been a big fan of the books. The criminal organization SPECTRE had been mentioned in *Dr. No*, and that thread, as well as such series mainstays as Bond's favorite martini and, probably less important to Bond, some of the supporting characters were utilized again here in order to get audiences to remember the last film and anticipate the next one. Furthermore, many Bond films would literally end with the on-screen promise, "James Bond will return . . ."

Posed publicity still of Eunice Gayson, Zena Marshall, Sean Connery, and Ursula Andress on the set of *Dr. No* (1963). *Photofest*

And it worked, brilliantly. Each film's audience, and box office, become significantly larger than the last, with one Bond film creating awareness of and expectations for the next. The box office receipts just keep compounding throughout the 1960s.

Everyone was also impressed with Sean Connery's debonair but brutal James Bond. No one had ever seen such a ruthless, coldblooded character on-screen who also, inexplicably, was the hero of the film. The series was bigger even than Connery's massive Bond-owed stardom. Weary of the role, Connery said "never again" for the first time in 1969 and was replaced by Australian George Lazenby, for *On Her Majesty's Secret Service.* Box office receipts dropped, briefly, but the series survived. Eventually Connery would return to the role—twice more, as it worked out. Of less consequence, to the general public at least, the series also survived the death of Ian Fleming in 1964 and the departure of Harry Saltzman in 1974. None of this mattered; James Bond himself was the star.

More consequential for the series, although no one realized it at the time, in 1965 Eon Productions finally got around to filming *Thunderball*, although they had to give screen credit to both McClory and Whittingham as part of the settlement in order to do so. In that settlement, Kevin McClory also retained future filming rights to the book *Thunderball*, which he used many years later, in 1983, for a loose remake of the property, now ironically retitled *Never Say Never Again*.

McClory's "outlaw" Bond, as it was then referred to, also succeeded in bringing back Sean Connery, this time really for the last time. That film was successfully released, surely infuriatingly so to Eon, not by MGM and not by United Artists but by Warner Bros. Eon got the last laugh, however; their "official Bond" film *Octopussy*, with Roger Moore, came out the same year and ultimately outgrossed, albeit narrowly, *Never Say Never Again*.

Around the same time (1981), United Artists, which with the exception of *Never Say Never Again* and a spoofy Columbia Pictures feature version of *Casino Royale* (1967) had released all the previous James Bond films, was purchased outright by MGM. Therefore, *Octopussy*, in addition to successfully fighting off Kevin McClory, would also be the first true-from-the-get-go MGM/UA Bond film. However, the United Artists name would be kept on the films by the parent company until *Tomorrow Never Dies* (1997).

In 1989, after the release of *License to Kill* (with Timothy Dalton now playing the spy), the series went into an unexpected six-year hiatus. One reason for this unprecedented break is MGM's perilous financial difficulties during this period. But that wasn't the only reason. The other explanation for the hiatus is that Kevin McClory had announced that he was making yet another version of *Thunderball*, this time with Columbia Pictures, who also still owned *Casino Royale* due to their 1960s spoof version. MGM consequently sued McClory, and Columbia, who of course countersued MGM.

But Columbia at the time was being purchased by electronics conglomerate Sony. Adding to the animosity between Sony/Columbia and MGM was the not-insignificant detail that they were about to take possession of MGM's old Culver City studio. Sony, it seems, intended to take both MGM's spy and their studio the same year.

They did take the studio, but the Bond litigation continued. It was not until 2001 that the case, and the subsequent cases that came out of the case, was finally settled—sort of. It was ruled that McClory could not make this particular version of the book *Thunderball*—not with Sony, and not at this time. But, with Sony still in tow, he could continue to assert his rights to do so in the future.

But what exactly were those rights? Yes, he could theoretically remake *Thunderball* in perpetuity, maybe. But did he have any rights to the *character* of James Bond or just to a single James Bond *adventure*? MGM's lawyers argued that new James Bond adventures not derivative of *Thunderball* were outside the scope of his original agreement. But McClory's lawyers were now claiming that he had actually co-created the cinematic James Bond, in total, with Fleming, and that MGM therefore owed him a percentage on every film—going all the way back to *Dr. No*.

Circling their wagons, in 1997 MGM acquired ownership of McClory's *Never Say Never Again* from Warner Bros. In 1999 they traded some old "Spider-Man" rights they were never going to use to Sony in exchange for the rights to *Casino Royale* the book, *Casino Royale* the movie, and even "Casino Royale" the forgotten TV episode. In 2006 they remade *Casino Royale* itself, with Daniel Craig now starring as the sixth official James Bond.

But Sony wasn't about to give up. They still very much wanted to control the franchise, but this time their lawyers decided that partnering with McClory was not the only way to go about it. Instead, in 2004, taking advantage of MGM's ever-precarious financial position, they purchased what amounted to a 20 percent stake in MGM itself. Some speculated at the time that this was primarily yet another attempt by the company to "own" James Bond. It didn't work. Sony's minority ownership, through a consortium they had put together for the sale, ended up being virtually powerless in the MGM boardroom. The only tangible Sony did get for their effort was the rights to distribute MGM product—including, finally, the Bond films—theatrically and on home video. Effectively now cut out of the deal was Kevin McClory, who still owned some largely intangible Bond rights he largely could no longer legally use.

And there were new, still-successful Bond films to distribute. MGM had successfully retuned to James Bond in 1995 with *GoldenEye* starring Pierce Brosnan. *GoldenEye* was also the last film produced by Albert R. Broccoli, who would pass away the following year. It was announced that the franchise would hereafter be shepherded by his daughter, Barbara Broccoli, and her half-brother, Michael G. Wilson. And by MGM.

On the other side of the battle lines, Kevin McClory died in 2006, although his ever-litigious subplot to the tale would continue, postmortem, until 2013. At that point, MGM/Eon/Danjaq, in order to keep the rights to the character safely in-house, finally acquired, for an undisclosed sum, all outside and remaining rights and interests in the character from McClory's estate.

Back in 1963, all of this was of course inconceivable and very far in the future. And so it's hard to look back at *Dr. No* and see it as it must have looked then. The 1960s "spy craze" this series singlehandedly ignited touched upon all phases of popular culture, including of course MGM's popular TV series *The Man from U.N.C.L.E.*, which itself spawned nearly a decade's worth of toys and spin-offs.

Ursula Andress seems slightly unsure whether she prefers the company of CIA agent Jack Lord (left) or MI6 spy Sean Connery. Ultimately, the British Empire would triumph. *Marc Wanamaker/Bison Archives*

Dr. No itself, though, is an interesting experience. For starters, the film is surprisingly gritty, almost more film noir than spy caper, as the rules of that genre had not really been worked out yet. There had been movies about spies, usually depicted as trench coat–wearing private eye types snooping around in bleak, often dark, European settings. The Cold War had introduced a new, vaguely Russian element, but Fleming had largely ignored this, opting instead for unaffiliated, megalomaniac villains bent on dominating both the East and the West with little regard for their respective political affiliations.

The tiny budget United Artists inflicted on the film is stretched out pretty well. Yes, the British MI6 headquarters look like a second-rate insurance company office and the scene where Bond is menaced by a spider(!) is ridiculously hokey, but Dr. No's headquarters, designed by Ken Adam, is appropriately massive and well stocked with uniformed minions waiting to watch things explode and then die on cue.

Director Terence Young introduces James Bond to the world with a great deal of visual style. Teasingly, we see his back and hands before, just as in Humphrey Bogart's famous entrance in *Casablanca,* the camera tilts up. The utilization of the soon to be world-famous "James Bond theme" here doesn't hurt either. The result of this stylish buildup is that Connery, or maybe it's Bond, is presented as being, like Bogart, a star already. He wasn't, not yet, although this scene certainly played a large part in making it happen.

Connery's charisma is a major asset, but the rest of the cast is fine too. Bernard Lee as "M" and Lois Maxwell as Miss Moneypenny, both of whom would stay with the series for decades, are already at their MI6 desks, but Desmond Llewelyn's wily "Q" would not show up until the series' sophomore effort, *From Russia with Love*, in 1963.

The title character of Dr. No, the series' first of what would be many would-be world-dominating villains, is played by Joseph Wiseman. Wiseman is aptly arch, but it's still a shame that Fleming's friend, writer Noel Coward, or his step-cousin, actor Christopher Lee, did not get to play the role.

Ursula Andress became an international star for her role as heroine Honey Ryder, introduced Venus-like emerging from the sea wearing a white bikini and a sheathed knife. That memorable scene was referenced decades later in *Die Another Day* (2002), in which Halle Berry has a similar effect on Pierce Brosnan's James Bond.

Jack Lord plays Felix Leiter, Bond's CIA counterpoint. Perhaps for the same reason the "Casino Royale" TV episode had Americanized James Bond, Broccoli and Saltzman maybe wanted to hedge their bets with their largely American audience, who might not have felt comfortable with such British material, by offering Lord as virtually a secondary James Bond. The two of them are presented as being equally capable and debonair. They look a lot alike here too. Director Young even dresses them both in identical white shirts and black ties and then frames them, mirrorlike, on either side of the same compositions. There were plans for Lord's "American Bond" to return for further adventures alongside his counterpart, but Connery ultimately had no problem whatsoever appealing to American audiences—especially female ones—and in subsequent films the Leiter character was played more comically, and by other actors. Jack Lord would have to wait several more years to become a star, on the long-running (1968–1980) *Hawaii Five-O* TV series.

Dr. No is the most influential and important MGM film that isn't really an MGM film ever made. No, the lion did not roar in front of the credits in 1962. But he does now. The studio long ago affixed their logo to the front of all circulating prints and video releases of this film, and on most other United Artists pictures as well. And this little bit of seeming vanity is neither surprising or inaccurate. After all, consider for a moment all the work, all the money, and all the years it took to be able to do so.

James Bond will return . . .

34

The Man from U.N.C.L.E. (1964–1968)

Lunch with Napoleon Solo

An essay by Stephen X. Sylvester

Because *The Man from U.N.C.L.E.* was my favorite television show, I just had to see where all that amazing action played out. During the summer of 1968, I was fortunate enough to take a tour of M-G-M studios, where the show was shot. The tour opened a door to a fascinating and surreal world I never knew existed. Anything you could ever imagine needed to tell fantastic stories on film was there within those walls, causing a complete sensory overload.

The tour of Lot One was a cornucopia of all the integral ingredients with multiple cavernous soundstages, a busting-at-the-seams prop house, a massive Wardrobe Department, vintage military vehicles from WWII, and the massive painted backdrops. Could it get any better than this? Yes, it could, and it did. Lot One was amazing, but now the tour would be bumped up a couple of notches from what was amazing to sheer incredibility.

Next on the tour agenda were the exterior backlot sets on Lot Two and Lot Three. What's a backlot? I had no idea but was about to find out, big time. Here were the most fascinating juxtapositions of architecture, culture, and location you could ever imagine. Grand Central Station next to the Great Wall of China, next to the Three Musketeers Court, next to the Northern Italian Village of Verona, Small Town Square

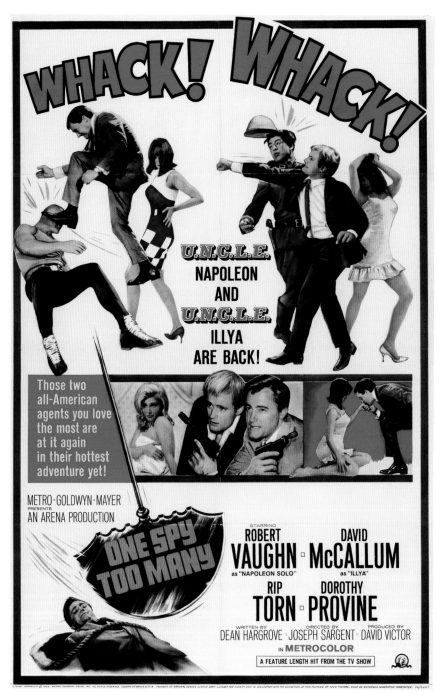

A theatrical poster for a TV show? *The Man from U.N.C.L.E.* was so popular that several episodes were reedited and released as popular feature films. *Stephen X. Sylvester*

at the southern end of New York's urban Fifth Avenue, and an ocean liner (facade) docked at a big-city harbor within a short walking distance of New England (Andy Hardy) Street.

Touring this acreage was truly a condensed trip around the world and a bombardment of visual delights. I kept wishing the bus driver would slow down. For a kid who loved magic, these were the ultimate full-sized illusions. No offense, but the trip to Disneyland the following week paled by comparison. So it was *The Man from U.N.C.L.E.* that would begin my keen interest in the studios of M-G-M and lead to the eventual collaboration on a book, *M-G-M: Hollywood's Greatest Backlot.* But hey, I digress.

By 1964 the studio of Metro-Goldwyn-Mayer was everything it would ever be, a compilation of forty years of being at the top of the Hollywood hierarchy of moviemaking. It was no secret that movie theater attendance had been on the decline since 1950. Much of the audience had turned their attention to that free, in-home form of entertainment, television. The grand movie factory was now in a deep slumber.

And M-G-M was late, like many of the other Hollywood studios, to enter into the then-new medium of television. Instead of figuring out how to own it, they first ignored it, fought it, and then lost out to it. Consequently, their first TV program was a rather lame attempt, broadcast on ABC-TV and titled *M-G-M Parade* (1955–56), described as "a look inside the world of moviemaking" and utilizing a combination of clips from their older movies and promotions for upcoming productions. Ultimately the audience was not impressed, and the show ended after a nine-month run.

The studio then tried television series adaptations of their previous popular movies like *Northwest Passage, The Thin Man, National Velvet, Father of the Bride*, and *The Asphalt Jungle.* But again the audience reaction was disappointing, with the exception of *Dr. Kildare*, which would become a solid ratings winner.

During the fall of 1962, television producer Norman Felton (*Pursuit, Dr. Kildare, The Lieutenant*) had approached Ian Fleming, author of the James Bond series, with a concept for a new television series based loosely on Alfred Hitchcock's hit *North by Northwest* (1959). Ironically, this proposed series would be yet another to have its conception rooted in an M-G-M movie. Felton's producing partner on the planned new series was the talented Sam Rolfe, the creator, producer, and writer of such acclaimed series as *Have Gun Will Travel*, *Playhouse 90*, and *The Eleventh Hour*.

On September 22, 1964, they premiered their new series, now titled *The Man from U.N.C.L.E.*, on NBC-TV in time to capitalize on the emerging spy craze, in large part fueled by the massive box-office success of *Dr. No* (1962) and *From Russia with Love* (1963), the first two in a series of James Bond movies based on Fleming's novels.

At that time many countries did not have the level of saturation of television sets as in the United States, and certainly not color TVs. Eight of the two-part TV episodes received a boost in budget for a few additional scenes and were edited into feature films that played to mostly international audiences. "The Alexander the Greater Affair" two-part TV episode played in movie theaters with the title *One Spy Too Many*. "The Bridge of Lions Affair" became *One of Our Spies Is Missing*. "The Concrete Overcoat Affair" became *The Spy in the Green Hat*. "The Five Daughters Affair" had a theatrical run as *The Karate Killers*. "The Prince

The *U.N.C.L.E.* cast, Robert Vaughn, David McCallum, and Leo G. Carroll, lend their likenesses to a comic book cover. *Stephen X. Sylvester*

of Darkness Affair" became *The Helicopter Spies,* and "The Seven Wonders of the World Affair" became *How to Steal the World* in movie theaters. They proved to be extremely popular in Europe (especially England) and Asia, making "*U.N.C.L.E.*" a worldwide phenomenon. National and international fan clubs were formed, with many surviving long after the series would go off the airwaves.

The series stars became pop sensations, much like Elvis Presley and The Beatles. Crowds followed them everywhere. Robert Vaughn (as Napoleon Solo) soon had young fans camped outside his house at all hours, some trying to get in. He eventually had to resort to a recording device broadcasting the sounds of a dog barking to keep the would-be trespassers at bay. David McCallum (who played Illya Kuryakin) received more fan mail at M-G-M than any of their past movie personalities, including the legendary Clark Gable. Leo G. Carroll (Alexander Waverly) added an element of class and sophistication to this show and, for that matter, everything else he appeared in. He was a favorite actor of director Alfred Hitchcock and was another connection to the Hitchcock classic *North by Northwest*. His role in the movie, simply referred to as The Professor, was an undeniable prequel to his future role as Mr. Waverly.

As popular as the series stars were, a fourth "star" of the series soon emerged: the U.N.C.L.E. Special, a futuristic combination of automatic pistol and rifle. The original concept for the weapon was to create a "breakaway" gun with attachments, based on a 1934 7.65 German Mauser pistol. The show's special effects team (Robert Murdock, Arnold Goode, Bill Graham) and the capable crew in the M-G-M gun room gave the pistol an extended barrel with horizontal foregrip, Bushnell scope with mount, custom anodized aluminum grips, an extended cartridge magazine, and a collapsible shoulder stock, creating an incredibly unique weapon. Adding an interesting twist to the story, artist, car, and motorcycle customizer Von Dutch (Kenny Howard) had considerable input on the overall design of the initial prototype.

Unfortunately, their impressive prototype was deemed too small, unbalanced in scale with the large attachments; even worse, it proved unreliable for firing blank cartridges. Fortunately, Manuel Zamora, "Gunsmith to the Stars" and manager of the M-G-M gun room, had a practical solution. Take the attachments from the Mauser and machine them to fit a much more reliable Walther P-38. This was a very common 9mm pistol at the time, surplus from WWII Germany, and the M-G-M gun room had an ample supply, extensively used on the *Combat!* TV series, also filmed at the studio.

The standard Walther P-38 automatic pistol was modified, the hammer bobbed and the barrel cut and threaded to accommodate both extended barrel and silencer attachments. In pistol form, a handmade flash-suppressor "bird cage" screwed into the internally threaded and bobbed barrel gave it balance and an unmistakable appearance. Soon after their creation appeared on-screen, a new star was born. And what a star it would become! The gun would get its share of weekly fan mail, up to five hundred letters a week.

So convincing were these weapons that they caught the attention of the US Treasury Department, which would fine M-G-M for the offense of manufacturing automatic weapons without a license. Ironic, given the fact that these guns could only fire blanks; with any internal threaded barrel attachment in place, the barrel was essentially blocked.

The idea for this unique weapon was tied concurrently to a potential toy version tie-in with the series. Stan Weston, president of Weston Merchandising Corporation licensing firm, was hired for the task partially because Weston had an established relationship with the Ideal Toy Corporation. The project design was given to an independent toy inventor, Reuben Klamer, and his staff at Toylab studios. The Toylab designers created a plastic toy "breakaway" cap-firing gun with barrel, scope, and shoulder stock that evoked the attachments found on the television series originals.

Replica of U.N.C.L.E.'s popular P-38 special, the much-admired second version of Napoleon Solo's favored weapon. *Stephen X. Sylvester*

Although the Ideal toy weapon only vaguely resembled the TV version, the Napoleon Solo gun set would become one of the biggest selling toys associated with a TV series in television history. A mint, in an original box example of the toy weapon has fetched over $1,000, a substantial increase from the original price of $3.99.

The legacy of the U.N.C.L.E. Special lives on; copies of this gun and its various versions have been available for five decades as toys. The gun would become especially popular in Japan, where private gun ownership is prohibited by law. Machinist-minded fans of the U.N.C.L.E. Special in the United States even took it one step further and manufactured versions capable of firing live rounds.

This successful merchandising strategy for the series was a bonanza for the studio and the show producers. The wide array of items included lunchboxes, bubble gum cards, books, paperbacks, Gold Key comics, car models, walkie-talkies, a shooting arcade, playing cards, View-Master reels, clothing, Halloween costumes, a Corgi "THRUSH Buster" car, board games, magic sets, action figures, and more. The toys were produced by major toy manufacturers including Ideal, Milton Bradley, Gilbert, Marx, and Lone Star. In total there were 55 licensees with 135 products, according to the Weston Merchandising Corporation. Stars Robert Vaughn and David McCallum were contractually obligated to receive a percentage of the merchandising proceeds (their likenesses on the packaging helped stimulate sales) but never received their promised cut of the action—further proof that some things in Hollywood never change.

The innovative and glossy series benefitted from every aspect of the M-G-M motto that boldly proclaimed, "Do it right, Do it big, Give it class!" In every episode of *The Man from U.N.C.L.E.*, elements of the stellar legacy of M-G-M could be found. After all, the series producers had the biggest and best toy chest at their disposal to bring their show to life.

All aspects of the vast studio assets were utilized during its production, giving the series its unique and impressive style. The rich, vivid color was supplied by the studio lab, home of the popular Metrocolor film stock, a budget-conscious option to the industry standard of Technicolor.

They had use of a selection of almost thirty soundstages, some of them the biggest in the industry at the time. Stages 10 and 28 were extensively used for the sets of *U.N.C.L.E.*, with Stage 10 containing the permanent interior sets of the organization's New York headquarters, hallways, entrance, and Mr. Waverly's state-of-the-art office. And when no one was paying too close attention, the series would on occasion "borrow" a standing set from an M-G-M feature, including *Get Yourself a College Girl* (1964), *The Unsinkable Molly Brown* (1964), and *Made in Paris* (1966).

The modern cinematography was a major element of the show's unique style. Cinematographer Fred Koenekamp and cameraman Til Gabani gave the series a unique look, utilizing colorful "whip pans" (which other television series would later emulate), dramatic freeze frames, tilted camera angles, and extensive use (for the time) of an Arriflex handheld camera.

The famous M-G-M commissary, home to the legendary chicken soup and dumpling, even got into the *U.N.C.L.E.* act, featuring a Robert Vaughn sandwich (hot pastrami on pumpernickel bread) and the David McCallum Special (a sliced chicken and avocado sandwich). The two main stars had dressing rooms above the M-G-M rehearsal hall where the likes of Fred Astaire, Gene Kelly, Cyd Charisse, and Debbie Reynolds had all danced their feet off.

The studio's Scenic Art Department had 2,500 painted backdrops to dress the sets on these stages, including the Manhattan backdrop seen from the windows of Mr. Waverly's office set.

The studio Art Department added to the overall "big picture value" and iconic M-G-M gloss to *The Man from U.N.C.L.E.* series. Here the show utilized the creative talents of many more M-G-M veterans, including set decorator Henry Grace; his association with the studio went back to 1934. Grace had worked on many of the studio's box-office hits from the previous decades, including *The Blackboard Jungle* (1955), *Jailhouse Rock* (1957), *Gigi* (1958), *North by Northwest* (1959), and *The Time Machine* (1960).

Among the art directors and set decorators that worked on the show were set decorator Keogh Gleason, who had a career at M-G-M lasting twenty-eight years, and art director Merrill Pye, whose career at M-G-M spanned forty-five years, beginning in 1926.

They, and talented others, had a treasure trove to work with, since M-G-M was considered the studio that never threw anything away. With furniture from every historical period and style, the Property Department gave the set decorators a massive selection of props to utilize, many from previous M-G-M features. Props from

Man from U.N.C.L.E.

$3.99

"MAN FROM U.N.C.L.E." GUN WITH HOLSTER.
This UNCLE cap-firing* basic .45 automatic
toy pistol looks ordinary until you convert it into
a special UNCLE rifle. Fast clip-loading .. clip
slides into pistol grip. Barrel extension has a
built-in silencer. Bi-pod legs attach to extended
barrel for extra balance. Slip on the Superscope
telescopic sight for accurate aiming and fire.
Smoke rolls from barrel when roll caps*are fired.
Authentically detailed in rugged plastic and
metal. UNCLE badge, I.D. card included.
48 T 3467—Ship. wt. 1 lb. 12 oz.......SET $3.99

Vintage, and decidedly non-PC, 1965 Sears catalog ad for a *Man from U.N.C.L.E.*–inspired assassin's rifle kit.
Stephen X. Sylvester

Forbidden Planet (1956) were used in "The Bridge of Lions Affair," props from *The Prodigal* (1955) used in "The Prince of Darkness Affair," and props from *Atlantis: The Lost Continent* (1961) used in "The Concrete Overcoat Affair," just to name a few. If, on the rare occasion, the vast inventory of the studio Property Department did not have what they needed, they had the facilities to manufacture it.

In recognition of their work creating unusual gadgets and props, including the automatic opening doors of U.N.C.L.E. Headquarters, THRUSH infrared sniper rifle, communicator cigarette case, communicator pens, and pistol cane, Robert Murdock, Arnold Goode, and their assistant, Bill Graham, were nominated in 1966 for an Individual Achievements in Art Direction and Allied Crafts—Mechanical Special Effects special Emmy award by the Television Academy.

The M-G-M Wardrobe Department boasted a collection of 250,000 costumes representing all styles of attire, from the dawn of man to the swinging sixties. Some of the most famous costume designers who applied their trade here included Adrian, Irene, Walter Plunkett, and Mary Ann Nyberg. With *U.N.C.L.E.* plots centered all around the world, a huge selection of ethnic costumes were also utilized by Gene Ostler and Rose Rockney.

The Portrait Studio, once used to photograph M-G-M's legendary galaxy of motion picture stars, was used for the multitude of publicity photos taken of stars Robert Vaughn, David McCallum, and Leo G. Carroll. Many of these photo shoots would feature the unique *U.N.C.L.E.* guns and would later appear on a wide range of series-related merchandising.

The studio casting office kept the M-G-M connection going by often casting past and present M-G-M contract players for roles in *The Man from U.N.C.L.E.* episodes. These performers included Joan Crawford in "The Five Daughters Affair";

Richard Anderson in "The Quadripartite Affair" and "The Candidate's Wife Affair"; Angela Lansbury in "The Deadly Toys Affair"; Ricardo Montalbán in "The Dove Affair" and "The King of Diamonds Affair"; Janet Leigh in "The Concrete Overcoat Affair"; Cesare Danova in "The When in Rome Affair"; Chad Everett in "The J for Judas Affair"; Leslie Nielsen and Barry Sullivan in "The Seven Wonders of the World Affair"; and Anne Francis in "The Quadripartite Affair" and "The Giuoco Piano Affair."

The series writers, including Peter Allan Fields and Dean Hargrove, kept a binder supplied by the Art Department of backlot sets on Lots Two and Three in their offices for inspiration to incorporate the plethora of available exterior settings into the scripts for each episode.

The show would utilize hundreds of backlot sets during its three-and-a-half-year run, constructed for classic M-G-M movies over the past three decades and spread over more than one hundred acres. This was not the biggest backlot in Hollywood; 20th Century Fox and Universal each had more acreage dedicated to their exterior sets, but the M-G-M backlot was used for more productions than any of the others.

Lot Two comprised thirty-seven acres featuring three train stations, a middle-class residential street, a grand Southern mansion, vast formal gardens, a swimming pool, a lake, streets of Italy and Paris, a New York commercial district, a loading dock with ocean liner, and an English estate. These facades helped give the series that international flair.

The Fifth Avenue set, built for *Wife vs. Secretary* (1936) and seen in *San Francisco* (1936) and *Royal Wedding* (1951), was used for "The Discotheque Affair" and "The Never, Never Affair." The Waterfront Street set built for *The Barretts of Wimpole Street* (1934) and seen in *Too Hot to Handle* (1938) and *An American in Paris* (1951) was used in "The Foxes and Hounds Affair." The Southern Mansion set built for *The Toy Wife* (1938) and seen in *Love Finds Andy Hardy* (1938), *Undercurrent* (1946), and *Good News* (1947) was used for "The Her Master's Voice Affair" and "The Take Me to Your Leader Affair." Quality Street, built for the film of the same name in 1927 and seen in *Queen Christina* (1933) and *Random Harvest* (1942), was used in "The Concrete Overcoat Affair." The Verona Square set built for *Romeo and Juliet* (1936) and seen in *Gaslight* (1944) and *The Bribe* (1949) was used in "The Double Affair" and "The Alexander the Greater Affair." The Spanish Street set built for *Susan Lenox (Her Fall and Rise)* (1931) and seen in *Viva Villa* (1934) and *Fiesta* (1947) was used for "The Prince of Darkness Affair." The Old Mill House set built for *When Ladies Meet* (1941) and seen in *Mrs. Miniver* (1942) and *The Last Time I Saw Paris* (1954) was used for "The Double Affair" and "The Vulcan Affair." The Formal Gardens set used for *Marie Antoinette* (1938) and *The White Cliffs of Dover* (1944) was seen in "The Bow Wow Affair."

Lot Three, less than a mile east of Lot Two, was spread over sixty-five acres and included a Dutch village, three Western towns, a street of Victorian mansions, a large lake and tropical jungle, a Salem seaport, a US Army base, and a massive water tank for processing miniatures. Standing sets used here for *The Man from U.N.C.L.E.* episodes included Ghost Town Street, built for *Boom Town* (1940) and seen in *Annie Get Your Gun* (1950) and *Westward the Women* (1952), was also used for "The Maze Affair." Dutch Street, built for *Seven Sweethearts* (1942) and seen in *Green Dolphin Street* (1947) and *Mutiny on the Bounty* (the 1962 remake), was used for "The Finney Foot Affair." The jungle set built for *Too Hot to Handle* (1938) and seen in *White Cargo* (1942) and *Never So Few* (1959) was used for "The My Friend the Gorilla Affair" and "The Seven Wonders of the World Affair." The US Army base built for *Escape* (1940) and seen in *Thirty Seconds Over Tokyo* (1944) and *What Next, Corporal Hargrove?* (1945) was used for "The Alexander the Greater Affair." The rock formations seen in *The Bad and the Beautiful* (1952) and *Jupiter's Darling* (1954) were used for "The Seven Wonders of the World Affair." The St. Louis Street built for *Meet Me in St. Louis* (1944), also seen in *Cass Timberlane* (1947) and *Excuse My Dust* (1951), was used for "The Vulcan Affair" and "The Prince of Darkness Affair."

The Man from U.N.C.L.E. was awarded a Golden Globe by the Hollywood Foreign Press Association for Best Television Series in 1966. That same year, Robert Vaughn and David McCallum were both nominated for Best Actor. The show was also nominated for a slew of Emmys in categories including Cinematography, Editing, Outstanding Dramatic Series, Set Direction, Outstanding Lead Actor, Outstanding Supporting Actor, and Sound Editing. The musical score was nominated for both a Primetime Emmy and a Grammy. Yet despite the numerous nominations, there were no wins for this TV phenomenon.

It's a worn cliché, I know, but nothing lasts forever, and all good things come to an end. Such too was the case with *The Man from U.N.C.L.E.* The show, influenced by the ratings success of *Batman*, became too comedic and campy for its own good, and the once-loyal audience started to tune out. A gallant attempt to reverse the ratings nosedive during the last season with a return to suspense and drama was too little, too late. All the fun and excitement of the series came to an end officially when the final episode aired on January 15, 1968.

Ironically, the show's demise was a foreboding of M-G-M's own demise, as the grand studio would soon be whittled away to a mere shadow of its former prestigious, worldwide empire. With new studio ownership, everything that could be sold was sold. Many of the props from this show ended up in the studio auction in 1970, which *The Hollywood Reporter* would call "the greatest rummage sale in history." The magical backlots would eventually become housing developments. Included in the wholesale disbursement of forty-five years of M-G-M assets were props and costumes from *The Man from U.N.C.L.E.* Some of the items offered to the highest bidder included furniture from Mr. Waverly's office, weapons (including the infamous U.N.C.L.E. guns and THRUSH rifles), pistol case, cigarette case and pen communicators, and THRUSH jumpsuits.

In this early, staged publicity still, Robert Vaughn seems to prefer an Eliot Ness–inspired tommy gun to his usual P-38. *Photofest*

Academy Award–winning makeup artist Robert Short, *The Incredible World of SPY-Fi* author Danny Biederman, and Stembridge Gun Rentals associate Mike Wetherell collected many of these items and have been very generous in displaying them for fans over the subsequent decades. Mr. Biederman's SPY-Fi Exhibit has been featured in venues that include the *Queen Mary*, Central Intelligence Agency Headquarters, the Ronald Reagan Presidential Library, and the Hollywood Heritage Museum.

Forty years after the show ended, I had the opportunity to meet and befriend my childhood hero, Napoleon Solo. I spent many enjoyable hours with Robert Vaughn, and one afternoon we had a memorable lunch at Hollywood's Musso & Frank Grill. In between the sourdough bread, French onion soup, and roast beef sandwich, he shared stories of making the series and other tales of his career, his childhood hero (the magnificent John Barrymore), his disdain of guns (how ironic), and his political evolution (from liberal to less liberal). During our conversation he mentioned that people were still constantly asking him about all the traveling he did during the filming of the *U.N.C.L.E.* series. He was always amused at their stunned reaction when he shared the fact that 95 percent of the series was shot at the M-G-M studio in Culver City, California—perhaps a testament to the authenticity of the M-G-M backlot!

The waiters there all knew him from their decades of taking his order at several famous Hollywood eateries past and present, including the long-gone Hollywood Brown Derby on Vine Street. Several asked if he still had his George Barris–customized 1964 Lincoln Continental convertible, bought with an early *U.N.C.L.E.* paycheck. Fortunately, he did, and with some encouragement from me, he later had it completely restored.

And as I sat there listening to his insightful tales, a voice inside me was crying out, "Hey everybody, look who's having lunch with Napoleon Solo!" But I played it cool and laid back, you know, just like a seasoned U.N.C.L.E. agent, despite the fact that the impressionable seven-year-old boy inside me was completely and totally ecstatic. They say, "Never meet your childhood hero; you'll only be disappointed." That was certainly not the case with me.

A few years later, after my book *M-G-M: Hollywood's Greatest Backlot* was published, he was the first person I sent a copy to at his home in Bridgeport, Connecticut. A few days later I got a call from him thanking me for the book. He confessed that he and his wife, Linda, had stayed up all night reading the text and studying the huge selection of studio photos and maps. And at the end of the conversation, he enthusiastically shared that he had learned a lot about the studio's history and it had brought back a lot of fond memories of his years working there. Many of those memories had not been tapped in over fifty years. And he realized what a great honor it was for him to have worked at a studio that was so steeped in Hollywood moviemaking history. It was all a big thrill for him. And sharing his overwhelming delight with the book was a big thrill for me.

Such is the lasting influence of M-G-M!

The author wishes to thank Danny Biederman, David Heilman, Jan Murree, Robert Short, and Mike Wetherell for their contributions to this essay.

35

Doctor Zhivago (1965)

Doctor Zhivago was, for its studio, one of those increasingly frequent do-or-die epics that needed to be a success if that studio were to survive. Fortunately, in this case the film *was* a success. The box-office proceeds eventually climbed above *Ben-Hur*, but below *Gone with the Wind*, in the pantheon of MGM blockbusters.

As befitting such a mammoth production, *Doctor Zhivago* had a long and convoluted gestation. The story began with a controversial but best-selling book by Boris Pasternak. Pasternak was a Soviet Union poet who, upon publication of this novel, found himself in trouble with his government over his book's perceived anti-communist bias. When the book was banned in his homeland but went on to be a bestseller in the West and win the Nobel Prize for Literature, Pasternak was forced to renounce the award.

Legendary director David Lean, in search of a project after his successful *Lawrence of Arabia* (1962), interested producer Carlo Ponti in a film adaptation. Ponti, ever in search of vehicles for his wife, Sophia Loren, convinced MGM to commit to the project for financing and distribution.

That project, for obvious reasons, could not be filmed in the USSR. Surprisingly, it was "sunny" Spain that was largely conscripted to impersonate revolutionary Russia, although Finland would ultimately stand in for the motherland for a few of the snowiest vistas. For one scene, 7,000 daffodils were meticulously planted, but because the Spanish winter was so mild that year, they sprouted early and had to be dug up and replanted when production was finally ready to photograph them.

Equally un-Russian was the cast. Peter O'Toole, from *Lawrence of Arabia*, was apparently Lean's original choice for Zhivago, but ultimately Egyptian actor Omar Sharif,

A LOVE CAUGHT IN THE FIRE OF REVOLUTION

Turbulent were the times and fiery was the love story of Zhivago, his wife... and the passionate, tender Lara.

METRO-GOLDWYN-MAYER PRESENTS A CARLO PONTI PRODUCTION

DAVID LEAN'S FILM OF BORIS PASTERNAK'S

DOCTOR ZHiVAGO

STARRING
GERALDINE CHAPLIN · JULIE CHRISTIE · TOM COURTENAY
ALEC GUINNESS · SIOBHAN McKENNA · RALPH RICHARDSON
OMAR SHARIF (AS ZHIVAGO) ROD STEIGER · RITA TUSHINGHAM

WINNER OF 6 ACADEMY AWARDS!

SCREEN PLAY BY ROBERT BOLT · DIRECTED BY DAVID LEAN · IN PANAVISION® AND METROCOLOR · MGM

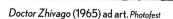

Doctor Zhivago (1965) ad art. *Photofest*

also a *Lawrence of Arabia* veteran, played the title role, supported by a largely British and American cast and crew.

The story of *Doctor Zhivago* is set during World War I and then the Russian Revolution. Yuri Zhivago is a physician who is also a poet, who is married to Tonya (Geraldine Chaplin), who also loves Lara (Julie Christie), and who is ultimately kept out of the arms of both by war, revolution, and fate.

Considering the Cold War the movie came out of, the story is not as politicized as one might expect. Although written by a disillusioned Russian and filmed in the West,

Alec Guinness and director David Lean enjoy a moment away from the Russian Revolution. *Photofest*

communism is never overtly condemned—although the horrors the Soviet Union was born of certainly are. The climax, which was not in the book, finds Yuri and Lara's daughter and her engineer husband enjoying their lives and operating a mighty hydraulic dam, which is visualized as framed in a rainbow. What's more, the couple are presumably happy under the current regime while bringing power to their people.

Upon its release, the film was initially neither a critical nor a box office success. The press carped that Lean had chosen to downplay the book's politics and nuance in order to concentrate on spectacle and romance. But the spectacle and romance were what the public eventually embraced about the film. And good word of mouth from the public is what ultimately pushed the film's grosses into the stratosphere. Maurice Jarre's music was similarly successful. In particular, one of his instrumental pieces from the score, "Lara's Theme," had lyrics added to its earworm melody and was a smash hit as "Somewhere My Love." The film received ten Oscar nominations, competing with Fox's *The Sound of Music*, which ultimately bested *Zhivago* for the Best Picture statuette, although, in a nice display of democratic détente, each film took exactly five trophies home.

Two of these Oscars were for the film's cinematography and art direction, which are among the best ever captured for a motion picture. David Lean's perfectionism, of course, is what made these images possible. For nearly a year he had kept his massive crew busy while the studio fumed ineffectually at his expensive excesses. This situation would never have been allowed to happen even a decade earlier, and that the studio allowed it here well illustrates how the power at MGM had shifted from the producers to the director.

Roger Mayer, a longtime executive at the studio, commented about this in 1992, pointing out:

> MGM was never what you would call a forward-looking studio in the sense of wanting to give the creator the control. David Lean was not used to that sort of relationship, and additionally, he was shooting on a distant location, so it was extremely hard for anybody to control him. But in any event Lean had gone out and filmed . . . all the flowers that you could possibly film, for days and days. Despite these many thousands of feet, David was not satisfied and wanted to go back and shoot at a later time. And that began to be a big contest. Finally, he won it, went back and shot some of the most gorgeous film there ever was. Did that make a difference in the picture? Probably.[1]

As Roger Mayer notes, however, those visuals David Lean eventually captured *were* beautiful. What's more, those visuals were not beautiful only for the sake of being beautiful. One of Lean's strengths as a director was his skill as a poet. A *visual* poet. This talent, though, occasionally worked to the detriment of his films. For his next picture, *Ryan's Daughter* (1970), Lean again held MGM hostage by again traveling to a remote location (Ireland, this time) and again toppling millions of dollars over budget and months over schedule while waiting for nature to supply him with perfect compositions. The resultant film again is beautiful and powerful, but the coastal setting and the intimate story that takes place in that setting is in fact swamped by those spectacular and this time, story-wise, largely unnecessary visuals.

For *Doctor Zhivago*, however, there is a potent thematic justification for Lean's excesses. Zhivago is, after all, characterized as a poet. Having him reading those poems on-screen to *show* he is a poet or showing him writing those poems, however, is not very interesting. It is a trap most movies about writers and poets fall into, which explains why there are so few good movies about writers and poets. Lean, however, instead of talking about Zhivago's verbal talents, finds visual equivalents to that poetry, like ice frosting over a window or wind blowing through those flowers. So when we finally do see Omar Sharif writing those poems, we immediately feel that we have experienced the passion that inspired his words, even though we haven't actually heard them.

This ten-acre replica of revolutionary Moscow, peopled with thousands of costumed extras, was constructed from the ground up on location in Spain. *Author's collection*

So, yes, at least here, those flowers Roger Mayer remembers the front office fuming over really did make a difference.

Boris Pasternak died in 1960, so he never saw the film based on his most-famous work, and of course he never saw that book published in his homeland. *Doctor Zhivago* would not be officially published in Russia until 1988. But the movie made from that book continues to be, especially among many people of a certain age, one of the great movie experiences of their lives.

Not surprisingly, other, lesser directors have tried to recapture or reinvent the property in the more than five decades since that movie opened. The story of Yuri and Tonya and Lara has been adapted for television, now even for Russian television, several times. It has also been the basis for (at least) two stage musicals, neither of which, due to legal restrictions, could include "Lara's Theme." But it took David Lean, MGM, and, yes, those acres of flowers to find Zhivago's and *Doctor Zhivago*'s poetry for the world.

36

Blow-Up (1966)

MGM never gets the credit for *Blow-Up,* one of the key 1960s movies, and the single biggest factor in toppling the decades-old production code.

If one watches the credits, though, *Blow-Up* was produced by something called Premier Productions. Although the on-screen copyright holder, in small text, is indeed MGM, the prints are by Metrocolor, and the end credits cite the film as being "presented by" MGM, whatever that means. MGM, however, provided more than just lab services. *Blow-Up* (the on-screen title is actually "Blowup") was produced by Carlo Ponti as part of his ongoing deal with the studio, which had in 1966 resulted in the blockbuster *Doctor Zhivago.* But unlike *Zhivago,* where Leo most definitely did roar, the studio here had to downplay its involvement because of its (founding) membership in the Motion Picture Association of America (MPAA). The film that director Michelangelo Antonioni allowed to be screened for Metro executives had a very strong sexual element, which those executives knew would have to be removed before the film could receive a MPAA seal—without which the studio would not be able to release it.

MGM had flirted with "dirty" movies before. Stanley Kubrick's *Lolita* (1962), which the studio distributed, had certainly challenged the aging production code in its depiction of a middle-aged man's infatuation with a teenager, but that film also had familiar stars in the cast and so somehow seemed less objectionable. After a few cuts and alterations it had been released, more or less intact. *Blow-Up,* however, which included actual on-screen nudity and an arty "foreign" director, possessed a whole new set of problems for studio brass to try, somehow, to overcome.

It is to the studio's, and those nameless executives', credit that rather than cut or reshape *Blow-Up* without its director's approval, they rather ingeniously created the pseudonyms and never-again-heard-from Premier Productions. *Blow-Up* could now be released, intact, without a seal. What could have been another *Greed* instead became an all too rare and harmonious collaboration between Hollywood commerce and art.

Long regarded as the most conservative of the major studios, MGM's involvement in such a daring project as *Blow-Up*, even veiled under a pseudonym, speaks well of the company's efforts at the time to remain a leader in an industry where it was rapidly being looked on as increasingly old-fashioned and moribund. Certainly the film's ultimate success both critically and commercially, and the respect it continues to command fifty-plus years on, reflects well on those efforts. It's a bit of a shame that this respect is all focused toward Antonioni himself rather than on the studio.

MGM released *Blow-Up* (1966) incognito in the United States due to its graphic content, but in overseas markets (Spain, in this case), Leo the Lion could roar without an alias. *Photofest*

Blow-Up was a game changer for the industry. It proved that movies, even movies from thinly disguised mainstream Hollywood, could be hip and sexy and could flaunt the rules and get away with it. Incidentally, or maybe not, *Blow-Up* is also considered to be the first commercially released American movie to (if fleetingly) depict pubic hair. Yet even with its disjointed narrative and pubic hair, *Blow-Up* played widely in the United States and worldwide and was well reviewed. And it accomplished all of this without an MPAA seal. That success subsequently destroyed the restrictive old production code, which had dictated what movies could and could not show us for decades. In 1968 the floundering code would be replaced entirely with the MPAA rating system that survives today.

But it might not have worked out that way. In the 1960s Michelangelo Antonioni was an internationally regarded director and screenwriter. He was also a maverick and a fiercely independent iconoclast. Many of his fans regarded it as a bit of a shock when, in 1965, he signed an agreement with Ponti to create three English-language films for MGM, of which *Blow-Up* would be the first, based on a script he had loosely adapted from a well-regarded Julio Cortázar short story and set in contemporary, swinging London. Former child actor David Hemmings took the lead role after the better-known and more bankable Sean Connery rejected the project as being incomprehensible. Hemmings would be supported on-screen by then-emerging stars Sarah Miles, Vanessa Redgrave, and Jane Birkin.

From available evidence, the project appears to have been a troubled one. Antonioni, who tended to favor tableaus and landscapes over the people who move through them, apparently enraged Ponti by largely disregarding his own, already confusing script and, even worse, going over budget while shooting that script. Out of time and resources, Antonioni never bothered to film much of the connective material that was supposed to have tied the narrative together and make it "accessible." As the film exists now, Hemmings, who plays a mod fashion photographer, comes to believe that he has inadvertently photographed a murder in London's Maryon Park.

Redgrave, who seems to be involved in this (maybe) homicide, subsequently and repeatedly tries to get the film back from him. But instead of making this thriller angle what the film is "about," *Blow-Up* then wanders off—frustratingly, fascinatingly—into other tangents, and the central mystery, if it is a mystery at all, is largely left unresolved. Louis B. Mayer would not have been pleased. Carlo Ponti was not pleased either.

Antonioni's camera instead spends the rest of the movie following Hemmings around an oddly empty yet very swinging London, a London apparently devoid of families, children, senior citizens,

David Hemmings looks like he himself is being observed, perhaps by the audience? *Author's collection*

Michelangelo Antonioni (center) directs *Blow-Up. Photofest*

or the police. He complains that he is so busy that he hasn't found time for his own appendectomy yet spends days driving through those empty streets, perusing antiques shops stocked with available women, having sex, and taking photos (one is equated with another). He also finds time to play an invisible tennis game with a troupe of white-faced mimes, which leaves modern viewers wondering if maybe mod London wasn't as much fun as we all thought it would be. Through it all, our man always seems to be trying—maybe he is—to put everything in context, to sort out his connection to his world and to reality itself. Is this why he then seizes upon the (imagined?) murder conspiracy, which is, at the very least, a way to do something "real"?

Hemmings repeatedly promises to give the mysterious Redgrave those (possibly) compromising photos, but he doesn't. Instead he obsesses over what those photos seem to contain. The scenes where Hemmings keeps cropping and enlarging (blowing up) these stills are suspenseful in a way the rest of the movie does not will itself to be. But do the photos point to a "real" murder? One does look like it contains a gun, maybe. Another picture seems to depict a body. But without some sort of context, what do the pixilated images *really* depict? 1960s-era kids who turned on to *Blow-Up* probably did not know that such a sequence had already been dramatized on-screen in the very "straight" drama *Call Northside 777* (1948). Those kids could not have foreseen that this trope would later be spoofed by Mel Brooks in *High Anxiety* (1977) either. In *Blade Runner* (1982), Harrison Ford discovers a clue the same way yet again, but this time he uses a computer to create the blow-up.

At the end of the movie, Hemmings goes to the swinging Ricky Tick Club (created for the production on a stage at MGM British Studios), where the band The Yardbirds loudly destroys an electric guitar on stage. Hemmings fights through the crowd, steals a piece of that broken guitar, and takes it outside. But like those photographs, outside of its context, its own reality, the guitar is now meaningless junk. He throws it away. And 1966 audiences marveled at the symbolism.

Vanessa Redgrave's frank, almost androgynous sex appeal contributed to her stardom among hip audiences in the 1960s. *Author's collection*

Sadly, the rest of Antonioni's English-language career would not be the arguably perfect storm that *Blow-Up*, at least financially, turned out to be. *Zabriskie Point* (1970), which again addressed aspects of the counterculture, was a box office failure and savaged by critics, although today it can lay claim to an ever-dwindling cult of tie-dyed fans. *The Passenger* (1975) had a more conventional narrative and a star, Jack Nicholson, but also was not financially successful. Nicholson now owns the distribution rights to the film, which he acquired as payment from MGM when a project he was developing there was canceled.

Unlike Antonioni's other "Hollywood" films, *Blow-Up* maintains its reputation as one of the very best alternative titles of its era, even as that era recedes into distant memory. One could even say that *Blow-Up* maintains its original value outside of its original context.

37

How the Grinch Stole Christmas! (1966)

Don't call it the Animation Department. The studio itself and the animators called it the Cartoon Department. Because they made funny pictures there.

In the late 1960s the Cartoon Department at MGM was in chaos and, in fact, was about to be shut down entirely—for the second time. Animated short subjects were no longer being made for theaters, and studios like MGM already had hundreds of such shorts in their vaults that could be rereleased had that market still existed, which it didn't.

Therefore, although *The Phantom Tollbooth* (1970) was MGM's first animated feature film, it was also destined to be the last. *Tollbooth* represented the end of a hand-drawn line that zigzagged backward, with a few eraser marks, to even before a mouse named Jerry met a cat named Tom. The studio closed their Cartoon Department after *The Phantom Tollbooth*, so it could be credibly argued that, as far as the studio was concerned, that film was the corporate hallmark.

I can't argue with this, but the truth is that *The Phantom Tollbooth* was not a success, although the reviews were okay, and anything by animation legend Chuck Jones is certainly worthy of some respect. But even had the film been an enormous success, the Cartoon Department probably would have been shuttered anyway, as all the studios except for the moribund post–Walt Disney Disney were doing, or had already done, at the time. Most of *Tollbooth* was made in 1968, but the studio apparently tortured Jones throughout production with their constant meddling and lack of confidence in the project and then dumped that final product into kiddie matinees, from which it never

emerged. A happier Jones-MGM collaboration was the short *Horton Hears
a Who!* (1970), which was spared this
indignity by premiering on television
about the time that *Phantom Tollbooth*
and Chuck Jones himself, as it turned
out, were being "released."

What is remarkable is that amid all
this dissent and bad feelings, a little
film somehow got made that, against
the odds, turned out to be a highlight
of the entire MGM filmography, as
well as a personal triumph for Jones
and everyone involved.

How the Grinch Stole Christmas!, a
children's book by Dr. Seuss (Theodor
Seuss Geisel), was published in 1957.
The author had not been happy with
his last Hollywood experience—the
live-action *5,000 Fingers of Dr. T*
(1953)—but he had worked with
Chuck Jones crafting training films
during World War II. Their shared,
slightly acidic view of human nature
convinced Dr. Seuss that his rather
dour original book—dour until the

The diabolical Grinch, at least in Dr. Seuss's original 1957
book, boasted no particular skin color. The famous green
pigmentation came later, perhaps as a nod to Boris Karloff's
Frankenstein's monster. *Photofest*

climax, that is—would be safe in Jones's non-sentimental hands.

Chuck Jones and MGM were then partnered with CBS, which had recently (1965)
scored a critical and financial success with *A Charlie Brown Christmas*, and was therefore anxious for a follow-up to air during the 1966 Christmas season. The budget for
this next animated special was reportedly set at $315,000, three times more than *A
Charlie Brown Christmas* and more than CBS, even with on-air sponsorship from a
bank, would be able to make back on the airing.

Boris Karloff, who was almost eighty years old at the time and Hollywood's most
venerable boogeyman, was cast as the voice of the Grinch, a green-colored Christmas-
hating loner who decides to steal the Christmas presents from the nearby residents

The good residents of Whoville celebrate Christmas in their own Seussian way. *Photofest*

of Whoville. Even Dr. Seuss reportedly thought Jones had gone too far in casting a horror film star as such a seemingly horrible character, reasoning that audiences would never buy into the Grinch's last-minute decision to return those presents. But Karloff or Jones—probably Jones—convinced the author that underneath the well-known Karloff lisp and snarl lay an ornate sweetness and wounded heart that for generations had endeared the actor to audiences, regardless of the countless dire skullduggeries they had witnessed that actor perpetrating on-screen. It was Jones before anyone else who seemingly realized that Karloff, creator of hundreds of on-screen inhuman monsters, was the one actor capable of humanizing the inhuman Grinch. There are photographs of the three of them—Seuss, Jones, and Karloff—happily working together during production. Their shared conversations must have been priceless.

As the special's credits oddly phrased it: "The sounds of the Grinch are by Boris Karloff . . . and read by Boris Karloff too." But it was actually Thurl Ravenscroft, the well-known voice of Tony the Tiger in television commercials, not Karloff, who sang "You're a Mean One, Mr. Grinch." Voice-over legend June Foray played Cindy Lou Who. Both were uncredited; therefore it was Karloff who subsequently received a 1968

Dr. Seuss, Boris Karloff and director Chuck Jones in the scoring stage. The conversations between these three icono-clasts must have been priceless. *Author's collection*

Grammy Award in the category of "Best Recording for Children." When the star, who apparently did not know what a Grammy was, saw his reward, he reportedly lisped, "It looks like a bloody doorstop."

When it aired on December 18, 1966, *How the Grinch Stole Christmas!* was immediately acclaimed as an instantaneous Christmas classic. Even Karloff, who had never allowed his impressionable grandchildren to watch his movies, called his daughter up that day to ask her and the kids to tune in with the rest of the country.

The next year's airing, in case you were worried, finally put the film solidly in the black. And it has been rerun profitably, annually, every year since. Syndication and countless home video releases have expanded the worldwide audience even more. Today *How the Grinch Stole Christmas!* may well be one of the most watched entertainments in the entire history of the human race. As even *Gone with the Wind* and *The Wizard of Oz* are now perceived by many to be dated by their attitudes and effects to the point where modern audiences are no longer as enthralled by their charms as they once were.

Today, *The Grinch* remains one of the only truly communal cross-generational entertainments still available, and still appreciated on its own terms, by us all. The very word "grinch" has entered the lexicon of our language. The *Merriam-Webster Dictionary* describes "grinch" as a "grumpy person who spoils the pleasures of others."

How the Grinch Stole Christmas! is about Christmas, of course, but unlike *A Charlie Brown Christmas,* for example, it also transcends the holiday. Like *A Christmas Carol* (which MGM had filmed in 1938), *How the Grinch Stole Christmas!* is really about how humanity and family and tradition, whatever form that tradition takes, can make anyone, even a cold-hearted grinch, a valuable member of the family of man.

That is not to say that *How the Grinch Stole Christmas!* is the *only* time the Grinch stole Christmas. We—meaning you and I and the Grinch—have since been subjected to sequels (1977 and 1982) and outright remakes (1992, 2000, and 2018).

None of these productions were directly from MGM, although the studio would dip its toes into animation intermittently in the upcoming decades. For most of these later projects, like *The Secret of NIMH* (1982) and *All Dogs Go to Heaven* (1989), the studio only financed or distributed. Decades later, the company also got involved in animated coproductions with other companies, resulting in *Igor* (2008) and two *Addams Family* comedies, in 2019 and 2021, among others. MGM has also, across disparate studio regimes, created animated films with live-action sequences, or live-action films with animated sequences. *The Phantom Tollbooth* contained "live" material, for example. As did *Pink Floyd—The Wall* (1982); as did, memorably, all the *Pink Panther* features.

But these later efforts will never approximate the alchemy that resulted at MGM in 1966, when three unique individuals named Seuss, Jones, and Karloff got together to make us a cartoon.

38

The Dirty Dozen (1967)

The Dirty Dozen was the antithesis of the traditional MGM war film. Instead of concentrating on heroism or the homefront, the focus here was the dirty business of war and the dirty policies of those who wage it. Not particularly well reviewed when it came out—some critics accused it of pandering to the basest instincts of its audience—*Dirty Dozen* was a major ($70 million worldwide gross) box office success and, ultimately, something of a mile marker in its studio's ultimate evolution.

The script, by Hollywood veterans Nunnally Johnson and Lukas Heller, was based on a book by novelist E. M. Nathanson. Nathanson based his book on an alleged World War II unit made up entirely of hardened criminals who were offered a pardon in return for their participation in an extremely dangerous mission. Unfortunately, although there had been an actual airborne demolition unit called the "Filthy Thirteen," Nathanson could find no documentation that such a company as described in his novel had ever really existed, so he admitted to basically borrowing the bones of what was probably a military urban legend and then making up the details to suit his purposes.

Even before reading the book, director Robert Aldrich immediately realized its film potential. He tried to option it, only to discover that MGM had already done so. He then successfully campaigned the studio for the chance to direct.

John Wayne was the obvious choice of everyone at that old-guard studio to star as the unit's commander, but for indeterminate reasons the role eventually went to Lee Marvin, who had recently won an Oscar for the comedic Western *Cat Ballou* (1965). Other roles, either as part of the dozen or their disapproving commanding officers,

Uncompleted ad art for *The Dirty Dozen* (1967) as depicted before the title and billing block were added, but already exciting. *Photofest*

eventually ended up going to pretty much all, except for Wayne, of the most masculine leading men of their generation.

There was an ongoing trend at the time for movies to place multiple leading men within the same film. *The Magnificent Seven* (1960) and *The Great Escape* (1963) had recently done this, and to great success, although in both examples, the expensive masculine cast had been padded out with familiar but less pricy character actors and young up-and-comers in order to keep costs down. The same thing would happen with *The Dirty Dozen*, which luckily also cast some future stars, like Charles Bronson, Donald Sutherland, and Telly Savalas, which today makes the film seem even more full of topliners than it did at the time. In 1967, aside from Marvin and character actors like Robert Ryan, Ernest Borgnine and George Kennedy, the most recognized names in the cast belonged to TV star Clint Walker; singer Trini Lopez, who had scored a pop/folk hit in 1965 with "Lemon Tree"; and Jim Brown, already one of the greatest professional football players of all time, in only his second feature film role.

Perhaps indicative of the era in which it was made, many of the cast were actual World War II veterans. Marvin, Ryan, and Robert Webber had all been Marines. Ernest

Borgnine and Ralph Meeker had served in the US Navy, Clint Walker as a Merchant Marine; and George Kennedy, Telly Savalas, and Charles Bronson in the US Army. Even director Aldrich had also served, if briefly, with the Air Force Motion Picture Unit. Lee Marvin, who had been wounded in the Pacific Theater, made it known during production to anyone who would listen that he thought the exaggerated Hollywood heroics in the script were somewhat silly, although he apparently got along well with his fellow veterans—all of whom, as well as he, undoubtably preferred these romanticized theatrics to the real thing.

In addition to the large, bawdy, almost entirely male cast. He had recently moderated the battles between Joan Crawford and Bette Davis on the set of *Whatever Happened to Baby Jane?* Consequently, like his cast, he found the make-believe battlefields of *The Dirty Dozen* much more to his liking. "When you are working with a male cast, you can use a few four-letter words to let off steam and nobody goes running to the dressing room,"[1] he commented gratefully.

In addition to the large, testosterone-fueled cast, MGM also lavished a great deal of money to release (if not shoot) *The Dirty Dozen* in 70mm. They also built, and then blew up, some expensive sets, including a fifty-foot-high "miniature" French château, all at their British studio in Borehamwood, where the film was shot.

Although the violence in *The Dirty Dozen* was stylized, it was also, as in a real war, abundant and very brutal. And in the climax, in which that château is blown up, German civilians, including women and servants, are depicted as being inside, collateral victims of the carnage. MGM's marketing department expertly fanned the flames of this controversy over what was perceived by liberal critics as a glorification of war crimes by using a very vivid tagline to describe the film's heroes: "Train them! Excite them! Arm them! . . . Then turn them loose on the Nazis!"

Those heroes, as noted, are mostly criminals, and Aldrich does not try to excuse their criminal behavior. Several of them, in fact, are depicted as being not just amoral but unbalanced, sometimes to the detriment of their mission. Savalas's Archer Maggot, for example, betrays his colleagues in order to engage in sexual assault and murder. Trini Lopez is described in the trailer as "crawling with hate!" John Cassavetes's repellent thug, Franko, who critic Bosley Crowther most memorably described as "wormy and noxious,"[2] scored the actor-director an Oscar nomination, apparently for being so good at being so reprehensible.

Crowther, in fact, found the whole film reprehensible. "A studied indulgence of sadism that is morbid and disgusting beyond words,"[3] he, again memorably, described *The Dirty Dozen* in the *New York Times,* whose primary critic he had been for

The dozen—or at least Jim Brown, Trini Lopez, and Donald Sutherland (all in foreground)—get ready to shoot something.
Photofest

twenty-seven years. Crowther had already written two books specifically about MGM: *The Lion's Share: The Story of an Entertainment Empire* (1957) and *Hollywood Rajah: The Life and Times of Louis B. Mayer* (1960), so to him the fact that MGM, that "his" studio, would lower itself to make a film with a title like *The Dirty Dozen* may well have felt like a personal slap in the face. Incidentally, Crowther's review of the same year's even more brutal *Bonnie and Clyde*—which he, not at all surprisingly, panned as being "reddened with blotches of violence of the most grisly sort"[4]—led to his dismissal from that long-held position at the *Times,* which, like the times themselves, was a-changing.

It is indeed interesting that MGM, the company known for decades for its depictions of home and hearth, should in 1967 be so criticized for glorifying violence and, by extension, those who practice it. For decades the studio, all the studios, had created pictures with a house style—a distinctive look and distinctive feeling that largely came from the same people deciding which films their studio would make and from the same people making them. Warner Bros. films, for example, often featured social realism and topical urban settings; Paramount had the sophisticated dramas and comedies; Universal created horror films and rural, or at least rural-appealing, comedies; Columbia specialized in populist dramas and lowbrow slapstick; 20th Century Fox was a slightly downscale version of MGM, with a lot of glossy musical and period pieces usually filling up their schedules.

It's not like that anymore. In the twenty-first century, only Disney films represent a consistent brand. So in the twenty-first century, a Paramount film looks exactly like a Warner Bros. film. No one outside the industry notices, or cares, what studio or conglomerate produces a film. But in 1967, it must have been shocking to a gentleman of Bosley Crowther's generation to watch Lee Marvin dropping grenades down a chute onto innocent people. The only thing more overtly offensive would have been if Mickey Rooney had played the part.

The Dirty Dozen is, as Crowther most dramatically warned us in 1967, indeed a violent movie, although today the carnage it revels in could be considered almost quaint, especially when compared to later war films like *The Deer Hunter* (1978) and *Saving Private Ryan* (1998) and the *Dozen*-derivative *Inglourious Basterds* (2009). Yet it's still hard to call the violence in *The Dirty Dozen* "cartoonish," because Aldrich and his cast at least pretend to treat their actions with appropriate gravitas. It's also probably difficult to compare this war film, or any war film, with any real war, which is why Lee Marvin and the other veterans on the set seem to have felt they were just dressing up and playing games.

At two and a half hours, the action in *The Dirty Dozen* does lag on occasion, particularly in the center section, where the amusing but completely unnecessary training and war simulations the men are subjected to ultimately contribute only to the film's running time. These scenes may have been inspired, weirdly, by some suspiciously similar sequences in a Disney film about the Boy Scouts (!) called *Follow Me, Boys!* that had come out the year before. Anyway, *Dozen's* redundant, yet apparently very well liked, war game scenes have since been spoofed—or perhaps inspired similar military hijinks—in service comedies like *Private Benjamin* (1980) and *Stripes* (1981).

Making up for this mid-film lag, however, is the protracted climax, which is appropriately boiling over with well-calculated suspense and explosions. It also breaks dramatically with war film tradition in that characters the audience has gotten to know and (sometimes) like start dying off violently, some even before they finish parachuting into the French countryside.

The all-male, and all manly, cast of *The Dirty Dozen* on display. *Author's collection*

In the end, although they have been promised to have their records wiped clean in exchange for their service, almost none of the dozen are still alive to take advantage of that deal. So that deal turns out to not be such a deal after all. Their mission is a military success, but it sure doesn't work out on a personal level. It's hard to figure out if the families of the deceased, when told that their black sheep loved ones had died "in the line of duty," would find that to be much of a consolation either. And maybe that was the point.

Despite the fact that the dozen is pretty much obliterated in the service of their country in the first film, MGM belatedly produced a sequel, for television, in 1985. *The Dirty Dozen: The Next Mission* brought back a now sixty-one-year-old Lee Marvin, as well as Borgnine and another survivor of the earlier film, Richard Jaeckel, for another bloody trip behind enemy lines. Although decades have passed in real time, this mission seemingly takes place right after the first film ends.

Only Borgnine's General Worden (who had been a major in the first film) returned for another sequel, *The Dirty Dozen: The Deadly Mission* (1987), also produced for MGM/UA television. Telly Savalas was back too, but as a new, more stable character. In this film it is he who is in charge of this new dozen. Yet a third installment, *The Dirty Dozen: The Fatal Mission* (1988), continued the saga, with Borgnine, Savalas, and MGM/UA television still directing the troops.

The first sequel, *The Next Mission*, had been shot largely in England, as the original had been. But subsequent adventures were filmed in Yugoslavia-Croatia to keep costs down. Jadran Films, a local company with inroads in the West, handled most of the physical production there.

This pattern continued for the inevitable *Dirty Dozen* TV series, which ran for twelve episodes in 1988. By the time of the series' production, no original stars were involved. The cast and crew were instead made up of expats from England and the United States. American actor Frank Marth, for example, played the equivalent of the Borgnine part, now renamed General Worth. The series, which aired on the Fox Network in the United States, was apparently canceled over a dispute between the network and MGM.

Wars, sadly, are still fought. Studios, and nations, still rise and fall. But successful franchises go on. Recently, Warner Bros., which now owns the rights to this particular franchise, has been reportedly developing a remake of the original movie.

Details are unknown. But the results are sure to be dirty.

39

2001: A Space Odyssey (1968)

"*2001: A Space Odyssey* was, at the time, the most experimental film ever released by a Hollywood studio." Patrick Stewart sonorously told us this was so in 1992's *MGM: When the Lion Roars*. And who could ever doubt anything told to us by Patrick Stewart? MGM, however, had also released the experimental game-changer *Blow-Up* in 1966, so it is revealing, even revolutionary, that the most conservative and old-fashioned of the seven studios in the 1960s was, in some ways, also the most forward-looking.

That said, it should again be mentioned that *Blow-Up* was really a Carlo Ponti production, which the lion had basically acquired as a negative pickup, partially in order to continue to secure the lucrative services of Ponti's wife, Sophia Loren. By contrast, *2001* was an in-house project from start to finish, although due to director Stanley Kubrick's remarkably one-sided contract, the studio's actual participation was largely restricted to providing facilities, financing, and distribution. So tying the resultant film into the rest of the studio's résumé is, at best, an iffy proposition.

We are going to do exactly that anyway.

To the studio's credit, *2001* was intended from its conception to be an experimental film. But it was also intended, or at least hoped by the studio, to be a potential blockbuster. Shot almost entirely at MGM Borehamwood in the UK, those expectations were nervously amplified when the budget eventually reached, and then considerably surpassed, the $10 million mark.

Like the similarly risky 1959 *Ben-Hur*, *2001* was filmed in the enormous MGM Camera 65 process. It was marketed as being in Cinerama as well, but wasn't. The

The general release artwork for *2001: A Space Odyssey* (1968) emphasized the film's straightforward science fiction and adventure elements. *Photofest*

Cinerama name was used, however, because MGM still owed the company a Cinerama picture, even though the cumbersome three-panel process from its *How the West Was Won* days had been replaced. Anyone who saw *2001* projected in a Cinerama theater probably didn't see the film at its best anyway, because the long tube-shaped spaceships Kubrick's technicians designed tended to bend into horseshoes as they crossed horizontally across the curved panels.

Fortunately for the studio, *2001: A Space Odyssey* turned out to be commercially worth the risk—the film, after a slow start, proved to be a major box office success, especially in college neighborhoods and with young audiences, many of whom returned to the theater to see it again and again for what the studio marketing department, *wink-wink*, termed the "ultimate trip."

Critics, however, were divided as to what the film was actually about.

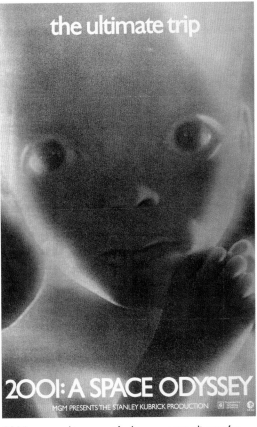

2001's more ambiguous art for hip, younger audiences featured the famous tagline "the ultimate trip." *Author's collection*

Andrew Sarris and Pauline Kael, two of the most respected film critics of their era, both panned the film, although Kael, interestingly, compared it to the studio's other arthouse hit, remarking that "*2001* is a movie that might have been made by the hero of *Blow-Up*, and it's fun to think about Kubrick really doing every dumb thing he wanted to do, building enormous science fiction sets and equipment, never even bothering to figure out what he was going to do with them."[1] In spite of Kael's barbed accusations, it is obvious that Kubrick knew *exactly* what he was doing in *2001*, even if large sections of his audience were not so sure.

Contrary to its reputation, the plot of *2001* is, in reality, fairly linear. That plot begins, as a subtitle tells us, with the "Dawn of Man," as primates are shown being endowed with the intelligence to become human by a monolith placed on Earth by some sort of extraterrestrial presence.

Centuries later, an identical monolith is discovered on the Moon by man, or rather by the descendants of those original primates, which leads man on an eventual mission to Jupiter. On the way, all but one of the astronauts on the ship are murdered by their onboard computer, HAL, although why HAL behaves this way is never clearly explained.

The last act of the film is the most controversial. The audience watches as that one surviving astronaut seemingly travels through a black hole and encounters an aged version of himself. And mankind seemingly enters the next stage of its evolution. Sarris—who, remember, disliked the film overall—called this sequence "a

Director Stanley Kubrick (right) confers with his team, who look more exasperated with the situation than he does. *Photofest*

mishmash of psychedelic self-indulgence for the special effects people and an exercise in mystifying abstract fantasy in the open temple of High Art."[2] But two years later, and rather admirably and to his credit, that same critic largely revised his opinion of the film, if not its finale, which he still dismissed as a "relatively conventional sojourn into psychedelia."[3]

A half century on, *2001* is still one of cinema's crowning, and most controversial, achievements. Although 2001 the year has long since come and gone, *2001* the movie has hardly dated at all, although decades of miniaturization in technology have rendered the film's oversize portrayals of telephones and cameras, and of HAL himself, monumentally quaint.

The special effects also, surprisingly, still convince, comparing favorably with the computer-generated visuals of today. And visually, it is these effects—the spaceships and moonscapes rather than the colors and lightshow of the climax, which, remember, is what displeased Sarris and overwhelmed so many stoners in 1968—that are most impressive today. Kubrick's camera also, intriguingly and (surely?) intentionally, catches lots of imagery of people stepping into spinning circles, often inside spinning circles. Like Hitchcock's *Vertigo*, the visuals here seem to evokes man's journey not into outer but rather into *inner* space: the ultimate trip?

The use of the song "Daisy Bell" as HAL is being shut down is probably a reference to the same song being "performed" by an actual computer in 1961—the first instance in history of that happening. But the song also evokes, unconsciously surely, MGM's gay '90s and turn-of-the-twentieth-century nostalgia films like *Meet Me in St. Louis* (1944), *Easter Parade* (1948), and *In the Good Old Summertime* (1949). The tune lends a level of nostalgic wistfulness to a film that is otherwise lacking in such sentiments—ironically, as it turns out, since the song is being performed by a dying, homicidal robot.

For MGM, *2001: A Space Odyssey* was a turning point of sorts for several reasons. Firstly, and for perhaps the last time (to date), the film's subsequent success and innovations would allow MGM to be perceived as an industry trendsetter, a leader rather than a follower floundering about in the backwash of its own past. Perhaps reflecting this, Leo the Lion does not make an appearance in *2001*'s opening. He is replaced instead by a stylized lion logo, which was so unpopular that after only one other film (*The Subject Was Roses*, also in 1968), the live, roaring Leo was brought back, although a version of this alternate logo still survives today as a mascot for the MGM resort chain.

Another loss to the company after this film came out was the studio where it was shot. In 1970 MGM Borehamwood, which MGM operated since 1936 and owned since 1944, was sold, closed, and subsequently demolished.

In 1971 Gary Lockwood, one of *2001*'s stars, would return to MGM to again play an astronaut, this time for a TV movie called *Earth II*, which was shot on the lot in Culver City. His *2001* partner, Keir Dullea, would also return to his spacesuit, and to MGM, for the official sequel: *2010: The Year We Make Contact* (1984), which was also shot in Culver City. At least two subsequent MGM productions, *The Strawberry Statement* (1970) and *Demon Seed* (1977) would reference *2001* as well, as would countless other outside movies, art, music, cartoons, television series, and, ironically, computer games.

40

Shaft (1971)

Shaft has one of the most iconic openings of any MGM movie. In footage of the real New York City—no backlot—and as well evidenced by the scuzzy grandeur of it all, Richard Roundtree's John Shaft prowls the mean streets, dodging between cars with the athleticism of a young Gene Kelly. Isaac Hayes's guitar and his aggressive vocals ("can ya dig it?") bob right along with him. The titles are red, and when that main, mean, big red title—*SHAFT*—zooms up into the forefront, filling the entire screen, it becomes clear that no one is going to mistake this MGM film for a Norma Shearer vehicle.

Shaft looms very large as an early modern blockbuster, and as charter member of the blaxploitation genre. And many still remember the film because Hayes's soundtrack would go on to win an Oscar (only the third African American win to that time in any competitive category). It has also been said that *Shaft*'s success singlehandedly saved the studio from bankruptcy. If only this were true.

MGM did make a killer profit from *Shaft*. It earned some $12 million in total, and on a half-million-dollar budget. But what is usually forgotten is that even without John Shaft's broad, Black shoulders doing their part, in 1971 MGM, far from being on the edge of bankruptcy as has been reported, actually publicly posted its largest profits since 1946! Although most of this windfall came not from the box office—or from *Shaft* at all.

The profit came instead from asset sales, specifically generated through the infamous studio auction, the sale of multiple overseas theater chains, and the sale of office suites in New York. Lastly, perhaps most tragically, these remarkable profits were culled from the methodical parceling off of the British studio lot and the first parts of the Culver City plant too.

Yet aside from *Shaft*, and from the profits generated by these shortsighted, high-stakes yard sales, the company, whatever that year's stockholders' reports indicated, was collapsing into itself. So during this period, Gordon Parks, *Shaft*'s talented director, was undoubtably glad to be far away in New York, working on a tiny budget and under the radar. Parks had earlier been the first African American director to helm a Hollywood film (1969's *The Learning Tree*, at Warner Bros.), but here he was, without knowing it, creating a whole new genre.

Blaxploitation was the name given—like film noir, after the fact—to low-budget urban films with an outsider Black protagonist who is often pitted against White society. *Sweet Sweetback's Baadasssss Song*, which had come out early the same year, was an independent

Richard Roundtree is, of course, *Shaft* (1971). *Photofest*

film, as many blaxploitation films would be, but *Shaft* had Hollywood financing, even if that financier was rapidly withering into an outsider itself.

Shockingly, if not surprisingly, considering the timidity of Hollywood in matters of race, *Shaft* was originally supposed to be a White dude. It has been printed more than once that the 1970 novel by Ernest Tidyman on which the movie is based featured a Caucasian John Shaft. This is untrue, although Tidyman himself was White. It is true, though, that when buying the book, the studio apparently intended to make the protagonist a White detective—probably along the lines of Steve McQueen's *Bullitt* (1968) or Paul Newman's *Harper* (1966) characters.

That all changed when Parks came on board, and to the studio's credit, or perhaps its ultimate disinterest, there were apparently no internal objections to his hiring Hayes and the then-unknown (and consequently inexpensive) actor Richard Roundtree.

Parks did not politicize the project, as might have been expected. He probably knew that doing so would have drawn unwelcome interest from Culver City. So, unlike in *Sweet Sweetback*, where the enemies are White—where the enemies are enemies *because* they are White—*Shaft* features both White and Black villains.

Shaft's client is a Black gangster (Moses Gunn), who hires him to look for his kidnapped daughter, although it is obvious that Shaft has no more respect for this thug than he has for the Italian mafiosi he has to fight in order to get the daughter back. Incidentally, Shaft also has a fruitful friendship, or at least a mutually convenient partnership, with a police detective (Charles Cioffi), who happens to be White.

What audiences of all colors responded to in the material was what Parks, and Roundtree, slyly did to the character of John Shaft himself. The dude is so cool that, as the credits show us, he can cross through traffic in 1970s New York and survive. He has a cool theme song; a cool wardrobe, including a leather overcoat; and lots of turtleneck sweaters. Women, White and Black, throw themselves at him like he is James Bond. Unlike most other movie detectives, he also seems to do very well financially. While Harper and Bullit live in shabby apartments with no food in the refrigerator, Shaft seems to have the benefit of an (undoubtably female) interior designer in his pad. His walls are covered with expensive-looking art and books; his fridge is so well stocked, he even keeps a spare gun in the freezer section. Although he has trouble getting White cab drivers to stop for him, even his many enemies, including those who try to kill him, respect John Shaft.

This might have been subversive, even racist, if the movie insisted that Shaft was better than anyone else *because* he is Black. But none of the people around him, of any race, even come close to his level of coolness. He wears his ethnicity like he wears his overcoat. Like Popeye, he is who he is. And he's proud of, but not at all defined by his blackness. Unlike Sidney Poitier, who had to demand (nicely) what he was owed by White society, or *Sweet Sweetback*'s angry Melvin Van Peebles, who had to kill to keep from being marginalized, Shaft strides through his world—because it *is* his world. Accept it man. Or get outa his way.

That's actually good and bad. Certainly, commercially, Parks's decision to make Shaft a Black Superman was the right one, because Black ghetto audiences loved the film as much as suburban White ones did. But this embrace of one very cool individual over his society, or over his own race, makes the film today less audacious than other, less-well-made but more politicized blaxploitation films.

In some ways Shaft (and *Shaft*) fits in comfortably with other cop/vigilante characters in films like *The French Connection* (which came out the same year as *Shaft* and

An iconic *Shaft* moment features the character literally swinging into action, gun blazing of course. *Author's collection*

was also based on a book by Tidyman), *Dirty Harry* (again in 1972; notice a pattern?), *The Seven-Ups* and *Serpico* (both 1973), and *Death Wish* (1974). All these movies explored a yearning for a superior being to come and catch or, better yet, kill all the bad guys. But in the angrier, lower-budgeted blaxploitation films, the good guys and the bad guys were often defined by their race. Here they are just bad guys. Just movie bad guys.

It should also be said that as a film, *Shaft* is actually pretty tame today. There is a lot of talk, and the action scenes, when they come, are brief and cheap. The big action climax—which the studio was so proud of that they featured it on the film's poster—involves Shaft breaking a window! And like those action scenes, the language the characters use, even the sex they engage in, is rather restrained, even quaint, especially when compared to the hyperactive content of any R-rated action film of today. All of this makes one wonder if audiences, even young urban audiences, were really so patient then as to wait so long for the big climax, even if it wasn't so big, in 1971? Yes, apparently, they were. What in the hell has since happened to us all, anyway?

Times change, but *Shaft* struts on. Here director John Singleton supervises a 2000 sequel, also called *Shaft,* but this time for Paramount. *Photofest*

For some modern audiences, *Shaft* also contains the sociological fascination of seeing New York as it looked in all its gritty glory back in the early 1970s, and was it ever a mess. Parks, of course, never dreamed his film would become a time capsule into an era, but along with the swaggering Roundtree, this aspect of the film's appeal keeps things interesting today—although, if *Shaft*'s art director is to be believed, every interior in New York City in the early 1970s had the same red walls and looked a lot like the inside of a steak house.

Shaft's success led MGM to jump onto the blaxploitation bandwagon. For the first time in decades, the studio, thanks to *Shaft,* found itself in the position of being the instigator of a trend instead of, as then usually happened, following in that trend's wake. And they immediately made the best of their position. *Cool Breeze,* a Black remake of *The Asphalt Jungle,* came out the next year (1972), as did *Melinda* and *Hit Man,* the latter of which had the good sense to give the lead role to Pam Grier, arguably blaxploitation's most talented and charismatic discovery.

Also in 1972 came the inevitable *Shaft's Big Score,* with Roundtree, Parks, Tidyman, and Moses Gunn returning to their familiar roles. Here Shaft was presented, if possible, as being even more all-powerful than in the original. Audiences again responded enthusiastically.

The series' 1973 entry, *Shaft in Africa*, teamed Roundtree with (White) director John Guillermin and added James Bond–style foreign locations and a bigger budget, which of course robbed the series of the urban grit that had made the, let's admit it, rather improbable character of John Shaft seem so realistic to begin with. After that, not surprisingly, there was nowhere for the series, and Roundtree, to go but television, where, as just another cool TV P.I., he lasted for only seven episodes.

Against all odds, the franchise was rebooted in 2000 by noted director John Singleton and Paramount Pictures. Although the title was again just *Shaft*, this one was actually a sequel, with Samuel L. Jackson playing the original Shaft's nephew. Richard Roundtree, fortunately, was still on board for credibility. Another sequel, again just called *Shaft*, and again with Roundtree and Jackson, came out in 2019.

It's worth noting that by the time of this latest *Shaft*, Richard Roundtree had been playing the same cool cat, although not continuously, for forty-eight years! For comparison, only Leonard Nimoy's *Star Trek* "Spock" character, which he played on and off from 1964 to 2013 — a total of forty-nine years in those pointy ears — now surpasses, barely, Roundtree's reign in a single filmed, non–soap opera role over the most years. Sylvester Stallone, who has been playing Rocky since 1976, isn't even close!

Can ya dig it? Who knows, would anyone be interested in seeing Richard Roundtree in *Shaft: 2030*?

41

Hollywood: The Dream Factory (1972)

In spite of its misleading title, the fifty-one-minute, Emmy Award–winning television documentary *Hollywood: The Dream Factory* is not about Hollywood in general but concerns itself specifically with MGM, although the script makes the point subtly, and truthfully, that the two are largely interchangeable and that our concept of what we consider to be Hollywood was actually milled at, and by, MGM. Irwin Rosten's script, which is by turns witty, sarcastic, and sentimental, manages to touch all the highlights of the studio's story despite the brief running time. In fact, the later documentaries *That's Entertainment!* (and its sequels) and *MGM: When the Lion Roars*, despite their undeniable charms, could ultimately only repeat the formula created here—sometimes, as we shall see, in shockingly blatant ways.

Hollywood: The Dream Factory did more than that, however. It created, or rather first represented on-screen, the early 1970s nostalgia boom for all things Hollywood, which in turn led the studio to the very successful *That's Entertainment* franchise as well as to the less lucrative *Hearts of the West* and *The Sunshine Boys* (both 1975). Other studios quickly jumped onto this quickly crowded bandwagon, which eventually included *Nickelodeon* (Columbia 1975), *The Wild Party* (AIP 1975), *Inserts* (United Artists 1975), *The Day of the Locust* (Paramount 1975), *Won Ton Ton: The Dog Who Saved Hollywood* (Paramount 1976), *Gable and Lombard* (Universal 1976), *The Last Tycoon* (Paramount 1976), *Silent Movie* (20th Century Fox 1976), *W. C. Fields and Me* (Universal 1976), and *The World's Greatest Lover* (20th Century Fox 1977). There were also seemingly countless TV movies along the same lines,

Its title may have inferred that it was about the movie business in general, but *Hollywood: The Dream Factory* (1972) was all about MGM. *Author's collection*

including (as we shall soon see) MGMs own, and very bizarre, *The Phantom of Hollywood* in 1974.

By far the most successful of these films was *That's Entertainment!* But the trend actually started here. All these projects, as well as books, cartoons, and popular opinions about classic Hollywood, good and bad, were crystalized, and plagiarized almost entirely, from *Hollywood: The Dream Factory.*

Hollywood: The Dream Factory was the perfect summation of one era, crystalized for the benefit of another, presumably hipper era. Rosten's script succeeds because it both mocks and romanticizes the studio system. It depicts the legendary 1970 MGM auction as being the sacrilegious abomination it was, even though both the film and the auction were instigated by MGM, which financed the production. It also somehow depicts "old-timey" stars like W. C. Fields and the Marx Brothers as being both nostalgic and wickedly counterculture at the same time. And it presents Hollywood as being some sort of early twentieth-century Shangri-la, which later twentieth-century denizens could celebrate and fetishize. Check out, for example, Dick Cavett's very wry opening narration:

Footage from the infamous MGM auctions of 1970 were used as a bittersweet framing device for *Hollywood: The Dream Factory*. *Brainard Miller*

Once upon a time, in the place called California, there was an enchanted kingdom. It was said the streets were paved with gold and it was inhabited by gods and goddesses, sorcerers and elves, wise men, jesters, and kings. For three decades the kingdom flourished, it was loved, for it offered human multitudes a rare and precious gift—escape from the mortal coil into wonderous flights of fantasy.

It should be noted that this Hollywood as Camelot routine was not, of course, completely original. Christopher Isherwood, in his 1945 novel *Prater Violet*, for example, had remarked that "the film studio of today is really the palace of the 16th century. There one sees what Shakespeare saw. The absolute power of the tyrant. The courtiers, the flatterers, the jesters, the cunningly ambitious intriguers. There are fantastically beautiful women. There are incompetent favorites."[1]

If Isherwood was being ironic, Cavett/Rosten was too. But no one noticed. Rosten's script is uniformly witty, which is remarkable considering that he was best known at the time not for any particular insights into popular culture but rather for writing

The MGM backlot, specifically (at least here) Lot Three, was given a final, slightly fuzzy on-screen shout-out in
Hollywood: The Dream Factory. Author's collection

numerous *National Geographic* specials and for an undoubtably spellbinding episode
of *The Undersea World of Jacques Cousteau* that was about underwater habitats.

On smoking in the movies, for example, host Cavett dryly intones: "It is fair to say
that at least two generations grew up believing that a successful approach to the opposite sex somehow requires the holding of a cylinder of dried leaves between the lips
and lighting them." On the overall influence of the movies and their makers, Rosten/
Cavett also tells us: "Mayer will be called Hollywood's rajah. Supreme among movie
magnates. The highest paid man in America for ten straight years, and a power in both
entertainment and politics. Before the two fields merged years later."

The film does make a few missteps, however. Scenes from movies made in color are
occasionally and inexplicably shown in black and white, which perhaps makes sense
stylistically for the phony "trailer" that opens the film. But this dubious technique
is carried over into the rest of the program as well, although why? Later, footage of

the Grand Central Station backlot set on Lot Two is misrepresented as being used in *Goodbye, Mr. Chips* (it wasn't), and simulated silent film footage is used to represent real silent film footage (huh?).

Also, it must be said that fifty-one busy minutes just isn't enough time to encompass fifty busy years. In its *Variety* review of the special, an anonymous critic, signing off as "Tone," agreed in a remarkably syntax-free review that the "problem of how to squeeze all that material into a one-hour spec was never satisfactorily resolved—there's just too much—but what there was kept topping what had come before. Like looking through the ol' family album, there were many memories. Many forgotten moments, and much tugging of heartstrings."[2]

The sad thing is that Irwin Rosten (who died in 2010) probably never realized just how much his work had influenced our collective impressions regarding MGM, regarding Hollywood, and regarding the dream factory.

Or maybe he did. Rosten closed his special with the following heart-tugging narration regarding what had been, and what had been lost. I first heard this epilogue when I saw the film in a Cinema 101 class in college. It changed my life, as frankly, I've never forgotten it: "Hollywood, the dream factory, at its worst," Cavett poignantly tells us, "it was spendthrift, crass, and vulgar. But at its best it offered a rich, compelling world of illusion. While no one can be certain, the world probably will not see anything quite like it again."

Apparently, I'm not the only one who remembered Rosten's words either. Two years later, in the more widely seen and acclaimed *That's Entertainment!* Frank Sinatra's writers somehow came up with a similar line for the crooner to utter: "You can wait around and hope. But I'll tell you, you'll never see the likes of this again."

Even more overtly, decades after, in *That's Entertainment III*, Gene Kelly—in the last words of his last appearance on-screen—closed that film with a by now most-familiar sentiment: "MGM's dream factory created a rich, romantic, compelling world of illusion. And although we may not see anything like it again, we're blessed with memories, and miles and miles of film. In the words of Irving Berlin, 'The song is ended but the melody lingers on.'"

Sound familiar?

42

The Phantom of Hollywood (1974)

A version of the following essay was printed in the Fall 2010 issue of Filmfax *magazine, and is reprinted here with the kind permission of publisher Mike Stein.*

Since the very beginning, the movies have been attracted to tales about endings. Last stands, lost causes, empires falling, frontiers closing, lonely people at the end of their tethers, and rulers abdicating their crowns for love or for the guillotine have long been popular in Hollywood and with audiences.

These movies, however, always looked to far-off lands and long-ago eras. The kingdoms and regimes collapsing into ash were always far distant and safely removed from Hollywood itself. With one exception, that is.

Movies have usually been justifiably cynical about the movie "business"—but only one film has ever addressed what would happen if Hollywood itself should cease to exist. That movie was a lowly and decidedly odd TV film called *The Phantom of Hollywood* from 1974. The story it told, and how that story came to be told, is both weird and remarkable. Because for a little while, it really did look like it was all going to come true.

In the early 1970s the American film industry was in deplorable condition. Business had been steadily decreasing since the end of World War II, when audience indifference, television, and Supreme Court decrees had broken the back of the original studio system. By the 1960s the aged moguls who had created a business dynamic that had worked so well for so many years were dying off, retiring, or hopelessly out of touch with audiences who were more inclined to respond to the likes of *Easy Rider* (1969)

The horror movie–style title art for one of the most meta, exploitive, insurgent, provocative, and self-loathing things ever produced inside the American studio system, 1974. *Author's collection*

than traditional Hollywood fare like *Doctor Dolittle* (1967). Print media of the time actually prophesized that within a few years, Hollywood, as an industry, might well no longer exist.

It might have happened. 20th Century Fox had sold off hundreds of acres of valuable studio property in the early 1960s in order to pay off debts. Columbia and Warner Bros. were, by 1972, sharing a single studio lot, and that property was in danger of being sold as well. Universal was surviving only through television productions. Paramount was looking for a buyer. RKO and Republic no longer existed except on the late, late show, and Disney was apparently being operated via instructions left by Walt Disney himself—who unfortunately had died in 1966.

The studio that had fallen the farthest was MGM. For decades the mightiest force in the industry, MGM had been purchased in 1967 by investor Edgar Bronfman Sr. Roger Mayer, the studio's vice president of administration, later recalled, "This is what set the studio on its path to destruction. Bronfman tended to scale back rather than expand. It all became about the quick buck. Something MGM had never, ever done before."[1]

Bronfman's two-year reign set a business pattern that would be continued by the next owner, billionaire Kirk Kerkorian. Kerkorian, who as a teenager had been a manual laborer on the studio backlot, hired television executive James Aubrey to run the company.

Aubrey has taken a lot of abuse as the man who "destroyed" MGM. Some of the criticism is justified. His abrasive personality and cutthroat business practices undoubtedly contributed to the studio's downfall. But, as Mayer points out, "He did have a background of sorts in the entertainment industry, unlike a lot of people running Hollywood at the time. His tactics were ruthless, but I'm sure that's what he believed the company needed at the time. Maybe it did. But he went about it all wrong. Perhaps he was guilty of trying too hard to please Kerkorian by dragging the studio back into the black . . . at any cost."[2]

Aubrey's efforts to drag the studio into the black included fighting with and interfering with talent, closing studio departments that had been on the lot since the 1920s, and making fewer, and less-expensive pictures. In 1969 he turned his attention to selling the studio's storied backlots.

Studio backlots, which had been memorably referred to by F. Scott Fitzgerald as "thirty acres of fairyland" in *The Last Tycoon*, are by anyone's estimation the most recognizable and iconic sectors of any of Hollywood's studio lots. In fact, varied and vast architecture representing the entire world once stood at every studio. But by the late 1960s, backlots were something of a beloved anachronism. Lightweight camera and sound equipment had made shooting on actual locations a desired alternative, although audiences probably were seldom able to recognize the difference. In 1970 Aubrey sold off MGM's sixty-five-acre Lot Three backlot for $7,250,000. It was quickly bulldozed.

For an additional $5 million another deal was made to sell off Lot Two, a nearly forty-acre property across the street from Lot One, MGM's corporate offices and soundstages. With this sale it appeared that the story of this property, MGM's primary backlot and perhaps the most photographed real estate on the planet, was at an end. Yet oddly, and although no one could have known it when the checks were being signed, Lot Two still had a job to do.

In 1974 the studio (through United Artists) released *That's Entertainment!*, a salute to MGM's vintage musicals that felt more like a requiem than a tribute to an ongoing company. Reflecting the pessimism of the industry at large at the time, *Variety*'s review famously and morbidly predicted that "while many may ponder the future of Metro-Goldwyn-Mayer, nobody can deny that it has one hell of a past!"[3]

Part of the decidedly wistful aura that hung over *That's Entertainment!* came from the odd, and ultimately poignant decision to film linking sequences on Lot Two—which the studio, remember, no longer owned. Audiences were thus treated to vintage stars like Fred Astaire and Peter Lawford picking gingerly about the still-standing sets and reminiscing about their past triumphs exactly where the magic had originally happened. The desired nostalgia was tempered somewhat by the undeniable fact that the backlot, now undressed and unrepaired, and in fact slated for imminent demolition, looked not like a nostalgic and well-remembered friend but rather like a ghost town, dark and forlorn and sinister.

That's Entertainment! hadn't opened yet when there came about a most unusual decision by Aubrey and his people. On November 10, 1973, the *Los Angeles Times* announced that *The Phantom of Lot Two* about a "mysterious killer who roams the backlot of a motion picture studio"[4] had been announced by MGM Television and CBS.

"Actually, they originally intended for us to be a feature film," screenwriter George W. Schenck remembers. "*That's Entertainment!* looked like a hit, so they wanted us to do something similar utilizing the old stars and the studio. Later on, they maybe realized that what we were doing was somewhat critical of things that were happening on the lot, and so they '[reined] us in.' But we had already managed to get an unbelievable cast for a TV movie."[5]

According to the first treatment MGM commissioned, dated January 23, 1973, the original writer was Robert Thom (who died in 1979). Taking Aubrey's dictate about using the studio lot for what perhaps would be the last time, Thom came up with a variation on Gaston Leroux's 1910 novel, *The Phantom of the Opera*, substituting MGM for the novel's Paris Opera House setting. All of the assorted screenplay drafts, as well as the finished film, also bear some resemblance to *How to Make a Monster*, a 1958 AIP oddity about a forcibly retired makeup artist wreaking vengeance on a movie studio, as well as to a then recent (1973) episode of the TV series *Circle of Fear;* "Graveyard Shift," which was about a haunted movie studio. There was also a somewhat unsettling, perhaps unintended, parallel with real life. In 1971, just two years earlier, the trial had ended for Charles Manson, another maniac with a mission who had been captured after hiding out on a movie backlot—the Spahn Movie Ranch in the Santa Susana Mountains.

The first draft of the screenplay has the Phantom, a deranged actor living in the catacombs under the backlot, trying to stop the production of a remake of 1937's *Camille*—the original of which had starred his idol: Greta Garbo. Thom's treatment, oddly enough, included a cameo for Bette Davis—as herself—who, much to the Phantom's horror, is hired to play the role played by Lionel Barrymore in the original *Camille*!

The second treatment, also credited to Thom, is dated April 12. In this version, "new Hollywood" is represented as being even more vulgar. The *Camille* remake is now slated to be a sex film. One of the heads of the studio is a cross-dresser. And at the end, the hero and heroine—the stars of the *Camille* remake—are killed along with the Phantom as the backlot topples around them.

Schenck's revision was submitted on September 11. Now the Phantom, who had no particular political agenda or physical deformities in earlier drafts, is a scared, deranged actor, "Erich Vonner," whose career at the studio had been cut short in the thirties by a freak set accident—after which he had retreated into the bowels of the studio, which he has now vowed to protect.

"I went through the Depression with Wally Beery! I marched to war with Huston! Tracy! Oh, I knew them all! I wore their props! Their makeup! I knew their secrets," Vonner rhapsodizes in Schenck's script—giving his Phantom a poignancy and wider purpose beyond being the demented "Garbo freak" of earlier versions. In this draft the studio being demolished (and haunted) is most definitely identified as being MGM. In fact, here the Phantom even makes his last stand, *King Kong* like, atop the giant "Metro-Goldwyn-Mayer" sign on Stage 6, and from which he eventually falls to his death, presumably leaving Hollywood once again safe for studio executives.

Remarkably, or maybe not, these studio executives failed to notice, or failed to care, that they were greenlighting a project about the end of their own industry and which, furthermore, was targeting *them* as the craven villains letting it happen.

With a screenplay in place (the final draft was dated November 23), casting by director Gene Levitt could begin. Levitt, who also contributed to the screenplay, was primarily a television director, which perhaps indicates that the studio always intended the film to be a quickie production designed to fulfill an obligation to CBS. And yet, as Schenck wryly points out, the final talent list was odd and remarkable indeed. Bette Davis apparently was otherwise engaged; yet the rest of the cast, nearly without exception, is made up of Hollywood luminaries, well-known character actors, waxworks, and has-beens—all of whom would feel very much at home in coming weeks working a curtain call on Lot Two.

Jack Cassidy, cast as both Erich (now renamed Karl) Vonner, and his brother Otto, would be the Phantom. Cassidy's flamboyant, somewhat pompous demeanor would make him well-suited for the role of this insane, self-important, John

Barrymore–inspired character. In fact, Cassidy, who died in 1976, would be fated to play Barrymore that same year, in *W. C. Fields and Me*.

Former child star Jackie Coogan would play Jonathan, a longtime studio employee. Broderick Crawford, of course, would be the policeman investigating the case. Peter Lawford, fresh off of the not yet released *That's Entertainment!*, was cast as the suspiciously James Aubrey–like studio head. John Ireland, Allen Jenkins, Peter Haskell, Corinne Calvet, Billy Halop, Kent Taylor, John Lupton, Regis Toomey, and Fredd Wayne were also featured. Wayne, an actor with a distinguished career going back into the early 1950s, was cast by Levitt as one of the Phantom's victims. Wayne, who remembered his director as "a charming man," recalled the actual shoot as being somewhat "depressing

Jack Cassidy, as a fire- and madness-scarred Phantom pursues Skye Aubrey, as a hapless studio president's daughter, willy-nilly across the backlot. Cassidy would die of burn injuries within two years, and Ms. Aubrey really was the studio president's daughter. *Marc Wanamaker/Bison Archives*

and melancholy. It was just us, seemingly, in this vast, empty place."[6]

One member of the cast was not a Hollywood veteran at all, although, like her castmates, she did have an association of sorts with the backlot. Twenty-nine-year-old Skye Aubrey, who played Randy, the imperiled female lead, already had a rather extensive list of mostly television credits on her résumé. In 1970 she and fifty-one other starlets had posed on one of the sets on Lot Three (shortly before it was demolished) for a *Look* magazine spread about actresses in Hollywood. Unlike other ingenues trying to make it in the movies, however, Skye had an edge. Her father was James Aubrey. What's more, in *Phantom* she was cast, with interesting insensitivity, as the daughter of Lawford's studio head. Skye Aubrey was, in effect, playing herself.

According to MGM's daily production reports, the picture's scheduled thirteen-day shoot began on Monday, December 3, 1973. The helicopter sequences that open the film were done the following day. The company shot entirely on the backlot until

Thursday afternoon, when some sequences involving the studio streets and administration building (known before Aubrey's reign as the Thalberg Building) were filmed on Lot One. At eight p.m. the unit returned to Lot Two for night work.

Interiors involving the Phantom's underground lair and assorted studio departments were shot the next day on Stages 15 and 26 on Lot One. Starting Tuesday the eleventh and for the rest of that week, all production was at various Lot Two locations. A week later, on the eighteenth, the unit again crossed the road to shoot at the base of the studio's water tower and on Stage 26. The next couple days were occupied on Lot One as well.

The picture was a day over schedule on December 20 but did not wrap until 7:58 p.m. on the following day. Cassidy was called back for retakes on Christmas Eve and again on January 14. Interestingly, the production had only fallen behind during the sound-stage work. All the backlot photography came off without a hitch.

The Phantom of Lot Two opens with a TV news crew flying over the "Worldwide Pictures" backlot. The studio name change was a last-minute backpedaling measure designed apparently to protect the guilty. Regardless, signage can still be seen on-camera clearly identifying the studio as what it was: MGM. Additionally, all the films identified in the script as being "Worldwide Pictures" product are well-known MGM classics. Getting back to the movie, the commentator aboard the helicopter describes what we are seeing as his cameraman films the hundreds of familiar sets below. "Got enough?" he asks at the end of his spiel. "I could make a movie," the cameraman says.

This movie here does something interesting. Ghostlike, the camera again starts to wander across the myriad backlot sets, this time from ground level. The dozens and dozens of facades, familiar from a hundred late shows, are desolate, windswept, deserted. Weeds sprout up from cobblestone streets. Plaster-of-Paris tombstones are covered with vegetation and crumbling to dust.

Suddenly director Levitt, in an impassioned montage, starts intercutting these sequences, haunting enough in their own right, with black-and-white scenes from classic movies made on the same sets. Magically we are suddenly watching not the death throes of MGM but the silvery, enchanted earlier Hollywood of *Pride and Prejudice* (1940), *A Tale of Two Cities* (1935), *The Human Comedy* (1943), and *Waterloo Bridge* (1940). The effect is bittersweet and magical, and in a way that even *That's Entertainment!* would fail to be.

Next we see two teenagers breaking onto the lot and vandalizing a set, which is unidentified in the film but is actually the "Verona Square" location from *Romeo and Juliet* (1936). The boys are dispatched by the Phantom, described in the script as wearing Robert Taylor's 1952 *Ivanhoe* costume. Well, sort of.

The principals are introduced. It seems that studio chief Peter Lawford is dead set on selling off the "Worldwide" lot and doesn't want any scandal associated with the missing teens to get in the way of the sale. Lawford confided to reporters before filming that "old backlot number Two hadn't been touched in years . . . it's completely overgrown with vines and bushes."[7] But from his oily, spirited performance, it's clear that no moss has grown on *this* studio relic. In fact, Lawford is a little too charming for the film's good. It's hard to understand why this middle-aged hipster with the pretty daughter is so set on demolishing the studio. Inexplicably, his character disappears partway through the film. The expected and hoped-for face-off between him and the Phantom, sadly never comes to pass, although a pair of prone legs on the floor of his shag-carpeted office indicate that the two have indeed met, and that the meeting did not go well.

There are more murders. It seems that every time a construction worker, trespasser, or developer wanders onto Lot Two, he is never heard from again. Footage of Aubrey's infamous MGM studio auctions, during which millions of dollars of priceless props and costumes had been callously sold off at pennies on the dollar, are utilized here. Unfortunately, the actual auctions had been in 1970, nearly three years earlier! So we are forced to watch various characters view the proceedings on television or talk about "going down to the soundstage" where the historic auction was allegedly still taking place—yet never quite getting around to doing so. No matter. Usage of this legendary event, which Tom Walsh, a president of the Studio Art Director's Guild once referred to as "the defining moment when Rome was sacked and burned,"[8] does reinforce quite well the "end-of-an-era" feeling the screenplay is obviously attempting here.

More murders, more red herrings. This is the only *Phantom of the Opera* variation to date in which the title character shows no particular interest in the leading lady. He does stalk and eventually kidnap Randy, not because he's in love with her but to gain leverage against her father in his single-minded quest to save the backlot.

It doesn't work. The destruction of the sets, some of which were apparently staged just for the movie, is poignant in a way that the film itself hasn't really done anything to earn. These sequences also provide the picture with more production value than the budget for many a theatrical feature would allow. Enormous and substantial-looking buildings, wide city streets, and even an entire medieval-looking castle are seen to crumble and fold under the blades of a single Caterpillar tractor (operated by part-time actor Wert Cunningham). The effect is somehow both comically tacky and genuinely apocalyptic.

The climax takes place not atop the MGM sign but rather on the scaffolding high above the "New York Street" backlot. The Phantom has been chased there by the

The actual and ongoing destruction of the backlot was used to bittersweet and dramatic effect for *The Phantom of Hollywood*. *Marc Wanamaker/Bison Archives*

police and by the demolition equipment. Tearing off his mask he rages at the fools who would destroy his papier-mâché kingdom: "You will never find me! I live in a world of castles! In mansions! In palaces! In dreams! A world of make-believe. Far, far better than this! My world is invulnerable to your machines! To your progress!"

In the script his last line is "I will live there forever!" But in the film he instead shrieks, "You will never find me," before toppling to his death. As he falls, we see a multitude of flash cuts of the studio falling as well, of the sets there crashing down around us.

The Phantom of Hollywood (the last-minute name change an obvious improvement) aired on February 12, 1974. Cecil Smith in the *Los Angeles Times* remarked, "It's no great shakes of a movie unless you are one of those who get dewy-eyed about the destruction of the dream factories of old Hollywood." Smith also remarked that Skye Aubrey did lend an "authentic note" to the casting and called her a "luscious chick in anybody's back lot."⁹ Later on, an unidentified critic would call the picture a "treat for masochistic film buffs." But overall, the film, after its initial airing and occasional syndication revivals, would be quickly forgotten. There would be no home video release of any sort until 2010.

This *Phantom* would have little perceptible impact within the industry either. Aubrey resigned from his position shortly before the picture aired, his resignation resulting not from a dispute with a phantom but with Kerkorian, over the closing of the studio's distribution arm.

It was already too late to stop what he had started. But the demolition of Lot Two dragged on fitfully over years and through lawsuits and zoning regulations. Movies, amazingly, would continue to be shot on the still-standing sets during this period, and the property would remain "The MGM backlot," even though the studio was only a tenant, until 1980. "We realized right away we had made a mistake in selling off Lot Two," Roger Mayer reflects. "But it was too late to do anything about it."[10]

The continued use of Lot Two as a film location, even after it had been pronounced dead and, in fact, eulogized on-screen, was possibly one factor in the eventual renaissance of Hollywood as well. Eventually producers began to realize that there was, in fact, a certain value in creating a location from scratch on a backlot or in a soundstage—or, later on, inside a computer. They learned what Hollywood's first generation of moguls had always known, that entire worlds could be created and controlled on-lot. Worlds that on a real location could only be photographed as they were found. Slowly the studios, and their audiences, started to come back. Not to the levels of earlier decades perhaps, but enough to ensure that movies would remain Los Angeles's signature industry and the world's most popular art form.

The Phantom of Hollywood is a shadowy curio from the period it was made. Yet it reflected the torments of the time and the place in which it was produced, perhaps more bravely than any movie in history. And more than any movie in history, it pointed its anguished finger inward—at Hollywood itself. What's more, it actually bit the hand from which it fed not years after the fact, as is usually the way with Hollywood, but rather at that very moment in history when the wrongs it concerned itself with were being perpetuated. And from within the very studio, and under the nose of the very studio head, that was perpetuating these wrongs!

Ultimately the movie didn't change anything, of course. Lot Two was eventually destroyed. But Hollywood and even MGM survive to this day. Karl Vonner's tactics might have been flamboyant and extreme, but his cause, as history has proven, was ultimately a just one.

The Phantom is avenged!

43

That's Entertainment! (1974)

In 1974 MGM management was very leery of greenlighting a theatrical documentary. Even if what was being proposed to them by producer Jack Haley Jr. was a documentary about MGM, specifically a documentary about MGM musicals.

At the time, the studio was no longer even making musicals. Even Arthur Freed, who had recently (1973) died, had been unable to get a musical greenlit at the studio since 1960! The seemingly deathless Elvis Presley juggernaut had recently dried up, and the studio's last serious attempt at a traditional offering in that genre, *The Boy Friend*, had flopped in 1971. Other studios' musicals weren't performing either. Blockbusters like *West Side Story* (1961), *The Sound of Music* (1965), and *Oliver* (1968), all of which should have been made at MGM, hadn't been, and follow-ups like *Song of Norway* (1970) and *Lost Horizon* (1973) had been money-sucking embarrassments.

Somehow Haley—probably not exactly because he was the son of *The Wizard of Oz*'s Tin Man, although that probably didn't hurt—got the studio to commit to the project, realizing that they could then sell it to television if a big-screen release didn't work out.

The idea, to bring together old footage of the studio's greatest song and dance numbers, seemed foolproof—and cheap. But it didn't work out that way. For the first time many different types and formats of film, film aspect ratios, and sound elements had to be combined, enlarged, duped, restored, and then reproduced back onto 35mm film. The studio had not exactly been meticulous in maintaining their vaults either. Original negative material was often "unavailable," meaning missing or, worse yet, destroyed, or had been copied so many times that it was no longer usable. Ultimately, one of the glories of the final product is that many fans who had only seen these films on scratchy 16mm television prints got to see them on the big screen, beautifully but expensively brought back to an approximation of their original grandeur. One can't help but wonder how many film buffs and future filmmakers had their lives forever changed by this sight.

Late in the process, Haley certainly made no friends in the corporate offices when, on top of all these expensive technical issues, he decided that a star, an MGM star of course, would be needed to introduce this material on camera. Yet no one could decide which star that would be. Could you? Eventually it was decided that, instead, *all* of them, expensively, would need to make appearances—and not archivally, in those wonderful numbers, but as they were in 1974.

Despite the jubilant, celebratory nature of *That's Entertainment*'s one-sheet, in 1974 MGM was internally ripping itself into pieces, as evinced by the film's distribution being provided by United Artists, and its soundtrack album by MCA. *Photofest*

This was after all 1974. With the tragic exception of Judy Garland, who had died in 1969, virtually every major MGM musical star was still alive, many of them still singing and dancing, albeit some of them in summer stock and dinner theater. So ultimately, and alphabetically, Fred Astaire, Bing Crosby, Gene Kelly, Peter Lawford, Liza Minnelli (to pinch-hit for her mother), Donald O'Connor, Debbie Reynolds, Mickey Rooney, Frank Sinatra, James Stewart, and Elizabeth Taylor were brought back to the lot. Their participation (even though there were no new musical numbers) ultimately widened the film's value beyond its appeal as nostalgia. Their appearances coronated

That's Entertainment! as an actual, organic MGM musical, and as much more than the inadvertently postmortem and postmodern celebration of MGM musicals Haley had originally intended it to be.

So, where to film all these stars? Some were photographed wandering about Lot One, still little changed over the decades. Elizabeth Taylor's sequences were shot in a dressing room in Europe pretending to be a dressing room in Hollywood. The rest of these sequences were filmed on the backlot.

It's been said many times that this was the last time Lot Two was utilized in a feature film. Robert Osborne used to say this while introducing the film for screenings on Turner Classic Movies. But sorry, Robert, nothing could be further from the truth. MGM had worked out a deal to sell the property to the Levitt Housing Development Company in 1972, but the deal was never finalized. It would not be until 1978 that MGM renounced all ties to the property. And for two years after that—until the last very storied, very haunted facade had been leveled—it was still being used actively and consistently for production. So seeing the stars walking among these dilapidated facades as a symbolic eulogy was still a bit premature in 1974.

Premature, yes, but achingly effective.

It's hard to fault Haley and his army of archivists and editors for their selections of the clips these stars would introduce either, although, even at two and a quarter hours running time, ultimately there was just too much material available to include everybody's favorites.

Studio executives continued to doubt the property's viability almost until its release. Especially as that property's budget climbed north of $3 million. *The Boy Friend*, that recent, entirely new musical had cost less than $1 million—and that had been a flop.

Those executives needn't have worried. Upon its release in June 1974, *That's Entertainment!* instantaneously, inexplicably, was a colossal hit, the highest grossing movie the studio had released in years. The tag line "Boy, do we need it now" cannily summed up the appeal of the film for older audiences. Their children, most of whom would have been familiar only with MGM through *The Wizard of Oz*, were thus introduced to films, and to the stars of those films, they barely knew existed.

Ultimately *That's Entertainment*'s box-office take exceeded $25 million, making it the ninth-biggest grosser in the studio's history to that time. Adjusted for inflation, in 2022 that amount is equivalent to more than $140 million. That might not sound so impressive in these days of literal billion-dollar franchises. But remember, even today, documentaries never even come close to reaching this stratosphere. The highest-grossing documentary of all time, Michael Moore's *Fahrenheit 9/11*, for example, made

That's Entertainment? Amid the ruins of Esther Williams's old swimming pool, Donald O'Connor tries not to get lost in the weeds. *Marc Wanamaker/Bison Archives*

an impressive $119 million. But that was in 2004. So even today, adjusted for inflation, *That's Entertainment!* is the most successful documentary ever made.

Such successes of course always breed imitators. Haley did not participate in the inevitable follow-up *That's Entertainment, Part II* (1976). But anyone who believed the best of the studio's library had been exhausted after the first film were in for a surprise. This time Astaire and Kelly were the only hosts. And they even got to dance together, in new material, for the first time since *Ziegfeld Follies* (1945). Astaire was seventy-six at the time and Kelly sixty-three, but they realized that if they didn't dance together, people would assume they no longer were up to it. So they danced and spun about on camera a bit, creating a historic moment not because of that moment's particular merits, charming as they were, but because that moment, in 1976, could still exist at all.

That's Entertainment, Part II also contains the best opening credit sequence of any film ever made. Leo the Lion, for example is featured in a book taken off a shelf by an unseen hand (he doesn't roar). Then Kelly and Astaire are shown in old photographs on a shelf. Next, a marching band spells out the word "and," which leads to the rest of the cast's names, which are written in sand on a beach and unrolled on a parchment, which then catches fire. Next we are shown other stars' names—as stones in a pond, as fading into a sunset, as silver letters on velvet, in the pages of a book, as a message in a bottle, replacing the "no sale" key on a cash register, as pecked out on a typewriter, as the tabs on files in a cabinet, as burned into a piece of wood with a branding iron, spelled out in falling dominoes, and, finally, on the face of a gong. The actual title of the film is represented atop a snowcapped mountain.

All of these often-silly title ideas have been used in movies before; most of them have probably been used in MGM movies before. But none of them have ever been used in the *same* movie before.

Unlike its predecessor, which laser-focused on the studio's musicals, *That's Entertainment, Part II* also included non-musical asides with the likes of Spencer Tracy and Greta Garbo and comic sequences by the Marx Brothers, Abbott and Costello, Laurel & Hardy, W. C. Fields, and Jack Benny. As wonderful as these sequences are, their inclusion illustrates a certain unease on the part of the studio as to how much more musical nostalgia audiences would be able to take. Sure enough, *That's Entertainment, Part II*, although successful, made only about one-fifth as much money as its predecessor.

Jack Haley came back for *That's Dancing!* (1985), which attempted to appeal to younger audiences by incorporating footage of Mikhail Baryshnikov, who cohosted along with usual suspects Kelly, Liza Minnelli, Ray Bolger, and Sammy Davis Jr. For *That's Dancing!* MGM did at least try to do something new. In order to tell the story of dance on film, from Isadora Duncan to Michael Jackson, for the first time clips from non-MGM musicals were included, as well as footage of ballet, pop, disco, and breakdancing stars of the 1980s. The idea should have worked well as a fleet-footed bridge between the disparate eras. But the footage does not mesh as well as it should, perhaps because the modern stuff seems like an awkward annex rather than an organic outgrowth of what had come before. It's also rather unfair, frankly, to compare a 1985 music video with a 1945 feature film, if only because the budget, production facilities, and rehearsal period for the feature would have been substantially larger than for a three-minute television clip. It's like watching an elaborate dance number in a feature, which would have taken weeks to rehearse and choreograph and film, and then seeing that same number, perhaps even featuring the same artist, reproduced on a 1970s television variety series. There just isn't any fair way to compare the two. So the new material, probably to the delight of the film's older-skewing audience, not surprisingly

Moving on. *That's Entertainment, Part II* (1976) producer Saul Chaplin hangs with Gene Kelly and Fred Astaire. Note that Astaire is wearing a tie as a belt, just as he had in *Royal Wedding*, twenty-four years earlier. *Photofest*

comes off as condescended to and, ultimately, second best. The obvious bias against the newer segments in *That's Dancing!* is unfair. Even if these segments really *are* second best. At best.

In spite of the flat-footedness evident in *That's Dancing!* the studio tried one more time, for the company's seventieth anniversary, with *That's Entertainment III* (1994). This time, not surprisingly, the focus was once again squarely on MGM, and only on MGM musicals. Although now, in the wake of the 1986 Ted Turner buyout, the studio humiliatingly had to pay to license clips from their own movies. Highlights this time included unique footage from the vaults that had been cut from familiar films, including Judy Garland's memorable "Mr. Monotony" number from *Easter Parade* (1948) and a Lena Horne *Cabin in the Sky* (1943) number. The film also featured welcome new appearances as hosts by Horne, Esther Williams, Ann Miller, Howard Keel, June Allyson, and Cyd Charisse, none of whom had previously been involved in the series.

That's Entertainment III (1994). Mickey Rooney recalls past glories while pretending not to notice the garbage cans and Sony Pictures insignia behind him. *Photofest*

But that cast, and the audience that would have been interested in that cast, was dying off. And unlike in 1974, when younger crowds had enthusiastically responded to the material, in the mid-1990s a new *That's Entertainment* movie was as anachronistic as a minstrel show, although less inflammatory. Theatrically, the film failed to even make back its production expenses, although it did do significantly better on home video and cable television.

The most poignant part of *That's Entertainment III* is its very last scene. Host Gene Kelly, by then eighty-two years old—who we had just seen bounding about athletically for two hours, and who we had previously seen bounding about athletically for fifty years—here walks hesitantly, shakily, to a waiting director's chair and then gingerly, slowwwwwly, sits down, obviously exhausted by the effort. His long-ago costar, Debbie Reynolds, saw this, just as audiences and his fans surely did, as irrefutable evidence of an era's close. "It was sad for me to see Gene having trouble walking, when he could dance a million miles and not seem tired,"[1] she later admitted.

44

Rocky (1976)

In 2014 Leo the Lion was afforded the highest single honor possible in the entertainment industry when, on the occasion of MGM's ninetieth anniversary, the big cat put his big paws in a cement block in the forecourt of Grauman's Chinese Theatre on Hollywood Boulevard.

Aside from Leo (played here by a magnificent animal named Major), the *other* star in attendance that day was actor Sylvester Stallone. Stallone, in his remarks to the crowd, solemnly mentioned that the character of prizefighter Rocky Balboa, who he had been playing by that time for almost forty years, "was born under the MGM banner."

Not quite. The story behind the production of *Rocky* is one of Hollywood's all-time great underdog tales. Both for Rocky and for Stallone himself, who had effectively failed as an actor when he created the character and wrote the screenplay over a weekend, and when, according to him, he was days away from getting evicted from his tiny apartment on Hollywood Boulevard. Eventually he showed that script to his agent, who shopped it to, among others, producers Irwin Winkler and Robert Chartoff. Winkler-Chartoff then had a deal in place with United Artists. The rest, as the cliché goes, really is history.

The point, however, is that it was UA, a full five years before they would be purchased by MGM, under whose "banner" Rocky was if not born, then certainly nurtured.

Stallone's hastily-written screenplay, which United Artists liked so much, was nonetheless more than a little bit derivative. The "borrowed" material prominently included sections, situations, characters, and attitudes lifted from MGM's *The Champ* (1931), which, post-*Rocky*, that studio would hopefully if incompetently remake in 1981; *On the Waterfront* (1954); and *Somebody Up There Likes Me* (1956), which had been about real-life fighter Rocky Graziano. This particular Rocky's birth name by the way, had been, no, not Balboa, but the rather suspiciously similar-sounding Barbella.

That said, few UA executives in the 1970s would have noticed that *Rocky* was mining these clichés at all, as studio executives were nearly as woefully ignorant of their industry's past trends and successes then as they are now. In fact, in that cynical era, when even a thriller like *Jaws* contained a subplot about political corruption, Stallone's earnest "let's give an underdog a shot" story, and that underdog's innate, if

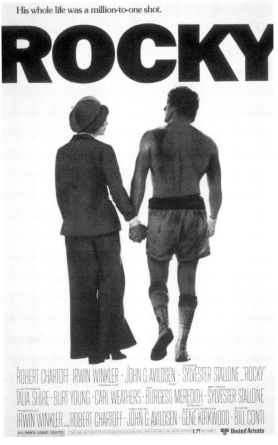

Rocky (1976). *Photofest*

not too bright sweetness, might have seemed fresh, even if it wasn't.

Unfortunately, although Stallone's script, familiar though it might have been, was well liked, nobody at UA liked the idea of Stallone—a complete unknown after all—as the lead. And they punched hard to hire a star, James Caan, perhaps, to play Rocky. But Stallone's early deal with Winkler-Chartoff had specified that he play the lead. And although the actor's financial situation was still dire, he refused to yield on this point, even though he could have made $300,000 up-front for the script alone versus the $75,000 (and points) he ultimately took into the ring with him as Rocky. Fortunately, United Artists eventually if cynically decided that Stallone's—and Rocky's—single-minded, do-or-die determination to go the distance would at least make for excellent publicity. It did.

With no star attached and because Winkler-Chartoff were contractually obligated to keep the budget low, *Rocky*'s negative cost ended up being only a little more than $1 million. By contrast, the same year's *King Kong* remake, filmed at MGM, and which *Rocky* eventually outgrossed, cost $25 million to produce. A few days filming with Stallone took place in Philadelphia, where the film was set, but in an attempt to control costs, most of the production was based at home in Los Angeles.

United Artists, for their part, realized that *Rocky* would need to be marketed in a big way in order to avoid getting lost in the Christmas 1976 cinema shuffle. Their self-serving ad campaign ultimately cost four times as much as their movie. Ironically, this campaign allowed, even encouraged, Stallone to emphasize the studio's evil step-mother role in trying to keep the actor from playing the role, thus focusing audience empathy on the actor and his own Rocky-style battle against corporate Hollywood to "go the distance." Stallone's studio-created persona—that of the little guy fighting for all of us and against larger forces, and which the actor still successfully uses today—is almost entirely due to United Artists' canny marketing of him as just such a crusader.

The gambit worked brilliantly too. United Artists at the time was even worse off than MGM among Hollywood studios in regard to marketing blunders, gaffs and goofs—perhaps exactly why MGM would eventually gobble them up. For example, Winkler-Chartoff's *New York New York*, and UA's own *A Bridge Too Far*—each of which cost two dozen times(!) as much as *Rocky*—were soon to be disastrously released in a UA-created quicksand of red ink. On the other hand, *Rocky* ultimately grossed more than $200 million at the box office. And it won the Academy Award for, among other things, the best picture of its year. And Sylvester Stallone became a star, a title he retains even today, decades later.

This is ironic indeed, because until this point, unlike every other equivalent studio, UA had never been able to create a star. The company had been created *by* stars, back in 1919, and had distributed countless star vehicles, but unlike MGM, which had by then created a hundred stars, United Artists only ever created this one, in its twilight: Stallone.

Thanks to United Artists, Sylvester Stallone rocketed from being an out-of-work actor allegedly unable to pay his rent and barely able to feed his family to an undisputed superstar almost literally overnight. He received Oscar nominations for both his *Rocky* performance and his *Rocky* screenplay. Critics in 1976, perhaps unaware they were being manipulated by United Artists' marketing department, literally fell over themselves that year comparing the actor to a young Marlon Brando.

Rocky of course has also spawned a franchise that produced substantial profits then, and which continues to do so today. The first sequel, inevitably titled *Rocky II*, came

When Sylvester Stallone as Rocky Balboa climbed the steps of the Philadelphia Museum of Art in 1976, audiences cried and cheered. They still do. *Author's collection*

out in 1979. This follow-up, with ever-underdog Rocky again going the distance, was again distributed by a happy United Artists and was again a huge box office success. Stallone, now much more of a master of his fate than before, directed this one.

Unfortunately, UA in 1979 was still in relative financial freefall, which would not abate until February 1981, when Kirk Kerkorian/MGM bought the beleaguered company's assets for $380 million. An undisputed crown jewel among these assets of course was previous—and future—*Rocky* films.

The first of those, *Rocky III*, with MGM now holding the purse strings, came out in 1982. Once again audiences responded enthusiastically to the character's increasingly farfetched adventures in the ring. Not that the superstar probably cared, but by this time, no one, certainly not critics, was comparing Stallone to Brando anymore. Incidentally, it was in that same year that the actor first portrayed his *other* iconic character—mumbling, misunderstood Vietnam vet John Rambo—in *First Blood*. This Stallone blockbuster was distributed by Orion Pictures, which, again, following a pattern, MGM would acquire in 1997.

The next sequel, *Rocky IV* (1985), pitted the character against a robotic Russian boxer. To hedge his bets, this time Rocky was also tossed into a symbolic battle with the entire population of the USSR. And at the end of the film, those Russians are depicted as cheering not for their own team but for Rocky! This latest fantasy was again a huge success—at least outside of the Soviet Bloc.

Predictably, Stallone and his studio followed up with *Rocky V* in 1990. This time they wisely tried to return the character, who was now more superhero than underdog, to his grittier roots via a contrived subplot in which Rocky's money is embezzled by his unscrupulous business manager. They also brought back John G. Avildsen, who had directed the first film more than a decade earlier and had won an Oscar for doing so. Unfortunately, by this time the character of Rocky had been knocked down and gotten up more times than even MGM itself, and for the first-time audiences were relatively indifferent to seeing him do so again. *Rocky V* made only about a third of the US box office that *Rocky IV* had. Any other franchise would have petered out, seemingly forever, here. Rocky, however, was not yet down for the count.

Post *Rocky V*, and post Rocky, Sylvester Stallone and MGM each moved on with their own hits and misses until 2006, sixteen years after *Rocky V*, with the release of *Rocky Balboa*. Stallone, who hadn't had a big success since *Cliffhanger* (1993), for obvious reasons still felt a great deal of sentiment toward the big lug and had for years been telling anyone who would listen that he felt that he "owed" Rocky and Rocky's fans a coda.

Unlike earlier Rocky adventures, for which UA, MGM/UA, or MGM had been eager participants, this time studio executives, none of whom had probably been there in 1976, were less than thrilled about chronicling the adventures of a sixty-year-old, washed-up prizefighter, as played by a sixty-year-old washed-up star.

Stallone, for his part, had no other option than MGM because they and Chartoff-Winkler, not he, owned the rights to the character. Eventually the studio came around, although, again echoing the first production, much of the filming was kept in Los Angeles, and the budget for that filming was carefully kept to a then relatively modest $25 million.

Rocky Balboa was a hit with audiences and even with critics, who had stopped taking Stallone seriously as an actor as far back as the 1970s. It turned out that fans, including fans not born during the era of the first film or even at the release of the last film had apparently made Rocky's acquaintance on home video or cable television, still really *did* want to see what the big marble-mouthed palooka had been up to since 1990. The *Rocky* saga, by all laws of nature and Hollywood, could have ended nicely with the unexpected success of *Rocky Balboa*.

This bronze Rocky statue was used as a prop in *Rocky III* (1982) and then gifted to the Philadelphia Museum of Art, where millions of visitors admire it every year. *Photofest*

But it didn't.

In 2013 Ryan Coogler was a young director who had just had a breakout with the critically acclaimed indie *Fruitville Station*. Coogler's father, like a lot of fathers from that generation, had been a big fan of the *Rocky* series. When the older man had been stricken with a neuromuscular disease, Coogler had amused his dad by telling him Rocky-centric stories. The younger Coogler was, however, very skeptical about turning this fan-fiction into his next actual project, even though he eventually, and reluctantly, pitched the project to an enthusiastic MGM and then to Sylvester Stallone.

Stallone surprisingly agreed. "You know what?" he later said about the younger filmmaker. "Someone took a chance on me once. I'm just going to throw caution to the wind and let him run with it."[1] As generous as the actor was certainly being, however, it should be noted again that it was MGM, not Stallone, who actually owned the character. Coogler, having already made his deal with the studio, could then have proceeded with the film with or without "Rocky's" blessing and participation.

The result was 2015's *Creed*, which rather remarkably stands as one of the most audacious sequels ever in that it is a *Rocky* film that, at its heart, is not really a *Rocky* film. The story instead is told from the point of view of the illegitimate son of Apollo Creed, Rocky's frequent opponent and then friend from the original series, who seeks out the now-retired prizefighter, who subsequently becomes a surrogate father figure to him.

It was while *Creed* was in pre-production, and not long after Stallone had confirmed his participation in it, that the star made his appearance at Grauman's with Leo the Lion and there offered up the white lie regarding MGM's part in the origin of the franchise. Sly also used the opportunity to publicly praise Gary Barber, then the studio CEO, who also attended. "He has done an extraordinary job in restoring MGM to its former glory" a grinning Stallone, perhaps self-servingly, told the crowd.

When *Creed* opened in 2015, it was both a critical and financial success. It even led to a second Oscar nomination for Stallone as Rocky Balboa, almost forty years after his first—and to the inevitable, and equally successful *Creed II* (2018). A projected third installment, *Creed III*, is scheduled for 2023.

For *Rocky*, for Sylvester Stallone, for UA, and certainly for MGM, "going the distance" has turned out to be much farther than anticipated.

45

Coma (1978)

Coma is a crackerjack medical thriller, the second of two successful 1970s collaborations between the studio and director Michael Crichton. It is also the only film the then-owner of MGM ever took a personal interest in.

Crichton, who trained as a doctor, instead became a novelist and then a film director after his 1969 novel *The Andromeda Strain* attracted the attention of Hollywood. *Westworld* (1973), which he wrote and directed at MGM, followed, although the studio's reputation was so bad at the time that he was initially leery of even dealing with them. "There were too many stories of unreasonable pressure, arbitrary script changes, inadequate postproduction, and cavalier recutting of the final film. Nobody who had a choice made a picture at Metro, but then we didn't have a choice,"[1] he said later, although ultimately his experience at the studio was largely positive and the resultant film a success.

Crichton returned to the studio five years later for *Coma*, which was based on a novel by his friend, and fellow doctor, Robin Cook. Both the novel and Crichton's film are about a Boston hospital where patients are intentionally murdered so their organs can be harvested and sold. Farrah Fawcett-Majors was reputedly considered for the role in the film that eventually went to Geneviève Bujold, with Michael Douglas and Richard Widmark in support. Budgeted at less than $5 million, much of which was offset by a presale to television, *Coma* went into production in June 1977 and was released only six months later to good, if occasionally condescending reviews and very potent box office. An effective marketing campaign, highlighted by the memorable tagline: "Imagine your life hangs by a thread. Imagine your body hangs by a wire. Imagine you're not imagining," played a part in the film's popularity, as did the appealing cast and production and good word of mouth. All of this made *Coma*, in 1978, a very good example of efficient, quality, factory filmmaking—a model MGM, after all, had largely created but had remarkably, consistently, almost constantly been otherwise unable to live up to in the 1970s.

Michael Crichton's direction is another plus. Crichton, who sadly never worked at MGM again, was a wonderful idea man. Many of his stories and ideas are so high concept that Hollywood is still making millions off those ideas today. Look no further than his still-potent *Jurassic Park* franchise or the *Westworld* TV series. Yes, both of these properties are based on the same basic idea, if one cares to think about it. But it's a really *good* idea.

But Crichton was not a very innovative director, never displaying much visual flair from the director's chair. And he tended to treat his characters/actors as chess pieces,

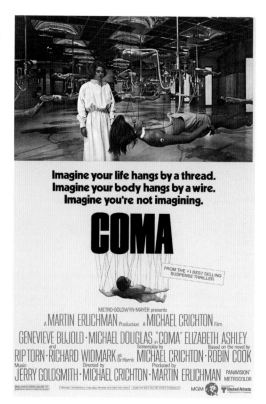

In 1978, *Coma's* provocative poster frightened both movie audiences and hospital patients. *Author's collection*

moving them around the board in support of his brilliant story ideas, which is probably why, after only four more films, he segued back into writing and producing.

Here, however, maybe for the only time, Crichton is the perfect man for the material. As a doctor, he was not creeped out by hospitals, blood, and corpses nearly as much as his audience was. So, unlike any other director—at least any other director without a medical degree—he brings an effectively cold dispassion to the shock scenes. When a body is viewed on a slab, for example, there are no crash cuts, dim lighting, or zoom-ins telling us what to think, and no burst of melodramatic music. In fact, the film doesn't bother with music at all for half its running time. During the autopsy and operation scenes, the surgeons make jokes and engage in chitchat while sawing out organs and cutting off limbs. Even the famous, and much discussed at the time, sequence involving comatose bodies warehoused, marionette-like, on wires is made eerily mundane by a nurse who pokes a still-living "patient" with her finger to demonstrate how fast the computer can compensate. After looking at the medical profession through Crichton's eyes, it is hard to ever look at it the same way again.

Paid assassin Michael Weston searches for Geneviève Bujold inside an uncomfortably well-stocked freezer full of corpses. *Photofest*

Another plus for *Coma* is its cast. Geneviève Bujold, as a young resident investigating the case, proves that she is one of the best actresses of her generation. She tears into her thin, Nancy Drew material with feral ferocity. Her adversarial cat-and-mouse scenes with veteran Widmark, as the hospital administrator, really crackle. Michael Douglas, then on the cusp of stardom, plays Bujold's boyfriend, effectively the reassuring girl Friday role had the lead been a man. He's effective enough, but his character, perhaps reflective of the time, and like every other male in the film, occasionally comes across as a bit of a chauvinist creep.

Actors Rip Torn and Elizabeth Ashley, who, respectively, play a doctor at the hospital and a nurse at the "warehouse," would already have been familiar faces to audiences in 1978, but the *Coma* cast contains a surprising number of soon-to-be familiar personalities as well. Sharp-eyed viewers will recognize future Bond Girl (*Moonraker*, 1979) Lois Chiles and future *Magnum P.I.* star Tom Selleck. Both play victims. A pre-stardom Ed Harris appears as a pathologist. *Very* sharp-eyed viewers might also be able to identify Philip Baker Hall, Joanna Kerns, and Lance LeGault roaming *Coma*'s creepy white corridors.

Another significant visitor to those *Coma* corridors was the owner of the studio, Kirk Kerkorian. Kerkorian, it should be noted, *never* visited the sets of his films. His profile on the lot was so low that he maintained only a tiny office and would not even allow his name to be painted on his parking space. Apparently, he enjoyed watching movies not in a personal screening room on the lot but in public theaters with audiences. And he showed absolutely no interest in seeing movies being made. Except for this one time.

Crew shot with director Michael Crichton, center, and his star Geneviève Bujold (to his left). Waiting for someone?
Author's collection

When this exceedingly hands-off boss requested to visit the set of *Coma*, then, everyone was astonished—astonished that he had even heard of *Coma* or knew *Coma* was shooting on his lot. According to executive Peter Bart, when Kerkorian's head of production, Richard Shepherd, asked about his interest, the boss only told him, "A friend told me about that movie; it sounds interesting."[2]

So one day, very late in production and at his boss's bidding, someone, probably *Coma*'s producer, Martin Erlichman, reportedly and certainly nervously piloted a golf cart with Kerkorian in the passenger seat to the stage where *Coma* was then shooting. Upon entering, an offer was made to introduce the mogul to Crichton and the cast, but Kerkorian demurred, saying he didn't want to bother anybody. Instead, presumably from the shadows behind the lights, the big boss watched for a few minutes then quietly slipped back outside.

Is anything to be made of this? Probably not. This visit, to this set, is probably a blip, just an anomaly in our story. But it's still worth mentioning that just a few months later, Kirk Kerkorian would release his infamous statement that "MGM is primarily a hotel company with comparatively insignificant interests in motion pictures."[3]

Coma is a relative high-water mark, commercially and artistically, during what was a very bleak era for MGM. Yet maybe, on that long-ago day in Culver City, Kirk Kerkorian didn't like what he saw.

46

Heaven's Gate (1980)

Heaven's Gate is the only film in history credited with single-handedly bringing down a studio.

That studio, of course, was not MGM but rather United Artists, which, after sixty-two years as an independent studio, was sold to MGM after this film disastrously premiered in 1980, was withdrawn and recut, and premiered again in 1981, again disastrously. When it became evident that *Heaven's Gate* was going to lose its entire (projected) $44 million budget, executives at UA's parent company, Transamerica, effectively threw up their hands and sold off the company, changing both companies' stories forever.

The story of *Heaven's Gate*, the story that intersected and entwined these two studios forever, has been told before of course. Steven Bach has written a book, *Final Cut: Dreams and Disaster in the Making of Heaven's Gate*, which he has updated and supplemented several times and was also involved in turning the story into a documentary. The story he tells about that story is well worth seeking out in any form.

As mentioned, *Heaven's Gate*, and the making of *Heaven's Gate*, has been much discussed, mocked, analyzed, and gossiped about—by Bach and many others—perhaps more than any other film, certainly more than any other film hardly anyone has actually bothered to watch. Most of these lurid legends—and, yes, some of those legends are certainly true—assert that once director Michael Cimino, who had recently directed the Oscar-winning *The Deer Hunter*, got to his remote Montana and Idaho locations, he could not be reined in by his bosses back home, and that those bosses could only stand by helplessly while the production hemorrhaged increasingly more money and resources.

The project, a Western about a range war between industrialists and settlers, had always been intended as a big, important production. So the budget for *Heaven's Gate*, and this we know, was originally set at about $12 million. But Cimino, his ego allegedly fueled by the success of *The Deer Hunter* and copious amounts of cocaine, kept envisioning his film as something even larger, even longer, and even more expensive than the studio had signed on for.

On location, Cimino immediately asserted his independence by forcing his cast to give him as many as fifty takes for even the simplest scene, all the while refusing to tell that cast exactly what they were doing wrong and why he was asking them to do it again, and then again. Unsurprisingly, by the fifth day of production, *Heaven's Gate* was already four days behind schedule.

Cimino instructed his cinematographer, Vilmos Zsigmond, to give him lots of smoke, clouds, and dust in his compo-

Christopher Walken, Isabelle Huppert, and Kris Kristofferson hover in the clouds. Some of *Heaven's Gate*'s advertising material proved to be as smoky as the movie (1980). *Photofest*

sitions, which made much of the resultant action prohibitively expensive, since smoke is difficult, and time-consuming, to control and light consistently. The director's constant dictate for more diffusion, even for scenes set indoors, runs completely opposed to a legendary David O. Selznick memo from the set of *Gone with the Wind* in which he scolded his crew for creating nearly the same effect. "If we can't get the artistry and clarity," he had said, "let's forget the artistry."[1]

At Cimino's urging, Zsigmond also shot much of the movie at dusk, during the elusive period sometimes called the golden hour by filmmakers, although contrary to its name, it lasts only a few minutes. The results were indeed striking. But those results were, again, prohibitively expensive and time-consuming to achieve and ultimately confusing to audiences, who must have wondered why the sun was always about to set but never actually did so.

Michael Cimino also kept tinkering with the huge sets United Artists let him build. Reportedly, his town square set, expensively constructed from scratch to his exacting specifications, still wasn't large enough to contain his cast, the backgrounds, and the forever-setting sun. Instead of disassembling one side of the street and moving it the required distance from the other to make it larger, however, the director had *both sides* demolished and then rebuilt, this time with the proper spacing between them—at a reported budget overage of $1.2 million.

Late in production, Cimino moved the beleaguered company to Oxford University in England to shoot a prologue set at Harvard University in Massachusetts, even though this sequence had no discernable narrative ties to the rest of the film. Inconveniently, however, neither Oxford nor God had thought to provide a tree in the spot where the director desired there to be one. So he—Cimino, not God—had a tree he liked found, uprooted, cut into pieces, and then reassembled on the campus, where he staged a spectacular outdoor ball with hundreds of waltzing extras. Confusingly, no one remembered to hire a band, so the source of the music these extras are dancing to was ultimately left unexplained, although some have speculated that the bandstand was—maybe—hidden behind the tree.

Snarky stories like this about the making of *Heaven's Gate* go on and on. Many of them are available courtesy of Bach's extensive autopsy of the production, and the now-aging cast and crew members who were there will probably keep telling and expanding on those firsthand stories for the rest of their lives. In fairness to Cimino, though, all these expensive debaucheries would have been immediately forgiven had the film he ultimately delivered been a financial, or even only a critical, success. After all, David Lean had very similarly held MGM captive while he was in Europe filming flowers blossoming for *Doctor Zhivago*. But Lean's movie had been a commercial triumph, ultimately worth the expense and the excess. UA executives surely must have hoped for a similar miracle with *Heaven's Gate*.

They didn't get it. As noted, somewhat like *Greed* decades earlier, *Heaven's Gate* was embarrassingly previewed, panned, withdrawn, recut, and rereleased, which, along with the uniformly bad—really, really bad—reviews and toxic word of mouth, kept audiences away by the millions.

And they have stayed away ever since. Even though the film's critical standing has improved somewhat in the forty-plus years since its release, and even after, in 2012, The Criterion Collection, whose stated mission is to bring to audiences "important classic and contemporary films from around the world" released a beautifully restored home video version. In publicity for this rerelease, the Criterion people charitably described the film as "among Hollywood's most ambitious and unorthodox epics." Even so, the film's reputation has still not markedly improved among audiences, perhaps because, to date, so few of those audiences have bothered to give *Heaven's Gate* a chance.

But *should* audiences give *Heaven's Gate* a chance? The truth is, because of all the scorn heaped on Michael Cimino and his expensive excesses at the time of his film's release, a sense of moral condemnation has long hung over the film, as heavy as the smoke in one of Zsigmond's compositions. Knowing what was occurring on the set and in the beleaguered UA boardroom as well while the film was being made, it's difficult, for reasons that now feel more ethical than aesthetic, to appreciate whatever positive qualities the film actually possesses.

This perhaps isn't fair. After all, audiences—at least those not invested in United Artists stock in 1980—were not being asked to help foot the bill for Cimino's film. Why should we care how much money *Heaven's Gate* cost, or lost, in 1980?

The truth is, even if one can lay aside its ruinous backstory, *Heaven's Gate* is a very hard movie to like. It's slowly paced. It's overlong. It's pretentious. The film's perspective, if indeed it really has one, seems to be that capitalism is corruptive, if not outright evil. This could be a valid "theme"—even if, like the ultimately horrified and disgraced United Artists' executives, you don't personally agree with that perspective. But that anti-capitalist theme is somewhat muddied by what actually happens on-screen. The settlers who are being exploited by the wealthy landowners ultimately want the same thing their oppressors do. They want to be wealthy landowners too. And if they became those wealthy landowners, you can bet those settlers will then exploit future settlers, and the environment, the air, and the water, just like those who had earlier exploited them.

Then there are those visuals. The look of the film is often too dark or too smoky to fully appreciate the care that obviously went into achieving that look. Although pictorially, the film probably played better, and undoubtably looked cleaner and sharper, on a big theater screen than on any home format, even the Criterion version, which is the only way most people will be able to see Zsigmond's careful, layered, and yes, smoky compositions today. However, even on television, much of the cinematography, when not defused to the point of abstraction, is stunning. That town square, for example,

The expensive sets constructed for *Heaven's Gate* included a large roller rink (left), which somewhat explains the film's title. *Photofest*

however wide its streets ended up being, is often framed with snowcapped mountains in the background and is breathtaking, as are assorted tableaus involving puffing loco-motives or wagons full of teeming immigrants waiting to be exploited.

It's curious that *Heaven's Gate*, perhaps because of its perceived anti-capitalist stance, is usually also considered to be some sort of an anti-Western or, even worse, not a Western at all. And yes, the film is one of the few (the only?) Westerns to contain sequences involving Harvard University, roller-skates, and yachts. Yet, anyone who takes the time to actually watch it will quickly realize that the script embraces more Western clichés than it rebukes.

In fact, *Heaven's Gate* is almost a remake of 1953's *Shane*, which no one has ever accused of being anti-capitalistic. Both films involve exploited little-guy settlers pitted against fat cat, big-guy settlers. In both cases an enigmatic hero rides into town and is forced to take sides, somewhat reluctantly, against the establishment. Admittedly, Kris Kristofferson's hero in Cimino's film is less of a literal "white hat" than *Shane*'s Alan Ladd is. And Shane, as far as we know, never had the benefit of a Harvard education.

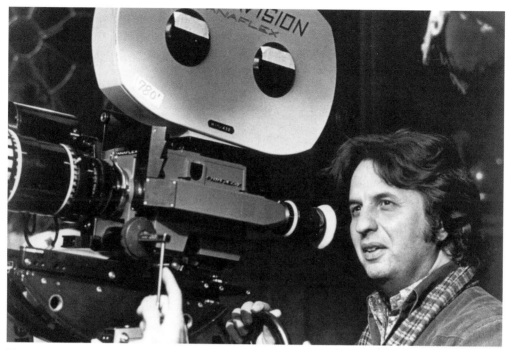

Maverick director Michael Cimino. Fiddling while Rome burns? *Photofest*

But Kristofferson's hero actually hoists his good-guy flag even earlier than Ladd does by rescuing an exploited settler being abused by establishment thugs mere moments after he rides into town.

Taking note of this, it's not hard to believe that Cimino was, in fact, a big fan of legendary Western director John Ford and of actor-director Clint Eastwood, with whom he had worked well most recently on *Thunderbolt and Lightfoot* (1974). It's also telling that at some point, Cimino, or maybe it was United Artists, reportedly considered John Wayne and later Steve McQueen for the Kristofferson role.

There are other "traditional" Western tropes to be found here too. Later on in the film, much later on—because, yes, this film does seem to go on for days—*Heaven's Gate*'s leading lady, Isabelle Huppert, who has demonstrated no particular aptitude for horsemanship in the all-too-many earlier hours of the plot, jumps off a speeding buckboard and onto the back of a runaway steed and then subdues it in a manner that would have made Dale Evans, if not John Wayne himself, proud. *Heaven's Gate* also ends, if you can make it that far, with a literal if ultimately misguided last-stand-ride-to-the-rescue cavalry charge—a charge that would surely have pleased Ford, Wayne, or D. W. Griffith.

The performances in *Heaven's Gate*, when you can see them through the dust, are fine. Actor-musician Kristofferson's career as a big-screen leading man all but ended with this film, although he would get plenty more chances to show off his talents in the future in both television and on the recording stage. His tired, been-up-all-night persona perhaps better evokes Robert Mitchum than Alan Ladd, but like Mitchum, he eventually proved equally at home in both TV Westerns (like a 1986 *Stagecoach* remake) and indie neo-noirs like *Trouble in Mind* (1985).

Christopher Walken, who here plays an enforcer pitted against Kristofferson, in the 1980s would very much find his fate entwined, for good or ill, with that of MGM. In rapid succession he costarred in both *Pennies from Heaven* (1981) and *Brainstorm* (1983) for the studio during this contentious period, and both films, along with *Heaven's Gate*, would play significant roles in the company's story moving forward. Post *Heaven's Gate*, Walken has continued a successful, quirky career. Incidentally, the actor credits his distinctive pompadour hairstyle to frequent MGM star Elvis Presley, whom he once portrayed on stage.

Isabelle Huppert, the third part of *Heaven's Gate*'s dusty love triangle, has, like Kristofferson and Walken, also enjoyed a long and distinguished career, although mostly in Europe, which Cimino's film ultimately did little to sidetrack. Her jumpy, exuberant performance here makes her stand out and is a bit out of key with the rest of the film's somber tone. And maybe that was Cimino's intention.

Michael Cimino suffered more collateral damage than anyone else involved in *Heaven's Gate*, with the notable exception of United Artists itself. Post-*Gate*, he directed only five more feature films over the next thirty-six years. None of these films was either a critical or box-office success.

Cimino also refused to participate in any of Steven Bach's literary or documentary postmortems of his film. In 2005, MGM screened a complete print of that film in Paris and then in New York, where it was finally acclaimed, by some, as a truly great movie. The BBC confirmed this opinion in a 2015 poll of the hundred best American films of all time, which was released a few months before the director's death. *Heaven's Gate* came in under the wire at number ninety-eight.

Just behind *Gone with the Wind*.

47

Hero at Large (1980), Being There (1979), or The Formula (1980)

Several movies and TV shows have laid claim to being the last to film on MGM's fabled backlots, as the "backlot" was in fact several different and unconnected properties.

In the late 1960s, studio president James Aubrey, backed by owner Kirk Kerkorian, conspired to eventually sell off the entire studio lot, beginning with Lot Three and its annexes. Consequently, in October 1970 the property was sold to the Levitt Housing company for $7.25 million. In August, just before the demolition, the studio held an unironically cheery "goodbye to Lot Three party." Production was still going on there as the bulldozers were being unloaded, and the crew probably had to deal with Caterpillar tractors circling vulturelike while they filmed, waiting to devour that set just moments after the crew drove away.

The thirty-seven-acre Lot Two was scheduled to go next. Yet, like the Chinese death of a thousand cuts, that property ultimately faced an even more inglorious, slower, and much more painful demise than Lot Three.

Unfortunately for Aubrey's year-end bonus, a proposed sale to the Levitt & Sons development company ultimately fell through. In 1973 the studio instead sold the land to a local scrap dealer for a little over $4 million, although Aubrey and then his successors, in order to satisfy contractual production requirements, had to go back and lease that same land back for the next *eight years*, even while the sets were being demolished, sometimes moments after being filmed.

Some of these last projects, like *The Phantom of Hollywood* (see entry), actually used the demolition to drive their story. Others took advantage of not having to pay to repair sets damaged during production. *The Stunt Man* (1980), for example, bulldozed tanks through the facades as part of a World War I battle sequence. Other projects just shot the sets as they were, presumably playing themselves. Orson Welles's long unfinished (until 2018!) *The Other Side of the Wind*, for example, used the property as-is in the late 1970s without any formal approval. Welles knew that any security on the property at the time would assume that the famous director was working there legitimately. Big-budget films for other studios, like *King Kong* (1976) and *Sergeant Pepper's Lonely Hearts Club Band* (1978), built new and expensive sets on the property, even while music videos for the songs "Hang On Sloopy" and "Stayin' Alive" shot their artists unironically performing amid the ancient ruins.

Peter Sellers seems to float inside his own silhouette for *Being There*'s poster art. At the time, MGM too was getting lost in its own shadow (1979). *Photofest*

Television also scurried amid the Caterpillars and hard hats. TV shows like *CHiPS, Buck Rogers in the 25th Century, Popi, Planet of the Apes,* and a 1978 *ABC Afterschool Special* all filmed amid the facades even as stacks of lumber were trucked in and stored for building the tract homes for which the land had been earmarked.

But what film was the final, last long goodbye for the MGM backlot?

That's hard to say, but there are three suspects. And the title of "last tenant on the backlot" almost certainly belongs to one of those three, although conflicting and sometimes missing production paperwork and conflicting and sometimes missing human memories tend to obscure the facts as to which one of these titles is our actual mile marker as to the true end of an era. Here are the facts as we know them.

On February 9, 1979, someone named "Stan," presumably working for, with, or at the behest of MGM, placed a singularly strange ad in the trade paper *Daily Variety*.

Being There's writer, Jerzy Kosinski, consults with director Hal Ashby. *Photofest*

"Attention Location Managers," it read. "Your last chance to shoot Fifth Avenue in Culver City. All buildings will be demolished in April." The studio itself was not named, as anyone reading that ad would have known that Fifth Avenue in Culver City was one of the last sections more or less still standing on that once mighty studio's once mighty backlot.

It's not known who responded specifically to this ad. But we do know that in early April, two months later, an MGM movie, *Hero at Large*, shot on these sets. *Hero at Large* starred the likable John Ritter as an out-of-work actor who inadvertently becomes a vigilante hero when he foils a robbery while wearing a superhero costume for a publicity gig. Most of the film was shot in New York, where it was set, but the climax featured Ritter, again in costume, rescuing tenants, including a child, from a burning building. For this very elaborate set piece, a solid month of prep on the old sets was required to rig the falling walls, collapsing fire escapes, and pyrotechnic effects required. The film ended

Harry Bellevar stands by as would-be superhero John Ritter signs autographs in *Hero at Large* (1980). Note future star Kevin Bacon meandering in the background. *Photofest*

with Ritter and his girlfriend, played by the equally likable Anne Archer, walking, just like a thousand cinematic couples before them, arm in arm through the facades portraying a contemporary New York for the last time. Fade to black.

Or maybe not. A few days later, on April 18, another project also shot on Lot Two—this one not on New York Street but on Copperfield Court, a Dickensian strip of real estate notable for an arched entrance connecting it to the nearby Waterfront Street. Most of Waterfront Street was gone by this time, owing to the Caterpillars and a 1976 lot fire. Most of Copperfield Court was gone too, but there were a few pieces of facade left that could serve as backgrounds for the contemporary Georgetown setting of Hal Ashby's *Being There*.

Being There was a Lorimar production and so, like Lorimar itself, was based on the lot. It is not known if "Stan's" earlier trade ad was responsible for its presence on Lot Two, because the decision might simply have been one of convenience or logistics instead. Again, several weeks of prep were needed to build the house and garden "Chance," played by Peter Sellers (in his penultimate role), is evicted from early in the film. The call sheets for the production, preserved for us by historian Donnie Norden, identify the location specifically as "Former MGM Lot #2, Overland Boulevard, Culver City."

Being There should then have been the last production on the property. It probably *was* the last production on the property. But maybe not.

There exists an internal MGM memo, dated December 20, 1979, *almost eight months later*, from Kevin Donnelly, who was then working as a production manager for another MGM film, *The Formula*. In this memo, addressed to the film's unit production manager, Ken Swor, Donnelly states:

Ben Cowitt has negotiated a rental price for the area selected as the bombed out set on Lot Two. Goldrich and Krest will charge $500.00 a day for construction and $2500.00 for the shooting day. Construction to start on 12/26, and shooting will be January 25th or 26th. There will be no charge for striking days.

On the face of it, this seems ironclad, although one has to wonder how much real estate would have still been standing on Lot Two this far into the demolition pattern. The month-plus prep time mentioned was also consistent with practices in the industry at that time and with, for example, what had recently happened there for both *Hero at Large* and *Being There*. Furthermore, it is known that a Ben Cowitt, presumably the same Ben Cowitt mentioned in the memo, did work in Studio Operations at MGM.

Then there is the intriguingly apt mention of property management company Goldrich & Kest Inc. (misspelled in the memo), who in 1978 had purchased those beleaguered Lot Two acres from Ching C. Lin, the scrap dealer who had generously, and profitably, been allowing MGM to use and then sublease the property. Goldrich & Kest, in spite of consistently making money on that property themselves, had also very greatly amped up the destruction-construction schedule, due no doubt to being very eager to develop the land into profitable tract houses, and perhaps to escape Hollywood's strange accounting practices and idiosyncrasies. Although here, at least according to this memo, they apparently had agreed to let production happen here one last time, for one last hurrah.

But did they? The "bombed out set" described in the memo was to be the rubble of a besieged, late–World War II Berlin, then ruined and in flames. The MGM backlot had of course once featured an array of suitably Germanic locations that could have been pressed into service for such a sequence, but by this time that same MGM backlot had largely been reduced to acre after acre of chaos or condominiums. Production designer Herman A. Blumenthal, who had most recently worked at the studio on the Dean

Hero at Large's John Ritter, trapped in a burning tenement, seems unconcerned with saying goodbye to the backlot. But note the false ceiling on that backlot just above his head. *Author's collection*

Martin vehicle *Mr. Ricco* (1975; in 1975 only MGM was still making Dean Martin vehicles), apparently walked the property and decided it might work, with night shooting and swastikas covering the holes in the walls.

Greg Gormick, who was on the lot at the time working in the Music Department on *Pennies from Heaven*, recalls:

> I was there. They burned the very last of the backlot for what may have been the opening scenes of *The Formula*—re-dressed to look like Berlin under siege by the Russians in April, 1945. When I started *on Pennies from Heaven* it was suggested by studio security guard Ken Hollywood (that really was his name) that I park on Lot Two because there was no space for us grunts on Lot One. But nobody cared who parked in the "war zone" on Lot Two. Although many employees who didn't know this instead had to rent spaces from businesses and homeowners all around the lot. But when they were about to do a controlled burn on the remains of Lot Two, he told me I would have to make other parking arrangements as well.[1]

The resultant scenes were short, ending on-screen at the same time as the film's opening credits, and for obvious reasons these scenes were photographed through low light or firelight to hide the preexisting damage and the very much American nature of the sets. But for all of that, the sequence gave the whole film an unintentionally impressionistic opening that the rest of the film, shot on the studio's soundstages and on actual, more-expensive locations, might have well benefitted from. Elephants, supposedly from the liberated Berlin Zoo, were also brought in as "extras" and lent an apocalyptic, almost biblical verisimilitude to the affair. One can only wish someone had thought to include a fleeing lion as well.

The problem is—maybe—it didn't happen.

"It *definitely* didn't happen," Donnie Norden tells us. "I was there every day and every night during that period. I was working security there, and if any production had been doing that much prep and then bringing elephants onto the lot, trust me, I would have noticed."[2]

Okay. But what about this seemingly irrefutable December 20 memo? "In the film industry," Donnie tells us, "a *lot* of paperwork is generated in production offices over production issues that sometimes never play out. About the same time, *Meteor* (1979) scouted the backlot as well. But they never shot there. It was a go, and then they didn't go. I'm sure *The Formula* too considered Lot Two; maybe they even paid for it. But they didn't shoot there. The burning buildings that employees on lot one saw over there were for *Hero at Large* back in April. I'm certain of it."[3]

Unfortunately, the decades that have passed since 1980 have also seen the passing of many crew members who could confirm or deny Lot Two's participation in *The Formula*. The two crew members I was privileged to speak to, script supervisor Ana Maria Quintana and camera operator Mike Benson, both agreed that *The Formula* had shot on Lot One in the soundstages, as well as on local locations and in Europe, but could not recall venturing across the street onto the backlot, although neither would definitely rule it out.

Much of the production paperwork for the film is also cryptic, vague, or nonexistent. Call Sheets or Daily Production Reports would have quickly and definitively solved the mystery, although unfortunately, they no longer seem to exist. What *Formula* paperwork survives, however, does tell us that on January 24, 1980, specifically, the production was actually out shooting something called "Ext: Pine Forests"—although on what continent, backlot, or soundstage this vague vegetation was to be found is, frustratingly, again not indicated.

Watching the film doesn't help much either, at least it didn't for me. Donnie Norden, however, is certain that "the film itself, if you watch it, doesn't match up at all to

Steve Shagan, producer of *The Formula* (1980), tries to keep his star, George C. Scott, from walking off the set. *Photofest*

anything then on Lot Two."⁴ Actually watching the film, with its burning, darkly lit city streets, it's vaguely possible they could be in Culver City. But they could be in Germany too, which, after all, is exactly what a backlot is *supposed* to do.

Watching the film(s) is ultimately all we are left with. Taken together, our three suspects—*Hero at Large*, *Being There*, and *The Formula*—illustrate all too well Hollywood's yin and yang of the era. Sadly, the best, and best remembered of them, *Being There*, is the one not produced by MGM. The film had been Peter Sellers's dream project for a decade, and he managed to finally get it made, and subsequently win an Oscar nomination for it, only shortly before his death. Sadly, the impact of Sellers's character—an idiot who everyone mistakes as brilliant—has been blunted by subsequent decades when actual idiots can be elected as our leaders and none-too-bright movie characters like Rocky and Forrest Gump can become our screen heroes.

Hero at Large, on the other hand, is at the very least an example of latter-day mid-level studio efficiency. The film, like its appealing cast, can be charming enough, although one can't help but wish that, like in *Being There*, director Martin Davidson had bothered to question even occasionally whether Ritter was deserving of the adoration he gets as a vigilante hero.

After all, like Chance, John Ritter only inadvertently and accidently becomes someone of note. Perhaps it is appropriate, then, that the two last verified films to be shot on the MGM backlot are both about those who are taken for something they really aren't. That is also about as good a summation of the place where both were shot as one is likely to find.

The Formula is the odd man out here. If *Being There* has an edgy new-Hollywood vibe and *Hero at Large* represents efficient old-school factory filmmaking, *The Formula* is that same factory veering off the rails and then expensively running amok. Superstar Marlon Brando is billed second but has only three scenes. He was paid almost $3 million for his very limited contribution to the film. The actual star of that film is George C. Scott, who, with his $1.25 million salary, received a million and a half less than Brando and had to work a lot harder for it. John Gielgud, Marthe Keller, and Beatrice Straight also appear long enough to cash hefty paychecks for tiny roles. Dominique Sanda, originally cast in Keller's part, was ultimately paid her entire salary, reportedly $350,000, even though she does not appear in the movie. Director John G. Avildsen, who four years earlier had won an Oscar for *Rocky*, repeatedly clashed with the studio and with Scott, and then reportedly attempted to have his name taken off the final $13.2 million film, unsuccessfully.

The story involves a shadowy conspiracy involving Nazi Germany's long-suppressed creation of a synthetic fuel substitute. *The Formula* was conceived and shot during the worst of the 1979 oil crisis, which had seen the price of crude oil more than double in the United States. Unfortunately, at least for MGM, by the time the film came out, this crisis had topped out; oil prices had started to drop again, which effectively dated the film before it was even in theaters, and certainly contributed to its ultimate and not unexpected, except to MGM, box-office failure.

Avildsen's direction, spotty and compromised as it is, does have its moments. At the very end, Scott is in Los Angeles. "I'm not an [advisor] anymore, I'm just a consumer," he growls about being unable to stop the conspiracy. At this point the camera looks above and past him at seemingly a million cars, all bumper to bumper on a freeway overpass. And here the movie—just like the backlot, and just like *How the West Was Won* almost two decades earlier—concludes.

The audience is left to ponder whether it was all worth it.

48

Pennies from Heaven (1981)

There are several candidates for the dubious and gloomy honor of being the last ever MGM musical. The studio could yet decide to make another one, after all. And the book is not really closed on this subject; it might happen.

That said, it is a tenacious uphill climb to connect *The Broadway Melody* in 1929 with a proposed musical version of *Rocky* (which has already happened on the stage) that could presumably, and frighteningly, be made sometime in the twenty-first century. Personal memory, corporate memory, even financial memory as copyrights and trademarks expire, only stretches so far. Arthur Freed had tried into the early 1970s to get one last MGM musical, "Say It with Music," greenlit. But even then there remained little residual goodwill for a genre the new Hollywood, and specifically the new MGM, already regarded as hopelessly antiquated. So tragically and not at all surprisingly, "Say It with Music" never got said. For that reason, some refer to Freed's Oscar-winning *Gigi* (1958) as a last, tuneful, studio curtain call.

And yet, throughout the 1960s and 1970s, and even into the 1980s, the studio, as the vanguard of the form, continued to flirt with it. In the 1960s of course there was Elvis, Elvis, and more Elvis, as well as Freed's *Bells Are Ringing* (1960), *The Unsinkable Molly Brown* (1964), *The Singing Nun* (1966), *The Boy Friend* (1971), and even an out-of-tune remake of *Goodbye, Mr. Chips* (1969). The successful *That's Entertainment!* (1974) had no original songs, so it was more a grave marker than a placeholder for the artform.

The studios' biggest original success in the genre during this era, or rather slightly past this era, was *Fame* (1980)—about New York's legendary High School of Performing

Arts, which sometimes uncomfortably bridged the gap between "realistic" studio musicals like *The Great Caruso* (1951), where the music generally occurs naturally, and the more fantastical Freed fantasies, even if director Alan Parker here didn't know that was what he was doing at the time. The mix and the music worked perfectly, however. *Fame* was a major success and led to a profitable TV series that ran on NBC and in first-run syndication from 1982 to 1987. A follow-up, *Fame LA*, ran during the 1987–88 season as well. Although this reimaging was undistinguished, it did include a very meta sequence where the aspiring stars/students literally scamper to the top of the Hollywood sign. A 2009 theatrical remake and several more television versions (including, of course, a reality series) have since been attempted on the subject.

Commercial illustrator Bob Peak's *Pennies from Heaven* (1981) artwork, like the film itself, manages to make Steve Martin, Bernadette Peters, and a toe-tapping chorus line all seem like real downers. *Author's collection*

Yes, Giorgio, which came out in 1982, was an attempt to make a beloved operatic superstar, Luciano Pavarotti, into a beloved movie superstar. Originally the project was designed as a remake of *The Great Caruso*, although Pavarotti, sadly for studio accountants, turned out to be no Mario Lanza, and the film was a major commercial flop. *Yes, Giorgio* did actually film at the studio, however, unlike the New York–based *Fame*, which must have been heartening for any old-timers still haunting the lot at the time.

The gender-bending *Victor/Victoria*, also in 1982, was an altogether happier experience. Superstar Julie Andrews here made her belated debut in an MGM musical; she had already acted at the studio, in *The Americanization of Emily* (1964), but had not sung there. Her *Emily* costar James Garner returned to the fold as well. Andrews's husband, Blake Edwards, directed with his usual light touch, although the film, sadly, was shot in England. Much like *Fame*, *Victor/Victoria* has had a long afterlife as a stage production.

Yentl (1983), from the United Artists side of the company, came out the next year. Critics carped at the time about star/director Barbra Streisand's ego as reflected by her singing the entire score all by herself. She played, *Victor/Victoria*–like, a girl pretending to be a boy, which, according to those same critics, the then forty-year-old star was just a bit long in the tooth to pull off, whatever gender she was supposed to be. No one noted that Streisand was actually seven years younger than Julie Andrews, who a year earlier had received raves and an Oscar nomination for the same kind of stunt. Barbra's fans didn't care in the slightest about the critics' opinions, and *Yentl* too was successful at the box office.

Between the cross-dressing antics of *Victor/Victoria* and *Yentl* was *Pink Floyd—The Wall* (1982), an audacious visualization of the band's mega-successful album. Although *The Wall* tells a story, it does not really fit into the larger whole of MGM musicals. Rather it sits more easily alongside concert films, which MGM or United Artists had recently been involved in, like *Elvis On Tour* (1972) and *The Last Waltz* (1976), and with music videos, which were then at their peak in popularity on television.

More traditional, and much later on, was *De-Lovely* (2004), a musical biography of composer Cole Porter, which again was largely filmed in England but was (partially) set in Hollywood and even at MGM. The picture was a passion project for producer Irwin Winkler, whose relationship with the studio went back to 1966. Kevin Kline played Porter, following in the footsteps of Cary Grant, who had portrayed the composer in *Night and Day* (1946) at Warner Bros, although it must be said that both Kline and Grant were probably more overtly debonair, and certainly taller, than the five-foot-six Porter actually was. *De-Lovely* was a minor commercial and critical success for Winkler, Kline, and for the studio.

For the most fitting send-off for the MGM musical, however, one has to go back again to 1981 and to an audacious oddity called *Pennies from Heaven.* The property began as a British-made, British-set 1978 miniseries about a 1930s sheet music salesman whose gray, working-class life keeps inexplicably slipping into the middle of Hollywood-style musical numbers. Or maybe he just imagines it is. The series was created by visionary writer Dennis Potter, who was brought to Hollywood to create a feature film based on the material.

At the time MGM was ever looking for financial stability, as had been the case for decades by this point. But the studio, admirably but perhaps ultimately unwisely, was also in search of some artistic respectability. In the early 1980s their slate of pictures included such (hopefully) prestigious releases as *The Formula* (1980), *Rich and Famous* (1981), and *Whose Life Is It Anyway?* (also 1981). But they also tried to mine their own past and their own library during this period with a remake of *The Champ* (1979) and a very belated sequel to 1942's *National Velvet* titled *International Velvet*, which finally came out in 1978. *Pennies from Heaven* would have seemed, then, to be a combination of both these strategies—an Oscar-baiting art film, but with elements of a traditional old-school MGM commodity as well.

In order to bring in a contemporary and younger audience, however, the studio hedged its bets by casting that wild and crazy comedian and newly-minted film star Steve Martin, who was then coming off a hit film (for another studio), *The Jerk* (1979). His costar, also from *The Jerk*, and also then from real life, was Bernadette Peters. Director Herbert Ross already had a relationship with the studio, having most recently directed *The Goodbye Girl* in 1977.

But good intentions only carried so far. The problems began when Potter was forced to rewrite his well-regarded script, repeatedly. And as was their habit at the time, the front office interfered and tinkered with the production throughout the shoot, which was largely on the lot, almost in sight of the Thalberg Building, where the front office was still located.

Unfortunately, the final result, at least to those in that front office, was not really worth the trouble it caused—the picture was a colossal box-office failure. Steve Martin went on *The Tonight Show* when it opened and rather desperately ran a clip from the film of himself lip-syncing—to a female voice. The audience, convinced that the film was a comedy, laughed. Neither Martin nor host Johnny Carson tried to convince the audience that this wasn't the case.

Critics were more respectful, although by no means ecstatic. Many of the trade reviews tiresomely remarked about how the film was only recouping "Pennies" for its studio, and that those pennies, even if they were from heaven, still wouldn't buy them very much.

Ultimately the film finally and forever closed the loop of MGM musicals, at least of those MGM musicals developed in-house. "The old MGM is dead," James Aubrey had repeatedly said. *Pennies from Heaven* ultimately proved him right.

The film itself, not that it ultimately mattered, is boldly audacious and bleakly uncompromising. Ross and Potter should be complimented for this, considering the amount of interference the film attracted during its production. Some fans of Potter prefer the British miniseries, but Americanizing the material does bring the songs home to where they were born. Although the irony of MGM, of all studios, subverting the material in this way is probably largely unintentional.

Bernadette Peters capably stomps out "Love Is Good for Anything That Ails You." *Photofest*

The contrast between the characters' bleak lives—Martin tries to sell frivolous sheet music in a Depression America where people can't even afford food, while Peters topples from school teacher to prostitute—is of course laid out in stark contrast with those toe-tapping numbers. For budgetary reasons, the original series was largely restricted to the characters lip-syncing to old records. But the movie could afford to indulge in full-scale "Hollywood" production numbers, and to do it on the very stages where many of those original numbers had actually been recorded. This is an irony that Ross either does not seem to understand or does not seem to know how to comment on.

Greg Gormick, a music advisor on the film, remembers that the director kept having him screen old musicals for "inspiration." Unfortunately, Ross, much like Robert Z. Leonard in *Dancing Lady* almost fifty years earlier, is ultimately only able to give us a couple Busby Berkeley–inspired kaleidoscope/crane shots, even though he possessed a musical (both ballet and Broadway) background.

Pennies from Heaven's director Herbert Ross and production designer Ken Adam meticulously (and expensively) re-created famous Depression-era artwork, such as Edward Hopper's *Nighthawks*, for the film. But to what end? *Photofest*

The relative lack of innovation in the musical numbers was not really the fault of the director, however. In the 1980s, as noted earlier, there was no longer an assembly line to create such numbers. MGM now lacked that long-standing army of technicians, in place and on payroll, who only worked on such numbers. Consequently, everything had to be innovated, created, or re-created, and completely from scratch. One can only wonder what the real Busby Berkeley, Arthur Freed, or Gene Kelly could have done with the same material in their and their studio's prime.

As a director, Ross seems to feel he is on firmer ground re-creating various Edward Hopper and Reginald Marsh paintings as backgrounds than he appears to be with the musical numbers. The technique is interesting, and the re-creations are dead on. But that said, unlike in the musical numbers, where the characters are possessed (or imagine they are possessed) by a better world, Hopper and Marsh's Depression-era landscapes represent exactly what these characters want to *escape*. The audience is apparently encouraged to recognize these *tableaux vivants* when they show up. Yet if that audience does so, the real world, like the musical one, becomes a fantasy landscape as well. Which kind of defeats the purpose.

Credit where due, Martin and Peters are troupers. They acquit themselves well enough with the material, although both are ultimately defeated by that material. Watching them dance, and dance well, one wonders if when possessed by those old songs, they are even *supposed* to perform them well or as soulless robots. The film never tells us.

It is not Martin's or Peters' earnest hoofing but rather "guest star" Christopher Walken's tap number, slyly performed to Cole Porter's "Let's Misbehave," that steals the show. Walken's adroit footwork even received praise from Fred Astaire, who otherwise hated *Pennies from Heaven*. Astaire's animosity toward the film could not have been helped when the aged star finally saw the whole film and noticed that MGM had incorporated a lengthy clip of him and Ginger Rogers, from RKO's *Follow the Fleet* (1936), and had neither informed him they were doing so nor asked his permission when they did.

Christopher Walken had recently had a very bad experience at the studio while working on the ill-fated *Brainstorm* (1983). His return to MGM must have been much happier for the actor. Although, sadly, Walken would not appear in another big-budget musical until 2007's *Hairspray*. His unquestioned affinity for such material has since been largely underutilized. Had Christopher Walken been a star in 1936, he might have had a very different career. All of which makes one wish for a world with more music, and more musicals, in it.

Just as the characters in *Pennies from Heaven* do.

49

Running Scared (1986)

The first feature film produced entirely for and at MGM under that name was *He Who Gets Slapped*, which shot for thirty-seven days in Culver City in 1924 and was successfully released in December of that year. Sixty-two years later, the last MGM film to roll off that very same assembly line was *Running Scared*, which shot for ninety-seven days in 1985 and was successfully released in June 1986. A few months later, on Friday, October 17, of that year, MGM sold its studio to Lorimar Telepictures, and it was all over. The announcement that it was all over came in the form of a memo, circulated among the staff via interoffice mail, which coldly said, "Over the weekend, Metro-Goldwyn-Mayer was purchased by Lorimar Productions. The studio will now be known as Lorimar Telepictures."

However, a bit of doggerel by an anonymous employee was even better circulated—copied and posted next to water coolers a few days later:

> There was a land of Cavalier Writers and Artists. That was called old MGM.
> Here in this pretty world, gallantry took its last bow. Here was the last ever to be seen of knights and Their ladies fair.
> Look for it only on the silver screen.
> For it is no more than a dream remembered. A Hollywood studio gone with the wind.

Employees, even if they had seen the writing on the wall, were stunned. "It's the end of an era," Ricci Rhodes, a cashier in the commissary, said, "and we've seen part of it.[1]

The company itself survived of course. Metro Goldwyn Mayer moved its staff and its brand to a glass office complex across the street, where that staff could still see their old studio and, for a little while, the 105-foot-long MGM sign, complete with its ironically-roaring Leo the Lion, on the roof of Stage 6. That sign was removed, along with a smaller one under it promoting *Running Scared* in November. The title *Running Scared* and even the words "running scared," under Leo's picture, in the studio's last days and even as it ran forever from its longtime home, were certainly apt.

"It was so very sad to see that big lion come down," remembers script supervisor Ana Maria Quintana, who was there. "I'm a Leo too."[2]

Poster art for *Running Scared* (1986) featured Gregory Hines and Billy Crystal as two cops trying to get out of town, just like the studio that made it. *Photofest*

The big sign wasn't the only thing that had to be removed. The name "MGM" had been stenciled or painted or sculpted onto walls and above doors and on studio maps and equipment across the lot to the point where it was impossible to eradicate it all. Particularly poignant was the day in which the two lions that had stood vigil outside the Thalberg Building for decades had to be removed. Eventually they were salvaged by actor Larry Hagman, of all people, who took them to his home in Ojai.

Lorimar's unenviable task of removing MGM from MGM was made harder by the attitude of the employees, many of whom had been on the lot for decades and retained their loyalty for the previous regime. The staffers who kept their jobs on that lot, and some two hundred others, would ultimately be laid off entirely, then proceeded—defiantly if passive-aggressively—to leave, even preserve the name "MGM," often with

Billy Crystal, Gregory Hines, and Joe Pantoliano are most definitely not singing in the rain. *Author's collection*

accompanying Leo artwork, wherever they could get away with it in their workplace, sometimes for decades. To this day, many set lighting units above the stages still say, in now-faded lettering, "MGM." They are there if you care to look.

As the stunned MGM employees went home, were repurposed, or reassigned to new quarters, some just couldn't believe what was happening. Shirley Englander, who had been on the lot for forty-two years at that point, told the *Los Angeles Times* in November, "It's sad the way the place has just been sort of carved up. It was once just a big happy family here."[3]

The studio commissary, where some of the staff had worked for decades, was hit particularly hard by the transition when Lorimar announced they would lease the operations of the restaurant to an outside company, meaning employees there would then become "outside contractors" and thus lose as much as $4 an hour in wages. Studio janitors, treated even worse, were offered a take-it-or-leave-it $8 an hour pay cut. "That was embarrassing, man," said Clarence Rogers, who had been employed there for eight years and who disgustingly told the *Los Angeles Times*, "Boy, am I glad I didn't buy into that house."[4]

Other employees who had not been on the lot for as long were affected as well. "I must have been one of the last people hired before it all ended," remembers future script coordinator David Bowen. "I was hired to work in MGM's mailroom just six months prior to Lorimar's acquisition. I'll always remember how proud I was to see my name in the studio newspaper, *MGM/UA Exclusive Story*, when I was hired. No one knew it would be, maybe, the last issue of that newsletter they would ever publish." After the acquisition, Bowen, who would be lucky enough to land a job at Lorimar, recalls, "I just remember the sadness everyone felt. Employees were wearing black armbands, including me. They hung a black bow over the entrance to the Costume Department. It was a sad, mournful time on the lot."[5]

The studio's existing physical resources had to be redistributed as well as its human resources. And once again there would be no room for these assets in an office complex. Expensive production equipment, costumes, props, lights, camera cranes, were largely abandoned, but the legendary film library could not be left behind. It would have to be removed from the studio's cavernous film vaults to go . . . somewhere. This did not physically happen until May 1987, after Ted Turner acquired the library and moved it to a nearby, cheaper storage complex on Jefferson Boulevard.

It's hard to really look at *Running Scared* outside of the extraneous fact that, like the (superior) *He Who Gets Slapped*, the film is more significant as a monument than a movie. Although, to be fair, as a movie it is not without its peculiarities and charms. Director Peter Hyams, who had recently directed *2010: The Year We Make Contact* for the studio, was apparently attracted to *Running Scared* because, although it was a gritty cop film, it also had a lot of humor, which he was interested in after his self-serious recent films. Gary DeVore's screenplay was originally about two older policemen on the verge of retirement, but Hyams and the studio wanted to attract younger stars and younger audiences. So Billy Crystal, following his breakout roles in the TV series *Soap* and *Saturday Night Live*, was eventually signed. This would be the actor/comedian's first leading role in a big-budget feature film.

Crystal's (top-billed) costar was Gregory Hines, who at the time was primarily known as one of the best tap dancers in the world. His own feature debut, 1981's *History of the World: Part 1*, in which he deftly played a role written for Richard Pryor, had proved that Hines had the comic chops to hold his own opposite scene-stealer Crystal.

Their fortunate, and probably accidental, chemistry and camaraderie proved to be the highlight of the movie. Crystal fires off one funny, sometimes adlibbed wisecrack after another. It's easy to see here how big a star he would soon become and why. Hines, although lacking his partner's street cred as a comic, makes up for it with lots of obvious charm and sad, Buster Keaton eyes. Hines would die in 2003.

November 1986. The new Lorimar Telepictures sign is on the roof of Stage 6. Leo the Lion is still there too, but not for long. *Marc Wanamaker/Bison Archives*

The rest of the cast is practically a roll call of 1980s crime film types, including frequent wise guys Steven Bauer, Dan Hedaya, and Jimmy Smits. Joe Pantoliano, "Joey Pants," is particularly amusing as a two-bit hood named, of course, "Snake," who exits (slithers?) out of the story all too soon, because he has a lot of rapport with the two leads.

The story still involves two buddy cops who hope to retire to Florida, although here it's burnout rather than age that is the motivation for a career change. But naturally, one last case has to be unraveled first.

Some of the filming took place in Chicago, although much of the "snow" for the Illinois scenes had to be simulated when the weather there would not cooperate. Hyams then came to California and shot the interiors at the soon-to-be-no-longer MGM Studios.

Upon release, *Running Scared* was a moderate box office success. It earned $5,227,757 on its opening weekend and eventually reached a worldwide gross of $38,500,726. That was good enough for the studio to desire a sequel, which, as often happened at MGM during this era, never quite came together.

What makes the film interesting today, however, aside from the bittersweet significance of it being the last film made at MGM while it was still MGM, is its significance as being one of the first of a genre that has become hugely successful and influential—at least for other studios. That genre could be called the "mismatched-comic-buddy-police-film." There had been other comedies involving the police, of course, going back to the Keystone Kops at least. But they were just that. They were comedies. Paramount's *48 Hrs.* (1982) is usually credited with being the originator of this sort of mostly serious procedural, which still mined big laughs off the comic interplay of its stars. Significantly, *48 Hrs.'* worldwide gross was $78,868,508, almost twice that of *Running Scared.* *Beverly Hills Cop* (1984), also from Paramount, would follow, earning an astounding $316,360,478. *Running Scared* should have performed in their league, as it had all the ingredients: action, comedy, chemistry. But like its studio at the time, at the end of the day, it just fell a little short.

Watching *Running Scared* today, even while being mildly amused, it's hard not to notice how the thing is also chock-full of then-topical, now-dated cultural shoutouts, mostly by Crystal, who even slips in a still-welcome Arnold Schwarzenegger–accented "I'll be back" at one point. Was this the first ever on-screen callout to 1984's *The Terminator*—a film to which MGM would later acquire distribution rights? That said, it should also be noted here that *48 Hrs.* and *Beverly Hills Cop* are now showing their age too. Has anyone actually watched *those* films recently?

Like those better remembered titles, *Running Scared* is also notably rampant with dated 1980s technology—cassette players and cinder block–sized cell phones, for example. It also includes now-nostalgic brand names like Pan American Airlines . . . and Metro Goldwyn Mayer Studios.

50

Get Shorty (1995)

By any standards, the low-water mark for MGM came in 1990 when, for $1.25 billion, Kirk Kerkorian sold the studio to Giancarlo Parretti, a former waiter and shady Italian financier with connections to the Italian Mafia. He had allegedly earned his bones as a gangster from one Don Graziano Verzotto. Verzotto had coached Parretti on the intricacies of organized crime and then trusted him to manage his business interests while in exile from Italy due to threats of arrest by the Italian government.

On the surface, Giancarlo Parretti was a rather comical figure—stout, prone to wearing too-flashy suits and wide neckties, and, perhaps heralding back to his days as a waiter, constantly trying to offer food to his associates, leading one of those associates to later refer to him, although not to his face, as "an Italian Ralph Kramden."[1] But there was nothing comical about Parretti's cut-and-burn business practices, or his volcanic temper.

Parretti was interested in the movie industry, and not the stopgap Italian version but Hollywood, with its trappings, its rituals, and its starlets. To that end he acquired the Cannon Group, an ambitious production company there in 1989 and folded it into his own company, Pathé Communications. But that was not enough. The big fish, the biggest fish in Hollywood, in name if not then in size, was of course MGM, which Kerkorian, apparently more than comfortable working with organized crime figures from his years in Las Vegas, all too quickly agreed to sell to him.

Parretti's regime as a Hollywood player was a disaster, even by the low bar previous MGM owners had positioned there for him. He brought over a capable Cannon executive, Alan Ladd Jr. (son of the movie star), to run the company but then proceeded to interfere with him every step of the way. Furthermore, Parretti possessed neither the patience nor the tact to be a studio boss. He insulted and repelled the male talent and chased even the most powerful female stars in the world around his big desk as if they were starlets, ever incensed that they would not let themselves be cornered by him, no matter what fabulous roles he offered them in return.

Unsurprisingly to no one, except maybe Parretti himself, in June 1991 Crédit Lyonnais, the respected French bank that had financed Parretti's grand Hollywood adventure, seized control of the studio's assets and sued its owner for gross misappropriation of their funds, both in California and in Delaware, where the studio had been incorporated back in 1924. The

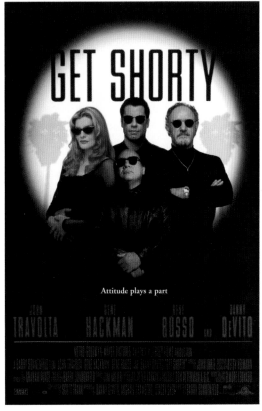

The successful and Hollywood-set *Get Shorty* (1995) contained numerous callouts to its studio's recent, and well-publicized, waltz with the Italian Mafia. *Photofest*

then-CEO of said company eventually fled the country, an indignity the patriotic-above-all-else L. B. Mayer certainly had never had to face. Giancarlo Parretti is, as of last reports, living in exile somewhere in Europe, having, like his mentor Graziano Verzotto, received an in absentia jail sentence, which he has yet to serve, for misuse of corporate funds.

In 1995 MGM, then still on life support via Crédit Lyonnais, produced a film called *Get Shorty*—based on a well-respected 1990 Elmore Leonard novel but certainly inspired by the company's recent, reluctant brush with the Mob. Ironically, the story deals with getting a single film greenlit at a studio, not with taking over that studio itself, which proves, or maybe not, that in Hollywood anyway, truth really is stranger than fiction.

Get Shorty starred John Travolta as Chili Palmer, a Mafia enforcer who comes to Los Angeles on a job and quickly realizes he is smarter than any of the Tinseltown

The charismatic John Travolta and Rene Russo help make immorality fun in Get Shorty. Photofest

power players he meets there. Consequently, he maneuvers and bluffs and schemes his way into the Hollywood hierarchy, and ultimately ends up becoming part of that hierarchy.

Travolta, then flush from the recent success of *Pulp Fiction* (1994), hadn't wanted to play Chili Palmer, feeling, perhaps, that the part was too easy in that the character was basically a more benign version of the dangerous thug he had played in the earlier film. It couldn't have been lost on the actor, either, that both characters are gangsters who just happen to also be ardent movie fans. Eventually he relented, and so John Travolta, for the second time in as many years, did the impossible by making being a film nerd also seem cool. There is no payoff for his character's movie fanaticism in *Pulp Fiction*, however, other than giving that film's director, Quentin Tarantino, a mouthpiece for his far-reaching views on cinema. But Chili Palmer, who is presented as knowing more about the movies than anyone he meets in Hollywood, uses this knowledge to eventually become a player there.

Unlike independent maverick Tarantino, *Get Shorty*'s director, Barry Sonnenfeld, is very much in the mold of studio directors of earlier eras, who managed to put a

The former MGM and current Sony/Columbia Studios was an ironic and bittersweet location for *Get Shorty.*
Author's collection

personal stamp on any sort of project in any genre, although quirky comedies like *The Addams Family* and *Men in Black* franchises have proven to be his specialty. Sonnenfeld's light touch is evident in his affectionate handling of material and characters who, if one stops to think about it, are amoral, profane, and violent, yet somehow likable. Chili Palmer, for example, is a street-smart lowlife, not really unlike, well, Giancarlo Parretti. But unlike Parretti, Chili dresses better and has an affection for Hollywood, and Hollywood people, beyond just trying to get whatever he can wrestle from them. Undoubtably, Frank Mancuso, who had recently replaced Alan Ladd Jr. as MGM CEO, and who would greenlight other studio hits like *GoldenEye* (1995) and *The Birdcage* (1996), wished, like Ladd before him surely must have, that Parretti had been half the movie lover that Chili Palmer turns out to be.

Yet ultimately, the most "meta" thing about the very meta production of *Get Shorty* was, possibly, unintentional. The climax of the film is an epilogue showing the production of the film that Chili and his friends ultimately get to make. The movie ends with Chili and company walking out the doors of a soundstage and the camera pulling up to reveal . . . MGM. Well, Sony Pictures Studio, actually, which is what the former MGM had eventually been renamed after that studio had been displaced.

One has to wonder. In 1995, in order to show a film being made in corporate Hollywood, MGM could have rented any suitable soundstage in town. There was no incentive whatsoever to go to Sony in particular. They could also have rented a stage in Canada or New Mexico and then *said* it was in Hollywood; no one outside the industry would have cared or known the difference. But they didn't. Instead, for this one film, MGM returned, specifically, to MGM.

In 1996, shortly after *Get Shorty*'s successful release, Crédit Lyonnais sold MGM back to Kirk Kerkorian, this time for a "reduced" $870 million. Kirk would keep the company until 2004, when a consortium of investors—which, ironically enough, included Sony—purchased it from him, this time for $4.8 billion, although Sony's actual involvement in MGM's business trajectory turned out to be minimal.

The following year this new iteration of MGM produced a *Get Shorty* sequel called *Be Cool*, which featured Travolta's Chili Palmer now taking on the music industry. This time the film was neither a critical nor commercial success, although that didn't stop the company from returning to Elmore Leonard territory one more time with a *Get Shorty* TV series, which ran for two seasons starting in 2017. The series was set in Hollywood, of course, but this time much of it *was* shot in New Mexico.

In 2021 MGM was purchased by retail giant Amazon for $8.45 billion. Amazon had recently consolidated their Los Angeles operations, in Culver City of all places, and like Giancarlo Parretti had been looking for inroads into the entertainment industry there. After all, as *Get Shorty*, and Chili Palmer, had told us, "What is the point of living in L.A. if you're not in the movie business?"

Appendix: Fifty More Times the Lion Roared

The problem with making a list of anything isn't those items that make that list, it's those that for one reason or another fail to do so. Therefore, in order to make up for any inadvertent omissions, slights, or sacrileges, what follows is a *second* fifty notable, for one reason or another, MGM films, each with a brief description/explanation justifying its inclusion here.

For this particular half hundred, however, we have loosened the requirements for making the cut just a bit. Once again, a film's ripple effect through studio and popular culture is a major consideration for inclusion, but an attempt has also been made to make up for past wrongs by including films that highlight a particular series, trend, or star that may have inadvertently been short-shrifted before. Included as well are a few one-off pictures that should have done more for their creators, their studio, or posterity than they did; that time has rather unfairly forgotten; or that were unfairly remembered only after the fact and only after it was too late to make a difference.

Most of the films below, even aside from their historic significance, are well worth watching, by the way. A few are masterpieces, and even the ones that fail for one reason or another are well worth a look as examples of a larger trend or, yes, even on their own merits. Although they don't all, I should hasten to add, contribute equally to the concept of "art for the sake of art," a few certainly do. You can decide for yourself which ones they are.

1. *The Crowd* (1927). King Vidor's silent masterpiece, like his *The Big Parade*, deals with an individual's sometimes reluctant assimilation into a larger collective, here

represented by James Murray's little-guy battles against corporate New York rather than the earlier film's depiction of integration through military might. This Vidor film also anticipates later corporate America takedowns like *The Man in the Gray Flannel Suit*, *The Apartment*, and TV's *Mad Men*, although the irony of corporate Hollywood condemning corporate America is just as ridiculous today as it was in 1927. Incidentally, Murray himself was an early victim of that big brother omnipotence. He became a homeless alcoholic and died in 1936, an apparent suicide.

2. *Show People* (1928). Marion Davies was an important star on early MGM rosters. Most of her films, however, were period pieces, which failed to show the very contemporary (in the 1920s) Davies at her best but which her mentor-boyfriend, millionaire William Randolph Hearst, seemed to prefer. Fortunately, King Vidor's (yes, him again) *Show People* bucked this trend and gave the ever-game star one of her better roles, as well as the opportunity to send up Hollywood without all the usual angst studios, then as well as now, seem to think is necessary when dealing with themselves as subject. MGM was not then much into angst, however, and would buck the trend and return to this formula later in *Bombshell* (1933) and *Going Hollywood* (again in 1933 and again with Davies). They were still milking the happy Hollywood trope in *Singin' in the Rain* (1951) and beyond. Bonus: Marion contributes amusing impressions of several Hollywood stars, and several Hollywood stars contribute amusing impressions of themselves.

Show People (1928) is one of the best movies built around making movies, and one of the best movies built around Marion Davies. *Photofest*

3. *Anna Christie* (1930). Garbo Talks! Which alone is perhaps enough to get this one a slot on the list. The film itself is a bit of a slog, although when the Divine One enters and tells a bartender to "Gimme a whisky, ginger ale on the side, and don't be stingy, baby!" a viewer, now or in 1930, can hardly help but be aware that cinema history is occurring before one's eyes, and ears.

4. *Manhattan Melodrama* (1934). A good enough gangster film, and the cast—Clark Gable, Myrna Loy, and William Powell—keep things lively enough. But its place in history comes courtesy of real-life gangster John Dillinger, who crept out of hiding to see this film, partially based on his life, and was gunned down in Chicago by FBI agents as he left the theater.

5. *The Thin Man* (1934) MGM's most prestigious film series rather ironically began with this low-budget, twelve-day programmer courtesy of the ever-game Woody Van Dyke and went on to become an audience favorite and led to numerous sequels and William Powell–Myrna Loy team-ups—and has influenced smart romantic banter between men and women, on-screen and off, ever since. The plot here, as in its five sequels, involves solving a mystery, although the sleuthing is really just something to do while this most glamorous of couples trade innuendos and consume copious amounts of alcohol, Prohibition having been repealed only six months before the first film's release.

Myrna Loy and William Powell as Nick and Nora Charles, seen with their dog, Asta, in *The Thin Man* (1934). Doubtlessly, one of them has just said something clever and sophisticated. *Photofest*

6. *David Copperfield* (1935). Arguably the best of David O. Selznick's big-budget literary adaptations, which he would continue to make even after he struck out on his own the same year as an independent producer. It's worth noting that, also that same year, before departing MGM, the tireless Selznick somehow gave us definitive versions of *A Tale of Two Cities* and *Anna Karenina* as well! All

In *Mutiny on the Bounty* (1935), the ship is seen making port in far-flung Tahiti. Unfortunately, an MGM film crew is already there waiting for them, and the supposed South Seas are being impersonated by Catalina Island, twenty-nine miles off the coast of Los Angeles. *Photofest*

are worth a look as examples of a genre that is largely extinct on the big screen in the twenty-first century.

7. *Mutiny on the Bounty* (1935). The winner of 1935's Best Picture Oscar brought the studio back to the South Seas by convincingly re-creating it on the backlot and in Catalina. Remembered today for terrific performances and a thrilling maritime story, the film also contains one of the most unlikely yet touching Christmas scenes ever filmed, with "God Rest Ye Merry, Gentlemen" performed simultaneously by the mutineers in Tahiti and merry carolers back home in snowy England, 9,500 miles away.

8. *A Night at the Opera* (1935). Before the 1960s, when the Marx Brothers were rediscovered by college audiences, this was universally considered to be their masterwork, and one of the greatest comedies ever made, owing to Thalberg's lavish production and to a plot that made the zany brothers sympathetic and gave them motivation for their lunacy. Today many consider those attributes to instead be liabilities, flaws that blunt the free-spirited anarchy of their humor. But come on,

does that make them any less funny? And is it really MGM's fault? Maybe instead it is the fault of us, and of the anarchic times in which we now live?

9. *Rose-Marie* (1936). The most famous and parodied of the eight on-screen musical pairings of Jeanette MacDonald and Nelson Eddy, and perhaps the best one to seek out if you want to sample their musical wares, although the couple's undoubted vocal and physical chemistry made even their weakest vehicles, well, sing. Woody Van Dyke directs, again proving there was no genre that guy couldn't handle. James Murray, of *The Crowd*, had starred (with Joan Crawford) in an earlier 1929 version, and supposedly he has a bit part here as well. A third remake in 1954 added nothing but color and Cinemascope to the mix. Although Howard Keel in the Murray/Eddy role did at least look good in that red Mountie uniform.

10. *The Great Ziegfeld* (1936). MGM scored its second Best Picture Oscar in a row for this gargantuan musical biography of impresario Florenz Ziegfeld Jr., which, just maybe, L. B. Mayer saw a little bit of his own life story in as well. Semi-sequels *Ziegfeld Girl* (1941) and *Ziegfeld Follies* (1946) would follow.

The lovely ladies of the chorus in *The Great Ziegfeld* (1936) offered champagne and skin to Depression-weary crowds.
Photofest

11. *Saratoga* (1937). Jean Harlow died while this film was in production, and the studio completed filming using a double (sometimes rather obviously) named Mary Dees. Ultimately the film managed to triumph over the perception that audiences were not interested in "last performances" by becoming a financial heavy-hitter. Decades later, MGM tried the same thing with *Brainstorm* (1983), which they released after star Natalie Wood's drowning. But this time that old adage held true—audiences stayed away.

12. *Marie Antoinette* (1938). Norma Shearer, after the death of husband Irving Thalberg, here had one last Irving Thalberg–styled hurrah under the all-Mayer regime as the doomed French queen, although she would remain at the studio until 1942, with predictably diminishing returns. So it is this film that marks the symbolic end of the Thalberg era. Norma would die in the Motion Picture Country Home in Woodland Hills, California, in 1983. In her declining years, she was remembered by the staff there for calling most of the male visitors to her bedside "Irving."

13. *Young Dr. Kildare* (1938). The first of nine Dr. Kildare films, which with assorted spinoffs would run until 1945. MGM would also make two TV series from the property—the 1961–1966 hit with Richard Chamberlain and a syndicated edition that ran less successfully in 1972. This original, with Lew Ayres, was the template for all of the good doctor's adventures to follow. Kildare DNA can also be found in other hospital-based properties, including MGM's own *Medical Center* (TV 1969–1976). Costar Lionel Barrymore, here and in later episodes, rolls off with the movie as the crusty, wheelchair-bound Dr. Gillespie.

14. *Goodbye, Mr. Chips* (1939). One of the most touching and well-remembered films of MGM's golden era was shot at the MGM British studios. Star Robert Donat, who possessed one of the finest voices of any actor in history, also achieved an unprecedented level of Hollywood

In *Goodbye, Mr. Chips* (1939) Terry Kilburn is seen pouring a spot of tea for an elderly Robert Donat. *Photofest*

stardom for an actor who never actually made a movie in Hollywood; lifelong health issues kept him from following other "British colony" actors to California. Donat's very odd, illness-plagued and erratic career peaked here; he won the Best Actor Oscar, beating out Clark Gable for *Gone with the Wind*. One wonders what would have happened had fate allowed Donat to go west, as Greer Garson, his costar here, would so successfully do.

The film itself, like the sad Mr. Donat, is wonderful, sentimental, charming, and unforgettable—although, frankly, my dear, Gable's Rhett Butler should have won the Oscar. Gable didn't because the studio supported Donat instead, reasoning that *Mr. Chips'* box office would benefit more from the win. Robert Donat's last words on-screen, delivered in that unforgettable voice, were in *The Inn of the Sixth Happiness* (1958): "We shall not see each other again, I think."

15. *The Philadelphia Story* (1940). Katharine Hepburn, who after a string of underperformers got herself labeled "box office poison," came back in a big way by securing the rights to a Broadway hit and then offering that vehicle to Hollywood, but only with her attached as its star.

L. B. Mayer took the bait, agreed to her choice of costars (Cary Grant *and* James Stewart), and then proceeded to give himself, her, them, and the studio one of their best, and best-remembered, vehicles. Audiences approved too. In 1956 MGM offered audiences a musical remake, *High Society*. Audiences once again approved.

16. *Lassie Come Home* (1943). Another of the studio's most-beloved successes is famous for introducing both a displaced collie named Lassie and a violet-eyed girl named Elizabeth Taylor to wide audiences, both of whom would affect the studio, and its bottom line, for decades. If you want to see only one Elizabeth Taylor film and you are over twelve, this might not be the one to seek out. But if you can tolerate only one *Lassie* film, whatever your age, come home to this one.

The "Lassie" franchise began as a 1938 novella by Eric Knight. Filmed in 1943, the collie's adventures would eventually be chronicled in other books, more movies, TV and radio programs, comics, and even a 2005 video game. *Photofest*

17. *Gaslight* (1944). This film and the (similarly set) *Waterloo Bridge* and *Dr Jekyll and Mr. Hyde* were all remakes of earlier, other studios' films, which MGM bought and then suppressed so as not to compete with their own adaptations. This regrettable and much-bemoaned censorship ultimately kept the original versions out of the public eye for decades, although in two out of three cases, the MGM version ultimately turned out to be the better one. (Paramount's 1931 *Dr Jekyll and Mr. Hyde*, with an Oscar-anointed Fredric March, did best MGM's 1941 Spencer Tracy version for thrills.) MGM's *Gaslight* was not only a suspenseful psychological thriller on its own, but its title also added a word to the English language—much used recently for manipulating a person or group into questioning their judgment or sanity. Alan Alda, for an episode of the *M*A*S*H* TV show, once did a spot-on impression of Charles Boyer, here gaslighting Ingrid Bergman, so there's also that.

18. *National Velvet* (1944). Elizabeth Taylor, then still best known for *Lassie Come Home*, returns, this time with a horse rather than a dog as the center of her obsession. More than one critic has remarked that the way Taylor's eyes spark and glisten here when talking about her horse is the exact same look she later affected when fixating on her on- (and off-) screen leading men. Mickey Rooney is her (human) costar here, although clearly, a new generation of juveniles, symbolized by Taylor, were now in the ascent. One can almost see Rooney fading into unwelcome Technicolor nostalgia here. *International Velvet*, a less than timely sequel, without either Taylor or Rooney, would follow in 1978.

A behind-the-scenes costume test for a young Elizabeth Taylor in *National Velvet* (1944). *Photofest*

19. *The Clock* (1945). While Mickey Rooney struggled with post-puberty and postwar obsolescence, his many-times costar Judy Garland here blossoms into a leading lady who does

not need to sing or dance to dominate the screen. She and Robert Walker play a couple who find love in New York's Grand Central Station. Winsome and wonderful.

The Yearling (1946) taught audiences, and young Claude Jarman Jr. (pictured), the fine points of deer raising. *Photofest*

20. *The Yearling* (1946). The last of MGM's influential trilogy of Technicolor animal odysseys (following *Lassie Come Home* and *National Velvet*) is more mature and tragic than the others, having been based on a Pulitzer Prize–winning novel about a little boy in rural Florida and his doomed fawn. The production was troubled and expensive, with Spencer Tracy originally cast in the lead. Gregory Peck, who ultimately played Tracy's role, is miscast but effective anyway, as is the rest of the cast, both two and four-legged. However, the film's large production costs would largely keep the studio away from non-Lassie-related animal films thereafter.

21. *Annie Get Your Gun* (1950). The studio's (then) invulnerability was proven, as if proof was (then) needed, by their callously firing Judy Garland—yes, Judy Garland, who had been on the payroll for more than a decade—and replacing her with Betty Hutton, and still being rewarded with a hit film. Although, in hindsight, we can see that the era in which the studio could do this was very soon to end.

In 1950 the Loews State Theater in New York premiered *Annie Get Your Gun*. The theater would be demolished in 1987. *Photofest*

Fred Astaire most unforgettably dances on the ceiling in *Royal Wedding* (1951). *Photofest*

22. *Royal Wedding* (1951). Stanley Donen's winning streak (recently inaugurated with *On the Town*) continued here. Jane Powell and Fred Astaire starred and danced, and so the world seemed, for the moment, to still be a good place to live in. Worth checking out today for the sheer amount of talent that routinely was pumped into this sort of thing. And for Astaire's gravity-defying dance on a ceiling.

23. *The Great Caruso* (1951). At the same time, on the other side of the lot and away from Freed, Minnelli, Donen, and their "artistic" innovations, a second cluster of musicals were being made by Joe Pasternak. This one was among the most successful, if not quite the best. Mario Lanza, who here played the famous title-role tenor, still has a cult following and a lively online presence among what now must be the grandchildren of his original fan base. Does anyone then looking down their noses at films like this from across the lot in the Freed Unit still have as robust a following after all these years?

Although MGM offered audiences a mini-version of *Show Boat* as part of *Till the Clouds Roll By* in 1946, they didn't film the whole story until 1951. Ava Gardner here lip-syncs to "Can't Help Lovin' Dat Man" for the later production. *Photofest*

24. *Show Boat* (1951). James Whale's 1936 production of *Show Boat* at Universal is widely considered to be the most faithful adaption of the 1927 Broadway triumph. But MGM's version, then as now, has always been the popular if not critical favorite. Again, MGM long suppressed the original version.

The song "Ol' Man River" is, of course, what people usually take away from either adaptation, and in that regard William Warfield's performance at MGM is actually superior to Paul Robeson's legendary interpretation at Universal (which Robeson races through as though he's late for a political meeting). Like Robeson, Warfield would continue to sing the dirge for the rest of his life, although by 2001, at a Hollywood Bowl *Show Boat* revival, his health would only allow him to narrate the production. William Warfield died the following year, depriving audiences of that astonishing voice and severing forever one more link to the classic era of MGM musicals.

Director (and MGM veteran) Mervyn LeRoy takes a moment from directing the masses to smile for a still photographer from the well-populated set of *Quo Vadis* (1951). *Photofest*

25. *Quo Vadis* (1951). The 1950s was the age of the cast-of-thousands epic. One of the first, and one of the best, was MGM's gargantuan, nearly three-hour gladiator epic *Quo Vadis.* Fortunately, the film was also a popular success, although it would set into motion a much less fortunate policy of gambling everything, including the studio's very survival, on the performance of a single film. *Quo Vadis* was also an early example of the studio's renting cheaper foreign locations, including soundstages, rather than using their own, which would never have happened before the war. The times were changing.

26. *Million Dollar Mermaid* (1952). Swimmer-actress Esther Williams deserves a mention here because she was such a success and for such a long time on the lot. It's hard to pick one of her films over another, though, because there are so many of them and because they are so similar. How many ways, after all, were there to get the girl into a swimsuit? *Million Dollar Mermaid*, at least, didn't have to try very hard to keep Esther wet because it was a fanciful biography of a swimming star from an earlier era—Annette Kellerman, who in addition to swimming the English Channel in 1905 had also acted and swum in silent movies, including

Lili (1953). Leslie Caron's gamine quality made her the perfect performer to spend nearly an entire movie interacting with puppets. Here human costar Mel Ferrer looks at her more wolfishly than the wolf puppet is able to do. *Photofest*

1914's *Neptune's Daughter*, which Williams had remade in 1949. *Million Dollar Mermaid* was well liked, even by Kellerman, who was hired as a technical advisor, and by Williams, who called it her favorite role. She borrowed the title for her 1999 memoir.

27. *Lili* (1953). A gossamer-thin but rather touching vehicle for Leslie Caron, this is also a very good musical for those who don't much like musicals, because it only has one song in it. Although, musical haters beware, there is some orchestrated dancing to sit through as well. The single song on the soundtrack, "Hi-Lili, Hi-Lo," has since been covered by everyone from Jimmy Durante to Richard Chamberlain, giving the song a long life outside the film, and outside MGM. That very minimalist score, by the way, won its studio an Oscar.

Lucille Ball offers a sitcom-worthy reaction to Desi Arnaz's handling of *The Long, Long Trailer* (1954). *Photofest*

28. *The Long, Long Trailer* (1954). Lucille Ball and Desi Arnaz here proved that the mega-success of their TV sitcom, *I Love Lucy*, was not confined to a tiny black-and-white monitor but worked just as well in color and on the big screen. Lucy and Desi had both worked at the studio in the past, but neither had quite found stardom there, although Lucy came very close. Vincente Minnelli directs. A follow-up, *Forever, Darling* (1956), failed to repeat the formula at the box office.

29. *Love Me or Leave Me* (1955). An atypical Joe Pasternak musical that would have been even more of an anomaly had Arthur Freed produced it instead. Doris Day plays actual torch singer Ruth Etting, who marries a man she does not love to get ahead in 1920s Chicago. James Cagney, as Martin "the Gimp" Snyder, brings his gangster persona over from Warner Bros., and his battles with the here anything-but-virginal Day create unexpected kinky sparks. The film was an important step in the maturation of the MGM musical, which unfortunately was just about to come crashing down even as it grew up.

30. *It's Always Fair Weather* (1955). Meanwhile, across the lot, the same cynicism that was so evident in *Love Me or Leave Me* was oozing out of the fissures at the Freed Unit as well. Intended as a sequel to *On the Town*, only Gene Kelly came back,

ultimately playing a different and somewhat more embittered veteran who reunites with his war buddies for a last fling. Kelly's roller-skating dance down the same New York–set backlot where he had earlier sung in the rain is a highlight, but the film itself, unlike *Love Me or Leave Me*, ultimately would lose money at ticket turnstiles.

31. *Guys and Dolls* (1955). A real anomaly in the MGM catalog, this was the only film ever released by Metro Goldwyn Mayer that was personally produced by Samuel Goldwyn, who had left Goldwyn Pictures in 1922, pre-merger. Make no mistake, though, this was first a Samuel Goldwyn film, with MGM providing distribution and little else. Goldwyn tried to secure Grace Kelly and Gene Kelly for the leads, and then was frustrated that his own distributer would not loan them out. Eventually, Marlon Brando and Frank Sinatra starred opposite Jean Simmons.

The script, from the Broadway sensation, was based on the writings of Damon Runyon, whose milieu of wise guys, gangsters, and gamblers Sinatra was well suited for. Brando, less so, although as the bigger star at the time, he was given the larger part and expected to sing most of the songs. The show's big hit, "Luck Be a Lady," would become a Sinatra standard he would consequently sing everywhere—

everywhere except in *Guys and Dolls*, where it was rather ineffectually masticated by Brando. Still, the film was a success and is well worth a look, although Sam Goldwyn, not surprisingly, then took his business elsewhere.

Guys and Dolls (1955) offered audiences Marlon Brando, Jean Simmons, Frank Sinatra, Vivian Blaine, and, off-stage, Samuel Goldwyn pulling their strings.
Photofest

Publicity still for *Gigi* (1958) with its stars, Louis Jourdan, Maurice Chevalier, Hermione Gingold, and Leslie Caron, in attendance. *Photofest*

32. *Gigi* (1958). Often called the last MGM musical, it was not of course. It was not even the last musical Arthur Freed produced at the studio, although after 1960's *Bells Are Ringing*, he would try for a decade for one last hurrah that was not to be. Even as a near-milepost, however, when considered as a movie, *Gigi* is a good one, winning the Best Picture Oscar that year. Leslie Caron plays a French girl being trained to be a courtesan. Audiences today may find this aspect of the plot a bit creepy, although in 1958 *Gigi* was considered to be acceptable family fare.

33. *The Time Machine* (1960). George Pal was a true visionary. He came to MGM in 1958 and while there specialized in science fiction cinema that managed to be, at its best, both thought-provoking and childlike. In some ways, his masterpiece is *The Seven Faces of Dr. Lao* (1964), which offers a fine, funny, melancholy performance by Tony Randall, an actor the studio often had a hard time casting but who excels here as all seven titular faces. That said, *Dr. Lao* was not a success, and after one more film (1968's *The Power*), Pal would leave the studio. *The Time Machine*, however, attracted popular and even some intellectual praise, perhaps due to the critical karma of original author H. G. Wells's literary pedigree. *The Time Machine* also represented an increasingly rare instance in which all of the studio's

Rod Taylor operates *The Time Machine* (1960). *Photofest*

then-underutilized departments pulled together, just like in the old days, to create cinematic magic. One of those units, the Special Effects Department, even snared an Oscar for their toils. Unfortunately, that department, like many others, would soon be closed down.

34. *Murder, She Said* (1962). When aged character actress Margaret Rutherford won an unexpected Oscar for *The V.I.P.s,* MGM attempted a very late, beneath-the-radar run at making a continuing mystery movie series along the lines of *The Thin Man* by casting Rutherford as Agatha Christie's beloved old lady detective, Miss Marple, in this, the first of four modest comic mysteries. Audiences liked them well enough, although Christie herself had mixed feelings about the series, which did feel like rather weak tea in an era when James Bond was ascendant.

35. *Ride the High Country* (1962). MGM, always somewhat clueless in marketing Westerns, abandoned Sam Peckinpah's sad eulogy to the frontier to second-run houses and the bottom halves of double bills, in spite of some good reviews and fine performances by Randolph Scott (his last) and Joel McCrea. *Ride the High Country* was at least a low-budget movie, reportedly costing less than $1 million

Joel McCrea and Randolph Scott search for a sunset to ride off into in Sam Peckinpah's magnificent *Ride the High Country* (1962). Mariette Hartley and Ron Starr follow in their wake. *Photofest*

to produce, but the studio also botched advertising expensive Westerns like *Wild Rovers* (1971), comic Westerns like *Advance to the Rear* (1964), and even fantasy Westerns like *The Seven Faces of Dr. Lao* (1964).

36. *The Pink Panther* (1963). Inspector Jacques Clouseau is one of those evergreen franchise characters that MGM inherited, along with James Bond, Rocky, RoboCop, assorted hobbits, and Hannibal Lecter—all of which they have benefitted from without actually instigating.

Clouseau is comic Peter Sellers's signature role, although here, in his debut (for United Artists), the good inspector has comparatively little screen time and is relatively subdued compared to the perfect idiot he would be portrayed as in the many sequels. MGM has kept the part alive in the twenty-first century, with Steve Martin playing the role, but even the animated title character (introduced in the credits here) has starred in his own series of theatrical and television shorts, all accompanied by a familiar Henry Mancini score.

37. *Where Were You When the Lights Went Out?* (1968). What is a forgotten, insignificant, and long-unavailable little Doris Day comedy doing here? Well, milestones are, as we have seen, made up of lasts as well as firsts. This was the last gasp of the (supposedly) sophisticated (usually) New York set, MGM-romantic comedy, which in the 1950s and 1960s was virtually a genre in and of itself. *The Tender Trap* (1955), *Designing Women* (1957), *Ask Any Girl* (1959), *It Started with a Kiss* (1959),

Where Were You When the Lights Went Out? (1968) featured Doris Day and Patrick O'Neal. In this scene those lights are still on. *Photofest*

The Mating Game (1959), *Please Don't Eat the Daisies* (1960), *Boys Night Out* (1962), *The Courtship of Eddie's Father* (1963), *Sunday in New York* (1963), *The Wheeler-Dealers* (1963), *Penelope* (1966), and *Doctor, You've Got to Be Kidding* (1967) being a few other MGM-made examples. But the formula, replete with wink-wink sex jokes, girls running about hotels wrapped in white bedsheets, and lots of martinis and misunderstandings, was almost as worn out as the backlot New York sets and the grainy stock footage of Manhattan these films utilized. This one, as tired and flabby as could be expected, was also Doris Day's penultimate feature film—although, even at forty-six, trouper that she was, she seems game. Day once said that *Where Were You When the Lights Went Out?* was, unsurprisingly her least favorite of her films.

38. *Ryan's Daughter* (1970). David Lean's follow-up to his successful *Doctor Zhivago* followed the same bank-breaking pattern of runaway expenses while on a distant location his earlier film had, and that *Apocalypse Now* (1979) and *Heaven's Gate* (1980) would utilize in the future. Unfortunately, Lean's epic of war and romance in Ireland was unfairly savaged by the critics, and audiences ultimately weren't large enough to absorb the massive production costs. Back in Culver City, this failure triggered more than a decade of micromanagement in the boardroom and scared away most of the creative and innovative young filmmakers who revitalized the industry, at least at other studios, in the 1970s.

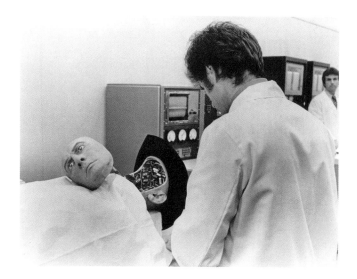

Yul Brynner re-creates his famous *Magnificent Seven* gunslinger character for *Westworld* (1973). Only this time, it now being the 1970s, he's a robot and has a removable face. *Photofest*

39. *Westworld* (1973). Michael Crichton was one of the few innovative young film-makers revitalizing the industry in the 1970s who *wasn't* afraid to work at MGM. His *Coma* has been discussed earlier, but *Westworld* deserves its due here too, if only because, at the time of production, the studio did not physically possess a "Westworld," having demolished their frontier sets in 1970. So here, for the first significant time ever, MGM had to rent a local Western backlot set from another studio, in this case Warner Bros., for one of their productions. And it would not be the last time either.

40. *The Sunshine Boys* (1975). The 1970s nostalgia boom, which had largely been insti-gated by *That's Entertainment!*, was probably also responsible for this warm Neil Simon comedy about two battling vaudevillians. The opening credits even featured, perhaps as a good luck charm, Nacio Herb Brown and Arthur Freed's "Make 'em Laugh," which of course had been one of the delights of *Singin' in the Rain*. Walter Matthau and (Oscar-winner) George Burns were sheer comic poetry in the leads, but the movie itself, like the following year's *That's Entertainment Part II*, underperformed, if slightly. The studio would return to the formula occasionally, sometimes well, as in 1982's *My Favorite Year*, but for now that little boom was a little bust.

41. *Network* (1976). A coproduction with (ironically) United Artists, *Network* was Hollywood's and screenwriter Paddy Chayefsky's satiric, or maybe not so satiric, dig at the television industry, the people in it, and those who consume it. The result netted critical acclaim and four Oscars, including in three of the four acting

Peter Finch rants eloquently in *Network* (1976). *Photofest*

categories. The following year, another coproduction, this time with Warner Bros., *The Goodbye Girl*, also won an acting Oscar, which unfortunately would not happen at the studio again for the next eleven years.

42. *Fame* (1980). This very late in the day musical hit, just like in the old days, was largely developed in-house rather than acquired after the fact. *Fame* also produced an ongoing franchise that has included (so far) stage adaptations, remakes, and several TV versions. Alan Parker's original is still the one to see, although the performing arts numbers are not always well integrated into the narrative—surprising since the story is all about a school for the performing arts.

43. *Poltergeist* (1982). MGM's best horror movie since *The Haunting* (1963) and Steven Spielberg's only MGM film, this very well-executed ghost story also stands as an almost too handy bridge between the old and new Hollywoods, which perhaps are not as dissimilar as one might assume. Spielberg, the film's producer, allegedly was not at all shy about flexing his creative muscle on set, sometimes to the detriment of Tobe Hooper, his director. Just like the old days? All ironies

Heather O'Rourke crosses into the light in *Poltergeist* (1982). Unfortunately, that light is from a television set. *Photofest*

aside, *Poltergeist* was also a huge critical and audience favorite in its day and would birth two sequels and a remake. The goth cult classic *The Hunger* (1983) would soon return the studio to the horror genre, but with less success.

44. *A Christmas Story* (1982). No MGM movie, save for *The Wizard of Oz*, has received as much adoration from audiences as director Bob Clark's tough-love look at Christmas past. Sadly, like *Oz*, this one took some time for those audiences to discover, in their hearts, how special to them it really was. So in 1982 the studio was not rewarded in dollars. Darren McGavin is particularly wonderful here as "The Old Man," a role allegedly conceived for Jack Nicholson!

45. *Moonstruck* (1987). Cher won an Osar for this well-liked romantic comedy, which, like earlier MGM versions of the same theme, is set in New York—although this is a tenement-infested, decidedly ethnic part of New York populated with characters even more eccentric than Tony Randall and where Doris Day would probably have been most uncomfortable. As in *On the Town*, some of the exteriors were indeed shot on location, but the soundstage used for the interiors, well, that was now in Toronto.

46. *Rain Man* (1988). Dustin Hoffman won an Oscar, as did the picture, director Barry Levinson, and the screenplay, although subsidiary United Artists rather than its parent company got to bask in the Oscar glory. However, as the highest-grossing film of its year, nobody at MGM is known to have complained. Tom Cruise, who would later run UA, costarred. A clip of Fred Astaire and Ginger Rogers as *The Barkleys of Broadway* (1949) with Fred singing "They Can't Take That Away from Me," in a scene where Valeria Golino teaches Hoffman's shy autistic savant to dance, was also a sweet, possibly unintentional, callback to an earlier era for the company.

Director Norman Jewison (in cap) confers with his leading lady, Cher, on the 1987 set of *Moonstruck. Photofest*

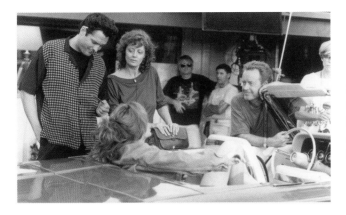

Behind the scenes on *Thelma and Louise* (1991) with Michael Madsen, Geena Davis (in car), and Susan Sarandon consulting with director Ridley Scott. *Photofest*

47. *Thelma and Louise* (1991). Several times over its history, just as it seemed MGM was retreating into safe nostalgia or sitcom platitudes, the company has dynamited those complacent cobwebs away and produced a piece of relevant-to-the-moment art that was widely discussed around water coolers and on the opinion pages of newspapers during its run. It had happened with *Blow-Up*, it had happened with *Network*, and it happened here with *Thelma and Louise*, a road movie about two feisty females on the run from both the law and assorted predatory males. Critics and audiences were divided, often along gender lines, by what they perceived to be the film's attributes and biases, which sometimes only tended to reveal their own.

48. *Leaving Las Vegas* (1995). Nicolas Cage scored an Oscar for this low-budget, 16mm chronicle of the last days of an alcoholic screenwriter. The studio's involvement in an indie-style, commercially off-putting project, almost the antithesis of what MGM had once been all about, was particularly commendable during a year when the ever-cash-strapped company was releasing artistically dubious titles like *Showgirls*, *Bio-Dome*, and *Cutthroat Island*. Fortunately, in this case their detour into arthouse territory paid off, both on Academy Award night and, more importantly, at the box office.

In *The Birdcage* (1996) Robin Williams and Nathan Lane both flattered and embraced gay (and beach) stereotypes, to the delight of audiences. *Photofest*

49. *The Birdcage* (1996). Like the later and equally loved *Legally Blonde* (2001), some of the studio's later-day

products, this one coming to us via United Artists, have been about having a good laugh too. Based on the French farce *La Cage aux Folles* (1978), Robin Williams and Nathan Lane play a gay couple trying, and not very well, to pretend they are straight. *Easter Parade* (1948) as well as studio alumni John Wayne and Judy Garland are all evoked. Incidentally, much of the soundstage filming took place at Paramount, which, unlike MGM, still *had* soundstages.

50. *Barbershop* (2002). Another successful comedy. This one, however, was also the inception for a series of theatrical and television sequels—in other words, an actual franchise, something the studio had not lucked into in decades (1994's *Stargate* and 1995's *Species*, both of which also spawned follow-ups, being semi-exceptions). The unexpected success of the series, which concerns itself with the customers and staff of a barbershop in a largely Black neighborhood, also steered MGM into other African American–cast comedies during the era, namely *Soul Plane* (2004), *Beauty Shop* (2005), *Who's Your Caddy?* (2007), and *Soul Men* (2008). Lena Horne, MGM's first African American star and still alive at the time, must have wished that, at least quantity-wise, she had been given so many opportunities at MGM.

Just in case your appetite for all things MGM-produced needs another fix, another fifty titles, without individual comments, follows below:

The Unholy Three (1925); *The Student Prince in Old Heidelberg* (1927); *The Wind* (1928); *The Cameraman* (1938); *The Hollywood Review* (1929); *The Big House* (1930); *Min and Bill* (1930); *Red Dust* (1932); *The Mask of Fu Manchu* (1932); *Dinner at Eight* (1933); *Queen Christina* (1933); *Viva Villa!* (1934); *A Tale of Two Cities* (1935); *Fury* (1936); *San Francisco* (1936); *Captains Courageous* (1937); *Boys Town* (1938); *The Women* (1939); *Ninotchka* (1939); *Babes in Arms* (1939); *The Shop Around the Corner* (1940); *Waterloo Bridge* (1940); *Third Dimensional Murder* (1941); *White Cargo* (1942); *Thirty Seconds Over Tokyo* (1944); *The Picture of Dorian Gray* (1945); *The Pirate* (1948); *They Were Expendable* (1945); *Easter Parade* (1948); *The Three Musketeers* (1948); *Father of the Bride* (1950); *An American in Paris* (1951); *Pat and Mike* (1952); *Julius Caesar* (1953); *The Band Wagon* (1954); *Bad Day at Black Rock* (1955); *High Society* (1956); *Some Came Running* (1958); *Village of the Damned* (1960); *The Haunting* (1963); *Advance to the Rear* (1964); *The Americanization of Emily* (1964); *The Night of the Iguana* (1964); *The Unsinkable Molly Brown* (1964); *Where Eagles Dare* (1968); *Elvis: That's the Way It Is* (1970); *Soylent Green* (1973); *Clash of the Titans* (1981); and *My Favorite Year* (1982).

Notes

2. Greed (1924)

1. Mark A. Vieira, *Hollywood Dreams Made Real: Irving Thalberg and the Rise of M-G-M* (New York: Abrams, 2008).

2. Karl Davis, *Hollywood* (episode 7, "Autocrats"), television documentary directed by Kevin Brownlow (London: BBC, 1980).

7. Hallelujah (1929)

1. John Baxter, *King Vidor* (New York: Monarch Press, 1976).

2. Stephen Bourne, "Nina Mae McKinney," *Films in Review,* January/February 1991.

8. Freaks (1932)

1. David J. Skall, *The Monster Show* (New York: Penguin Books, 1993).

2. Melvin E. Matthews Jr., *Fear Itself: Horror on Screen and in Reality During the Depression and World War II* (Jefferson, NC: McFarland, 2009).

3. David J. Skall, commentary, *Freaks* (DVD), directed by Tod Browning (Burbank, CA: Warner Home Video, 2005).

9. Tarzan the Ape Man (1932)

1. Johnny Weissmuller Jr., William Reed, and W. Craig Reed, *Tarzan, My Father* (Toronto, Canada: ECW Press, 2002).

10. Grand Hotel (1932)

1. John Bainbridge, "The Braveness to Be Herself," *Life*, January 24, 1955.

11. Dancing Lady (1933)

1. Ty Burr, *Old Movies for Families* (New York: Archer Books, 2007).

12. *The Good Earth* (1937)

1. Robert Osborne and Frank Miller, *Leading Men: The 50 Most Unforgettable Actors of the Studio Era* (San Francisco: Chronicle Books, 2006).

14. *The Wizard of Oz* (1939)

1. Danny Peary, *Cult Movies* (New York: Delacorte Press, 1981).
2. Otis Ferguson, "'The Wizard of Oz' and 'The Adventures of Sherlock Holmes' Reviewed," *The New Republic*, September 24, 1939.
3. Russell Maloney, "The Wizard of Hollywood," *The New Yorker*, August 12, 1939.
4. Les Perkins, interview with the author.
5. Ibid.

15. *Gone with the Wind* (1939)

1. Pat Conroy, *My Reading Life* (New York: Nan A. Talese, 2010).
2. Steven M. Aronson, "Look Inside Ted Turner's House in Florida," *Architectural Digest*, July 2004.

17. *Mrs. Miniver* (1942)

1. Vincent Canby, "Study of William Wyler Includes Documentary," *New York Times*, September 20, 1986.

18. *Song of Russia* (1944)

1. Robert Mayhew, "The Making of 'Song of Russia,'" *Film History*, vol. 16, no. 4, 2004.
2. Ibid.
3. Ibid.
4. Ibid.

20. *The Postman Always Rings Twice* (1946)

1. Lana Turner, *Lana: The Lady, The Legend, The Truth* (New York: E. P. Dutton, Inc., 1982).

21. *On the Town* (1949)

1. *American Masters: Gene Kelly: Anatomy of a Dancer,* directed by Robert Trachtenberg (Burbank, CA: Warner Home Video, 2002).
2. Ibid.
3. Kevin Jagernauth, "Review: Alex Gibney's 4-Hour Documentary, 'Sinatra: All or Nothing at All,'" *Indiewire*, April 3, 2015.

22. *Battleground* (1949) and 23. *The Red Badge of Courage* (1951)

1. Lillian Ross, *Picture*, New York NYRB Classics, reprint edition (2019); originally published 1952.
2. Ibid.
3. Robert Franklin and Joan Franklin, *Gottfried Reinhardt*, transcript of an oral history conducted 1959 by Robert and Joan Franklin, Columbia University, NY.
4. John Huston, *An Open Book* (New York: Alfred A. Knopf, 1980).
5. Peter Straub, *Ghost Story* (New York: Coward, McCann & Geoghegan, 1979).

29. Ben-Hur: A Tale of the Christ (1925) and 30. Ben-Hur (1959)

1. *Ben-Hur: The Epic That Changed Cinema,* directed by Gary Leva (Burbank, CA: Warner Home Video, 2005).

32. How the West Was Won (1962)

1. "How the West Was Won," *Daily Variety,* December 31, 1961.

35. Doctor Zhivago (1965)

1. *MGM: When the Lion Roars,* directed by Frank Martin (Burbank, CA: Warner Home Video, 2017).

38. The Dirty Dozen (1967)

1. Brian Hannan, "*The Dirty Dozen*: A 50th Anniversary Special," *Cinema Retro,* vol. 13, no. 38, 2017.
2. Bosley Crowther, "*The Dirty Dozen*," *New York Times,* June 16, 1967.
3. Ibid.
4. Bosley Crowther, "Bonnie and Clyde," *New York Times,* April 14, 1967.

39. 2001: A Space Odyssey (1968)

1. Pauline Kael, "Trash Art in the Cinema," *Harpers,* February 1969.
2. Andrew Sarris, "2001: A Space Odyssey," *Village Voice,* April 11, 1968.
3. Andrew Sarris, "2001: A Space Odyssey," *Village Voice,* May 7, 1970.

41. Hollywood: The Dream Factory (1972)

1. Christopher Isherwod, *Prater Violet* (New York: Farrar, Straus and Giroux, 1948).
2. "Telepic Review: Hollywood: The Dream Factory," *Daily Variety,* January 11, 1972.

42. The Phantom of Hollywood (1974)

1. Mayer, interview with author.
2. Ibid.
3. "That's Entertainment!" *Daily Variety,* December 31, 1973.
4. "MGM Set to Film 'Phantom of Lot 2,'" *Los Angeles Times,* November 10, 1973.
5. Schenck, interview with author.
6. Wayne, interview with author.
7. James Spada, *Peter Lawford: The Man Who Kept the Secrets* (New York: Bantam Books, 1991).
8. Walsh, interview with author.
9. Cecil Smith, "A Phantom with a Realistic Look," *Los Angeles Times,* February 12, 1974.
10. Mayer, interview with author.

43. That's Entertainment! (1974)

1. *American Masters: Gene Kelly: Anatomy of a Dancer,* directed by Robert Trachtenberg (Burbank, CA: Warner Home Video, 2002).

44. *Rocky* (1976)

1. "How Ryan Coogler Convinced Stallone to Make Creed," *Project Casting*, January 4, 2016.

45. *Coma* (1978)

1. Joseph Gelmis, "Author of 'Terminal Man' Building Nonterminal Career," *Los Angeles Times,* January 4, 1974.

2. Peter Bart, *Fade Out* (New York: Harper Collins, 1990).

3. *MGM: When the Lion Roars,* directed by Frank Martin (Burbank, CA: Warner Home Video, 2017).

46. *Heaven's Gate* (1980)

1. *The Making of a Legend: Gone with the Wind,* directed by David Hinton (Burbank, CA: Warner Home Video, 1988).

47. *Hero at Large* (1980), *Being There* (1979), or *The Formula* (1980)

1. Gormick, author interview.

2. Norden, author interview.

3. Ibid.

4. Ibid.

49. *Running Scared* (1986)

1. David T. Friendly, "Leo Roars His Last at the Old MGM Stand," *Los Angeles Times,* November 13, 1986.

2. Quintana, author interview.

3. Friendly.

4. Jeff Gottlieb, "Long Running Engagement Coming to an End at MGM," *Los Angeles Times,* November 9, 1986.

5. Bowen, author interview.

50. *Get Shorty* (1995)

1. Giovanni Di Stefano, *The MGM Connection* (independently published, 2013).

Selected Bibliography

BOOKS

Aylesworth, Thomas G. *The Best of MGM.* New York: Gallery Books, 1986.

Bach, Steven. *Final Cut: Art, Money, and Ego in the Making of Heaven's Gate, the Film That Sank United Artists.* New York: Newmarket Press, 1999.

Barbera, Joseph. *My Life in Toons: From Flatbush to Bedrock in Under a Century.* Atlanta: Turner Publishing, 1994.

Bart, Peter. *Fade Out.* New York: Harper Collins, 1990.

Baxter, John. *King Vidor.* New York: Monarch Press, 1976.

Benson, Michael. *Space Odyssey: Stanley Kubrick, Arthur C. Clarke and the Making of a Masterpiece.* New York: Simon & Schuster, 2018.

Bergen, Ronald. *The United Artists Story.* New York: Crown Publishers, 1986.

Biederman, Danny. *The Incredible World of Spy-Fi: Wild and Crazy Gadgets, Props and Artifacts from TV and the Movies.* San Francisco: Chronicle Books, 2004.

Bingen, Steven, Stephen X. Sylvester, and Michael Troyan. *MGM: Hollywood's Greatest Backlot.* Solana Beach, CA: Santa Monica Press, 2011.

Bizony, Piers. *The Making of Kubrick's 2001: A Space Odyssey.* Cologne, Germany: Taschen, 2020.

Blake, Michael F. *Lon Chaney: The Man Behind the Thousand Faces.* Lanham, MD: Vestal Press, 1997.

Burr, Ty. *Old Movies for Families.* New York: Archer Books, 2007.

Carey, Gary. *All the Stars in Heaven: Louis B. Mayer's MGM.* New York: E. P. Dutton, 1981.

Clarke, Gerald. *Get Happy: The Life of Judy Garland.* New York: Random House, 2000.

Conroy, Pat. *My Reading Life.* New York: Nan A. Talese, 2010.

Crowther, Bosley. *The Lion's Share: The Story of an Entertainment Empire.* New York: E. P. Dutton, 1957.

———. *Hollywood Rajah: The Life and Times of Louis B. Mayer.* New York: Dell Publishing Company, 1961.

Di Stefano, Giovanni. *The MGM Connection.* Independently published, 2013.

Eames, John Douglas. *The MGM Story.* New York: Crown Publishers, 1990.

Eyman, Scott. *Lion of Hollywood: The Life and Legend of Louis B. Mayer.* New York: Simon & Schuster, 2005.

Flamini, Roland. *Thalberg: The Last Tycoon and the World of M-G-M.* New York: Crown Publishers, Inc., 1994.

Fordin, Hugh. *M-G-M's Greatest Musicals: The Arthur Freed Unit* (originally published in 1975 as *The World of Entertainment! Hollywood's Greatest Musicals*). Boston: Da Capo Press, 1996.

Friedrich, Otto. *City of Nets: A Portrait of Hollywood in the 1940s.* New York: Harper & Row, 1986.

Gabler, Neil. *An Empire of Their Own: How the Jews Invented Hollywood.* New York: Doubleday & Company, 1988.

Gallagher, John Andrew, and Frank Thompson. *Nothing Sacred: The Cinema of William Wellman.* Asheville, NC: Men with Wings Press, 2018.

Gillespie, A. Arnold (Robert A. Welch, ed.). *The Wizard of MGM.* Orlando, FL: BearManor Media, 2012.

Griffin, Nancy, and Kim Masters. *Hit and Run: How Jon Peters and Peter Guber Took Sony for a Ride in Hollywood.* New York: Simon & Schuster, 1997.

Griffith, Richard, and Arthur Mayer. *The Movies: The Sixty-Year Story of the World of Hollywood and Its Effect on America.* New York: Bonanza, 1957.

Gutner, Howard. *Gowns by Adrian: The MGM Years (1928–1941).* New York: Harry N. Abrams, 2001.

———. *MGM Style.* Guilford, CT: Lyons Press, 2019.

Hanna, William. *A Cast of Friends.* Dallas, TX: Taylor Publishing, 1996.

Harmetz, Aljean. *The Making of The Wizard of Oz, 75th Anniversary Edition.* Chicago: Chicago Review Press, 2013.

Haver, Ronald. *David O. Selznick's Hollywood.* New York: Alfred A. Knopf, 1980.

Hay, Peter. *MGM: When the Lion Roars.* Atlanta, GA: Turner Publishing Company, 1991.

Hess, Earl J. *Singin' in the Rain: The Making of an American Masterpiece.* Lawrence, KS: University Press of Kansas, 2009.

Higham, Charles. *Merchant of Dreams: Louis B. Mayer, M.G.M. and the Secret Hollywood.* New York: Donald J. Fine, Inc., 1993.

Huston, John. *An Open Book.* New York: Alfred A. Knopf, 1980.

Isherwood, Christopher. *Prater Violet.* New York: Farrar, Straus and Giroux, 1948.

Knowles, Eleanor. *The Films of Jeanette MacDonald and Nelson Eddy.* Lancaster, Lancashire, UK: Gazelle Book Services Ltd., 1976.

Knox, Donald. *The Magic Factory: How MGM Made An American in Paris.* Westport, CT: Praeger Publishers, 1973.

Koszarski, Richard. *The Man You Loved to Hate: Erich von Stroheim and Hollywood.* Oxford, UK: Oxford University Press, 1983.

Larkin, T. Lawrence. *In Search of Marie-Antoinette in the 1930s: Stefan Zweig, Irving Thalberg, and Norma Shearer.* London, UK: Palgrave Macmillan, 2019.

Matukonis-Adkins, Richard. *Adrian: American Designer, Hollywood Original.* Independently published, 2020.

Maltin, Leonard (ed). *Hollywood: The Movie Factory.* New York: Popular Library, 1976.

Marx, Samuel. *Mayer and Thalberg: The Make-Believe Saints.* New York: Random House, 1975.

Matthews, Melvin E., Jr. *Fear Itself: Horror on Screen and in Reality during the Depression and World War II.* Jefferson, NC: McFarland, 2009.

Minnelli, Vincente. *I Remember It Well.* New York: Doubleday & Company, 1974.

Montgomery, Elizabeth Miles. *The Best of MGM.* Darby, PA: Bison Books Corporation, 1994.

Norden, Donald. *Phantom of the Backlots Present: Hole in the Fence.* Independently published, 2021.

Osborne, Robert, and Frank Miller. *Leading Men: The 50 Most Unforgettable Actors of the Studio Era.* San Francisco: Chronicle Books, 2006.

Parish, James Robert, et al. *Hollywood on Hollywood.* Metuchen, NJ: The Scarecrow Press, 1978.

——. *The MGM Stock Company.* New York: Arlington House Publishers, 1974.

——. *The Best of M-G-M: The Golden Years (1928–1959).* New York: Arlington House Publishers, 1981.

Peary, Danny. *Cult Movies*. New York: Delacorte Press, 1981.

Rempel, William C. *The Gambler: How Penniless Dropout Kirk Kerkorian Became the Greatest Deal Maker in Capitalist History.* New York: Dey Street Books, 2018.

Rich, Sharon. *Sweethearts: The Timeless Love Affair—On-Screen and Off—Between Jeanette MacDonald and Nelson Eddy: Updated 20th Anniversary Edition.* New York: Bell Harbour Press, 2014 (originally published in 1994).

——. *Jeanette MacDonald Autobiography: The Lost Manuscript.* New York: Bell Harbour Press, 2004.

Ross, Lillian. *Picture*. New York: NYRB Classics (originally published 1952), reprint edition, 2019.

Salzberg, Ana. *Produced by Irving Thalberg: Theory of Studio-Era Filmmaking.* Edinburgh, Scotland: Edinburgh University Press, 2020.

Scarfone, Jay, and William Stillman. *The Road to Oz: The Evolution, Creation, and Legacy of a Motion Picture Masterpiece.* Lanham, MD: Lyons Press, 2018.

Schary, Dore. *Heyday: An Autobiography.* Boston: Little Brown & Company, 1979.

Sellers, Robert. *The Battle for Bond.* UK: Tomahawk Press Publishers, 2007.

Selznick, David O. (Rudy Behlmer, ed). *Memo from David O. Selznick.* New York: Macmillan, 1972.

Selznick, Irene Mayer. *A Private View*. London, UK: Weidenfeld and Nicolson, 1983.

Silver, Alain, and Elizabeth Ward (eds.). *Film Noir, An Encyclopedic Reference to the American Style.* New York: The Overlook Press, 1979.

Skall, David J. *The Monster Show.* New York: Penguin Books, 1993.

——. *Dark Carnival: The Secret World of Tod Browning.* New York: Anchor Books/ Doubleday & Company, 1995.

Spada, James. *Peter Lawford: The Man Who Kept the Secrets.* New York: Bantam Books, 1991.

Straub, Peter. *Ghost Story.* New York: Coward, McCann & Geoghegan, 1979.

Thomas, Bob. *Thalberg: Life and Legend.* New York: Doubleday and Company, 1969.

Thomas, Lawrence B. *The MGM Years.* New York: Columbia House, 1971.

Troyan, Michael. *A Rose for Mrs. Miniver: The Life of Greer Garson.* Lexington, KY: The University Press of Kentucky, 1999.

Turner, George E. (ed.). *The Cinema of Adventure, Romance & Terror.* Los Angeles: ASC Press, 1989.

Turner, Lana. *Lana: The Lady, The Legend, The Truth.* New York: E. P. Dutton, Inc., 1982.

Urwand, Ben. *The Collaboration: Hollywood's Pact with Hitler.* Cambridge, MA: Belkamp Press, 2013.

Vieira, Mark A. *Hollywood Dreams Made Real: Irving Thalberg and the Rise of M-G-M.* New York: Abrams, 2008.

——. *Hollywood Horror: From Gothic to Cosmic.* New York: Harry N. Abrams, Inc., 2003.

——. *Irving Thalberg: Boy Wonder to Producer Prince.* Berkeley, CA: University of California Press, 2009.

Wayne, Jane Ellen. *The Golden Girls of MGM: Greta Garbo, Joan Crawford, Lana Turner, Judy Garland, Ava Gardner, Grace Kelly, and Others.* New York: Carroll & Graf Publishers, 2004.

——. *The Golden Guys of MGM: Privilege, Power and Pain.* London, UK: Chrysalis Books Group, 2004.

——. *The Leading Men of MGM.* Boston: Da Capo Press, 2006.

Weatherwax, Bob, and Richard Lester. *Four Feet to Fame—A Hollywood Dog Trainer's Journey.* Orlando, FL: BearManor Media, 2017.

Weinberg, Herman G. *The Complete Greed—Reconstruction of the Film in 348 Still Photos Following the Original Screenplay, Plus 52 Production Stills.* New York: E. P. Dutton & Company, 1973.

Weissmuller, Johnny, Jr., with Danton Burroughs and W. Craig Reed. *Tarzan, My Father.* Toronto, Canada: ECW Press, 2002.

Wellman, William A. *A Short Time for Insanity: An Autobiography.* New York: Hawthorn Books, Inc., 1974.

Williams, Esther, with Digby Diehl. *The Million Dollar Mermaid.* New York: Simon & Schuster, 1999.

ARTICLES

Aronson, Steven M. "Look Inside Ted Turner's House in Florida." *Architectural Digest,* July 2004.

Bainbridge, John. "The Braveness to Be Herself." *Life,* January 24, 1955.

Bingen, Steven. "Ghosts of the Backlot: Art Imitates Life (and Death) in Hollywood's Own Backyard: The Phantom of Hollywood." *Filmfax,* Fall 2010.

Bourne, Stephen. "Nina Mae McKinney." *Films in Review,* January/February 1991.

Canby, Vincent. "Study of William Wyler Includes Documentary." *New York Times,* September 20, 1986.

Crichton Gelmis, Joseph. "Author of 'Terminal Man' Building Nonterminal Career." *Los Angeles Times*, January 4, 1974.

Crowther, Bosley. "The Dirty Dozen." *New York Times,* June 16, 1967.

——"Bonnie and Clyde." *New York Times,* April 14, 1967.

Ferguson, Otis. "*The Wizard of Oz* and *The Adventures of Sherlock Holmes*, Reviewed." *The New Republic*, September 24, 1939.

Friendly, David T. "Leo Roars His Last at the Old MGM Stand." *Los Angeles Times*, November 13, 1986.

Gottlieb, Jeff. "Long Running Engagement Coming to an End at MGM." *Los Angeles Times*, November 9, 1986.

Hannan, Brian. "*The Dirty Dozen:* A 50th Anniversary Special." *Cinema Retro*, vol. 13, no. 38, 2017.

"How Ryan Coogler Convinced Stallone to Make Creed." *Project Casting*, January 4, 2016.

"How the West Was Won." *Daily Variety,* December 31, 1961.

Jagernauth, Kevin. "Review: Alex Gibney's 4-Hour Documentary *Sinatra: All or Nothing at All.*" *Indiewire*, April 3, 2015.

Kael, Pauline. "Trash Art in the Cinema." *Harpers*, February, 1969.

Maloney, Russell. "The Wizard of Hollywood." *The New Yorker*, August 12, 1939.

Mayhew, Robert. "The Making of 'Song of Russia.'" *Film History*, vol. 16, no. 4, 2004.

"MGM Set to Film 'Phantom of Lot 2.'" *Los Angeles Times*, November 10, 1973.

Sarris, Andrew, "2001: A Space Odyssey." *The Village Voice*, April 11, 1968.

——. "2001: A Space Odyssey." *The Village Voice*, May 7, 1970.

Smith, Cecil. "A Phantom with a Realistic Look." *Los Angeles Times*, February 12, 1974.

Telepic Review: "Hollywood: The Dream Factory." *Daily Variety*, January 11, 1972.

"That's Entertainment!" *Daily Variety,* December 31, 1973.

Thomas, Ryes. "The Ruby Slippers: A Journey to the Land of Oz." *Los Angeles Times*, March 13, 1988.

ORAL HISTORY TRANSCRIPTS

Behlmer, Rudy. *J.J. Cohn*. Transcript of an oral history conducted 1987 by Rudy Behlmer.

Franklin, Robert, and Joan Franklin. *Gottfried Reinhardt*. Transcript of an oral history conducted 1959 by Robert and Joan Franklin. Columbia University, NY.

MOVIES AND HOME VIDEO SPECIAL CONTENT

Most of the movies discussed in the text are available for streaming or on home video through Warner Home Video, MGM Home Video, or their licensed subsidiaries. For the following titles, however, special content included with feature films was consulted or quoted. Several freestanding documentaries are also here acknowledged.

An American in Paris (multiple documentaries included on 2008 DVD, including 2002's *American Masters: Gene Kelly: Anatomy of a Dancer*).

Ben-Hur: Fiftieth Anniversary Edition (2009, includes 2005 documentary *Ben-Hur: The Epic That Changed Cinema*).

A Christmas Story (commentary and documentaries on 2008 DVD).

Freaks (documentary and David J. Skall commentary on 2005 DVD).

Final Cut: The Making and Unmaking of Heaven's Gate (2004 documentary; not available on home video/streaming).

Gone with the Wind (multiple documentaries including 1988's *The Making of a Legend: Gone with the Wind* and Rudy Behlmer's commentary, included on 2009 DVD/Blu-ray).

Hollywood (Kevin Brownlow's 1980 documentary miniseries; in particular, episode 7, "Autocrats"; not available on home video/streaming).

How the Grinch Stole Christmas (included documentary on 2018 DVD/Blu-ray set).

Meet Me in St. Louis (2020 DVD/Blu-ray special features, including 1972's *Hollywood: The Dream Factory*).

MGM: When the Lion Roars (1992 documentary miniseries released on DVD in 2017).

Singin' in the Rain (multiple documentaries and commentary included on 2012 DVD/Blu-ray).

The Tarzan Collection (included on 2005 DVD set is documentary, *Silver Screen Kings of the Jungle*).

That's Entertainment! The Complete Collection (assorted documentaries and historic material on 2004 DVD set).

The Wizard of Oz (multiple documentaries and John Fricke commentary included on 2014 DVD/Blu-ray).

SELECTED BIBLIOGRAPHY

WEBSITES

Andy Hardy: Ultimate Movie Rankings regarding Andy Hardy series box office information: www.ultimatemovierankings.com.

Blow-Up locations: https://sites.google.com/a/blowupthenandnow.com/blowup-then-now.

Elvis at the box office: https://theconversation.com/elvis-presley-was-paid-a-kings-ransom-for-sub-par-movies-because-they-were-marketing-gold-81586.

Gone with the Wind's continuing appeal: https://today.yougov.com/topics/politics/articles-reports/2014/09/28/gone-with-the-wind.

How the West Was Won restoration: https://movieweb.com/exclusive-george-feltenstein-talks-how-the-west-was-won.

Leo the Lion at Grauman's Chinese Theatre: www.youtube.com/watch?v=1ApROSSSLMs&t=9s.

"There Is No Moral Difference between 'Gone with the Wind' and 'Malcolm X,'" 2006 Breitbart article by John Nolte: www.breitbart.com/entertainment/2015/06/29/there-is-no-moral-difference-between-malcolm-x-and-gone-with-the-wind.

INTERVIEWS

Mike Benson (2021)

David Bowen (2021)

Greg Gormick (2021)

Roger Mayer (2010)

Donnie Norden (2021)

Les Perkins (2020)

Ana Maria Quintana (2021)

George W. Schenck (2010)

Tom Walsh (2010)

Fredd Wayne (2010)

Charles Ziarko (2021)